Unholy Hungers

UNHOLY HUNGERS

ENCOUNTERING THE PSYCHIC VAMPIRE IN OURSELVES AND OTHERS

Barbara E. Hort, Ph.D.

SHAMBHALA
Boston & London
1996

Shambhala Publications, Inc.
Horticultural Hall
300 Massachusetts Avenue
Boston, Massachusetts 02115

9 8 7 6 5 4 3 2 1

First Edition
Printed in the United States of America
⊗ This edition is printed on acid-free paper that meets the
American National Standards Institute z39.48 Standard.
Distributed in the United States by Random House, Inc.,
and in Canada by Random House of Canada Ltd

Library of Congress Cataloging-in-Publication Data
Hort, Barbara E.,
Unholy hungers: encountering the vampire in ourselves and others
/Barbara E. Hort. — 1st ed.
p. cm.
Includes bibliographical references and index.
ISBN 1-57062-181-0 (pbk.: alk. paper)
1. Manipulative behavior. 2. Control (Psychology)
3. Interpersonal relations. 4. Jungian psychology. 5. Vampires—
Psychological aspects. I. Title.
BF632.5.H67 1996   95-25783
158'.2—dc20   CIP

This book is dedicated to the living spirit of

Aldous Huxley,

whose breadth of vision inspired me to take
on more than I thought I could handle, and whose
brave new path encouraged me to move forward
through a treacherous land where wiser souls
might have feared to tread . . .

and to the goddess whom the Greeks called

Hecate,

the taskmistress, paraclete, and midwife,
who also dwells at our dangerous crossroads
but who, unlike the vampire, brings us to a living
dawn beyond every dark night of the soul.

CONTENTS

CONTENTS

MEETING THE PSYCHIC VAMPIRE

THE BEAST has always been with us. For as long as our hearts have pumped blood, for as long as our souls have glowed with life, for as long as we have yearned for love, the beast has always been there. Sneering and stalking, drooling and scheming, it licks its full, soft lips in anticipation of its next warm meal. For the beast is essentially a feeding thing. Oh, yes, it has many faces, all of them human, and it has our endearing manners as well. But those human graces are a camouflage born of necessity—they are the disguise that enables the beast to prevail. Beneath its veneer of humanity, the core of the beast is hunger, and survival is its only goal.

The beast hungers for survival, but not for life as we know it, since life implies the warmth of a beating heart and the light of a shining soul. The beast has neither heart nor soul. It has only a clever mind and an insatiable hunger. To survive, the beast must appease its hunger, and it can feed only on the thing it lacks—the essence of life. So the beast must prey upon us, the living. It must suck our lifeblood and drain our force.

If we are lucky, we will merely die. If we are less fortunate, we will succumb to the deepest horror of the beast's predation, which is that most of its victims will *not* die. Instead, we will become the thing to which we have fallen prey, and we will be compelled to feed in the same parasitic way. Thus the feeding frenzy spreads, swelling into a bestial legion whose progenitors haunted prehistory. The beast is ancient and global and growing. It has many stories, and shapes without number, and all are like shadows—elusive and dim. But the name that we call the beast itself is clear and cold and precise. We call the beast *vampire*.

The story of the vampire is as old, as tangled, and as evil as any on earth. Our contemporary model for the vampire is the beast whom we call Dracula, so I will begin my storytelling with Dracula's tale. But first I must warn you. Do not be deceived into thinking that Dracula's truth is the only truth of the vampire. Do not believe that the lurid details of blood and fangs and bats and garlic are the sum of the vampire's existence. For if you believe that these bits of lore can capture its essence, then you are in danger of arming yourself against only the literal incarnation of the beast, and you risk falling victim to another kind of vampire—the one who can infect and exhaust our souls.

Dracula himself tells us that he is only one member (and certainly not the last) of a vast and ancient race. Now consider this: the creeping thing that we call *vampire* in English- and French-speaking countries is called *kukuthi* in Albania; *bhuta* in India; *vampiric* in Holland; *adze* and *obayifo* in West Africa; *vampiro* in Spain and Italy; *algul* in Arab countries; *wampior* in Poland; *hannya* in Japan; *mora* and *upir* in Slavic countries; *mrart* among the Australian aborigines; *upior* and *wampir* in the Ukraine; *civatateo* among the Aztecs; *vampir* and *vudkolak* in Serbia; *swawmx* in Burma; *Blutsauger, Neintöter,* and *Dubbelsüger* in Germany; *mara* in Scandinavia; *ramanga* in Madagascar; *strygia, wukodalak, vurkulada,* and *vrykolaka* in Greece; *katakhaná* in Crete; *dearg-due* and *leanhuam-shee* in Ireland; *aswang* in the Philippines; *ubour* in Bulgaria; *veripard* in Estonia; *bruxsas* in Portugal; *tu* and *talamaur* in Polynesia; *moroii, varcolaci, zmeu, murony, strigoi, priccolitch,* and *nosferatu* in Romania; *bajang, penanggalan,* and *langsuir* in Malaysia; *loogaroo* in the West Indies; *tlaciques* among the Nauhuatl; *estrie* in Israel; *chiang-shi* and *hsi-hsue-kuei* in China; *impundulu* in East Africa; *vieszcy* among the Kashubes of Poland; and *baobhan-sith* in Scotland.

So many, many names, and among them lies a hard truth. The vampire stalks the living in every corner of the human world. Dracula is only a single vampire among a global horde, and what's more, he is a young member of the clan, for he was born in the mind of Bram Stoker only one hundred years ago, and he was based on a warlord who lived less than six hundred years ago—a mere breath of time, considering it was more than three thousand years ago that the Assyrians and Babylonians described the monster *ekimmu,* an undead corpse who preyed upon the blood and flesh of the living in an effort to evade its own death. So it is between us and the vampire. Wherever we have lived, *when*ever we have lived, the beast has always been with us.

THE VAMPIRE AS ARCHETYPE AND HUMAN EXPERIENCE

What can account for the ancient, global presence of the vampire in myth and lore? Some authors have argued that the vampire myth is a superstition developed by tribal people to cope with the mysteries of contagious disease, untimely death, and bodily decomposition. This argument is compelling, but it does not explain the ongoing fascination with vampires in our age of modern medicine and sanitized death. Other authors consider the vampire story to be a folkloric treatment of sexual perversity and sadistic murder. This too is an interesting theory, but necrophilia and blood fetishism are only minor aspects of the vampire myth, relatively new and far from universal, so they cannot explain the vampire's long-standing presence in global lore. Still other authors have tried to establish the vampire's physical reality, documenting individuals who have allegedly stolen, drunk, or bathed in human blood. These authors themselves, however, admit that the incidence of literal vampirism is minuscule compared to the vampire's presence in myth and lore.

While the traditional approaches to the vampire's story are interesting, they are not persuasive explanations for the global proliferation of vampire myths throughout history. More importantly, the traditional vampire research does not hold any personal relevance for most of us, since few of us have ever had to exhume a body, engage in necrophilia, drink human blood, or endure sharp teeth entering our jugular veins. Why, then, are *we* so fascinated by the vampire? We find the vampire mesmerizing because, even though we lack literal experience with the undead, we have all met vampires in the course of our lives. It may seem outlandish to assert that every reader of this book has encountered a vampire, but a brief detour into the realm of psychology will help to justify my sensational claim.

For this discussion, I will use the model of the human psyche* developed by the Swiss psychoanalyst C. G. Jung. In Jung's model, every human psyche is composed of basic elements called *archetypes.* We can define archetypes as the constellations of energies or traits that make up our personalities; they are what we obtain when we carve the rich complexity of our internal experience at its natural joints. Thus, the images we use to symbolize archetypes can help us comprehend the whirling kaleidoscope of our psychic energies. Yet archetypes *feel* like much more than this neat definition. When our archetypal energies are activated, we feel as if we are moved by internal characters who are acting out gripping stories on the stages of our lives. Sometimes we feel that we possess these powerful psychic energies, and at other times it feels as if they have possessed us.

When we contemplate the archetypal energies that move us, it

---

*I use the term *psyche* to refer to the entire system of internal human experience, which comprises the mind, as the locus of conceptual knowledge; the heart, as the locus of emotional knowledge; the body, as the locus of sensory knowledge; the spirit, as the locus of our inherent divinity; and the soul, as the locus of the deep transpersonal knowledge and feeling that we may call intuition. Furthermore, I use the term *psychic* when referring to an aspect of the psyche (e.g., "psychic energy"). Even though this term has been borrowed by the television charlatans who vampirize the public with deceptive offers of nirvana, I am reclaiming the true meaning of *psychic* in this book, because the term *psychological* pertains more precisely to the study of psyche, rather than the experience of psyche.

seems as if each archetype has a distinct personality with positive and negative aspects, just like any other personality. Thus, as the Jungian analyst Marion Woodman has observed, the energies of our archetypes "can fill us with radiant light, or overwhelm us with destruction and despair. They are our gods within, spiritually and instinctually. Without access to them, life becomes a boring two-dimensional existence. Relating to them [consciously] allows us to work at incarnating our angels." I would add that relating to an archetype *unconsciously* leads us to incarnate our demons as well, which is consistent with Woodman's later observation that archetypes "are like hidden magnets [that] attract and repel. Gods and vampires, goddesses and witches are alarmingly close in this domain. They make us or break us, depending on our conscious relationship to them" (1992, 13).

A good translation of archetype theory into practical human psychology has been presented by the Jungian analyst Jean Shinoda Bolen. In her books *Goddesses in Everywoman* and *Gods in Everyman* Bolen uses the Greek deities to describe some of the archetypal energies that are important in Western civilizations. For example, Bolen employs the image of Artemis, the goddess of the hunt, to describe a kind of energy that is present in everyone who finds great meaning in physical daring and a connection to nature. When the archetypal energy of Artemis is activated in someone's psyche, he or she might be drawn to pursuits that involve an individual achievement, a contact with the wilds of nature, or a communion with the spiritual wildness that is present in us all. The energy of an archetype will influence what we do, but even more importantly, it will influence how we do it. A biologist in whom the energy of Artemis is activated will be likely to treat nature as home and animals as companions, and will probably view as sacred any contact with nature's elements. In contrast, a biologist in whom Artemis's energy is not active may view nature simply as a body of knowledge to be mastered or a terrain to be conquered.

Bolen, like Woodman, is careful to point out the grave danger in relating unconsciously to any archetype, no matter how attractive or helpful its potential may be. When this happens, we can become possessed by the archetype—that is, we take ourselves for the power itself. In our arrogance at playing god or goddess, we are apt to confuse our personal values with some absolute and exclusive version of the truth. For example, if we unconsciously identify with Artemis, we can become contemptuous of vulnerability, enraged at any perceived violation of nature, and merciless in our retribution. In this state, we forget that while Artemis shows us truth through nature, none of us *is* Artemis, and while Artemis's path is one path to truth, it is not the only path.

Archetypal energies can be activated in a variety of ways. A specific archetype can be activated in the psyche of one individual, but it can also be activated in the collective psyche of a group or a culture. Jung argued that when an archetype is activated in a group's collective psyche, the images of its energy will appear in the group's stories, myths, and folktales. He further believed that any story that has spread across the oceans and the millennia has done so only because it speaks to a psychological experience that is common to us all.

If Jung was right, then the vampire myth is much more than a byproduct of biological ignorance, sexual perversity, and a pathological taste for the macabre. The vampire's presence in lore from around the world and across the ages indicates, in the Jungian view, that the vampire archetype has haunted the human psyche since the dawn of history. Wherever we have lived, whenever we have lived, the vampire has always been with us, and with us in the most intimate way of all—psychically.

Because archetypes are simply the metaphors we use to think about different qualities of psychic energy, the myth of the vampire is merely a shape that we have developed to describe a particular kind of human psychic experience. We may have been psychically drained or infected by a vampiric person, but no individual *is* the archetype itself. That said, it must be admitted that there is something special about the vampire myth. It is unholy. It is prehistoric. It speaks of merciless predation and epidemic contamination. Most of all, the vampire myth exists worldwide: in Jungian terms, the vampire archetype is active on a global scale.

Thus, it appears that if we settle back into the saddles of our souls and look bravely into the perilous night, we are *all* likely to discover that we have been the victim of a psychic vampire. What's more, we are likely to realize that we have fulfilled the curse of the vampire's victim: at one time or another, in one way or another, we have acted the vampire ourselves. But I am jumping ahead of myself. It is too soon to hold up the dreadful mirror. Let's not talk about what is inside. Let's look first at what is outside. Let me tell you the story of a psychic vampire.

THE PROFILE OF A PSYCHIC VAMPIRE

Stories bestow enlightenment. They clarify our internal lives in the same way that the sun illuminates our external lives. Stories can bring a slow dawn of awakening, a fierce blaze of recognition, a dusky glow of wisdom. No corner of the mind is so dark, twisted, or well defended that a story cannot shine its beacon of consciousness into the musty hole. The storyteller's light is a dangerous tool in the telling of the vampire's story, because vampires hate the light. The vampire's nest lies in the blackest pit of the unconscious, where the foul thing broods on its ravenous gut. By shining my storyteller's light on the monster, I will awaken its wrath, for it would prefer to lurk in the shadow, to lull us in the night, to slip into our psyches under the velvet cover of darkness. Its shimmering fangs slide into our veins, its lips pull softly against our bare necks, and it sucks our blood with a desperate sweetness. The vampire promises us a mingling of fluid energies that swirl in a slow duet of passion. It invites us into a sinuous, pulsating dance that is consummated in a fusion of passion. All of time is in the moment, all of life is in the merging. There is no tomorrow. There is no dawn . . .

. . . or to be brutally precise, there is no dawn for the vampire. No bleak light falls on the ashes of its heart, for the vampire is gone before any cold dawn can chill the ecstasy of its union. It is we, the vampire's victims, who are left to take a grim accounting of the price we have paid for our fleeting moment of ecstasy. Drained and weary, we awaken into the bleak solitude of our mere mortality. It will take days, even weeks, to replenish the life that has been embezzled from us—unless the beast should return.

Lest you think that I am conjuring impossible ghouls in the psyches of ordinary mortals, or that I am running from the shadows in my closet, let me tell you about a real psychic vampire.

He was a powerful man, and a wealthy one.* Confidence and charm clung to him like a fragrant mist. He was larger than life, more capable and charismatic than the average man, and suddenly she realized that he was looking at *her,* a woman I will call Joan. The man seemed to savor Joan's attention as he recounted his exploits, confided his insights, and seasoned his story with wit. Joan hung on every word. The dinner was lovely, the evening divine—almost unreal in its brilliance and intensity. The next morning, however, Joan felt like she had a mild hangover. It wasn't one of those hangovers where her teeth felt loose and her hair hurt.

---

*This example, like all the examples in this book, is an amalgam of many real examples with which I am personally or vicariously familiar. Similarly, no dream or story is taken directly from the experience of one client or friend, although my images may incorporate theirs, and the theories I propose are based on my Jungian practice. I have deliberately written the book in this way so that I might minimize the possibility of vampirizing others in my very attempt to deactivate the beast. My decision does not imply that the use of clients' material is necessarily a vampiric act. But since the topic of this book made the danger of vampirism seem too likely, I decided to err on the most conservative side. Of course, other peoples' images have become so well integrated into mine that I could not completely exclude them without eviscerating the images themselves. So to all contributors I offer my deepest thanks and my hope that their material has been merely borrowed and not vampirized.

Her head was fine, her stomach sound; it was just a case of the blahs. Joan lay in bed feeling blah. Why bother getting out of bed to begin another day of boring mediocrity? Blah. But, thought Joan, I *like* my life. Still blah. How puzzling—she'd only had one glass of wine with dinner. Maybe she was getting sick. But she didn't have any identifiable symptoms. Still blah.

Joan dragged herself out of bed and shuffled to the mirror. Her face looked gray, her life looked gray, her future looked gray—all were tinged with the same bleak meaninglessness. Joan thought back to the glitter and glamour of the previous night, and she tried to imagine what the man would be doing this morning: eating a healthy breakfast, lounging in elegant bedclothes, jogging briskly (and attractively) in the crisp morning air. Joan trudged down to the kitchen and stared at her store-bought muffin from behind the strands of her limp morning hair. Her blahs got worse. She moped all morning in the blear of her blahs, which she tried to write off to the rain. Or a virus. Or something like that.

Joan saw the man again a few weeks later, as she was entering a restaurant that he was just leaving. The man was as charming as ever, exuding elegance and command in his every gesture. Joan and the man spoke for a few minutes, then went their separate ways, he to his car and she to the restroom to fluff before her luncheon meeting. As Joan brushed her hair, she thought it looked flat. She smoothed her attractive outfit, but she felt fat. What was the point in fluffing herself? Who was she fooling? Here she was, preening her two meager feathers, while exotic birds of magnificent plumage were populating the earth. Whatever led her to think of herself as something special? *The man* was special. She was just one of the mob. Joan felt that the man's attention to her was only flattery, an act of charity, a tribute to her doomed efforts at self-enhancement.

The truth, it seemed (if only she had the guts to accept it), was that specialness was not hers to own. *He* owned specialness, he and others like him—the beautiful people, the rich people, the smart people, the blessed people who glide through a life of carefree giftedness. Joan could bask but could not belong. Hers was the mud. They owned the stars. They could transcend life's petty dreariness and soar on the wings of beauty and wealth. They never smelled bad and they never got fat. They never felt despair. They never got sick and they never got scared. They were above all that. And Joan, in their presence, watched helplessly as her meager riches turned to gray dust alongside their rainbows of plenitude. No matter how brilliant, lovely, or accomplished she felt before she brushed against this special man and his special kin, once the encounter had occurred, Joan's self-esteem would evaporate, and only after days of focused effort would it reemerge, feeble and bruised.

Joan came to both yearn for and dread encounters with this special man. She yearned for the dazzling flight of their meetings and dreaded the demoralizing aftermath. She chided herself for her weak self-esteem and lectured herself about the beneficial effects of self-improvement programs. Joan told herself that she dreaded the man only because she was a slug, and that her malaise was her own damn fault. Then, one evening, during a gathering held at his house, the special man did something that gave Joan a liberating (though chilling) insight into his nature. He was holding forth at the head of a table covered with porcelain and silver and crystal, and he was delivering, with his customary magnetism, a discourse on the nature of scholars. The audience was mesmerized, and they complimented the perceptiveness and originality of his thesis. He accepted their accolades with his usual air of elegant entitlement. Then he pursued his point—but Joan was no longer paying attention.

Somewhere in the middle of the man's soliloquy, Joan had sensed something familiar in his logic. A few moments later, she realized that his argument was familiar because it was hers. Whether he had forgotten the source of his entertaining speech (which followed almost verbatim a monologue Joan had delivered over lunch a few months before), or whether he was drunk on the irresistible elixir of a rapt audience, Joan would never know. One thing was certain: he would not have intentionally exposed his vampiric methods in this way, for its effect on Joan was to shatter the mirrors and scatter the smoke on which the man's image depended. Without understanding how he managed his psychic sleight of hand, Joan suddenly realized that this man drew his specialness from others. Once he had the loot in hand, he instantly (and unconsciously) made it his own, leaving his victims to slump, as Joan often had, into a fog of dejected mediocrity.

The writer Algernon Blackwood has described the vampiric energy of a similar person, a man who

> drooped alone, but grew vital in a crowd—because he used their vitality. He was a supreme, unconscious artist in the science of taking the fruits of others' work and living—for his own advantage. . . . In the man's immediate neighborhood you felt his presence draining you; he took your ideas, your strength, your very words, and later used them for his own benefit and aggrandizement. Not evilly, of course; the man was good enough; but you felt that he was dangerous owing to the facile way he absorbed into himself all loose vitality that was to be had. . . . At first you would be conscious of taut resistance; this would slowly shade off into weariness . . . then you either moved away or yielded—agreed to all he said with a sense of weakness pressing ever closer upon the edges of collapse. . . . even the effort of resistance would generate force that *he* absorbed. . . . everything he said or did announced what I may dare to call the *suction* of his presence. (1912, 207–9)

Joan never confronted her vampiric acquaintance with his theft of her words and ideas, but she held the truth of his tactics close to her heart whenever she saw him after that revelatory dinner. The prevailing social situation required that she still be pleasant to him, but after a few encounters with Joan in her new state of awareness, the man no longer sought out her company as he used to. And when they were required to interact in a group, he never failed to comment to the others that a therapist (Joan) was present, and that they all had better watch how they conducted themselves, lest she should peek into their souls. Joan might have taken comfort in the man's behavior as a validation of her intuition. But in fact, she was never able to take any comfort from his behavior, not even self-congratulation. While Joan felt that her consciousness had thwarted his predation of her, she could never dismiss her disturbing recognition of the man's vampiric essence.

THE ESSENCE OF THE PSYCHIC VAMPIRE

In the opening scenes of Steven Spielberg's film *Jaws,* a young woman swims blissfully at midnight in the warm summer water of the Atlantic Ocean. She closes her eyes and savors the sensuous caress of the current against her skin. Then, from the cold, black depths, there rises the mindless predator, a shark lured by the vibrations of the unsuspecting life. Moving languorously, the young woman unwittingly draws the beast with every joyful kick. We see her from the eyes of the shark: she is nothing more than a lump of life, a morsel of flesh that will appease the predator's hunger and enable it to continue its incessant prowl. From above, we see her surrounded by the glistening water, an island of ecstasy embraced by the deceptively tranquil sea.

Suddenly, the young woman grunts with surprise, and for a surreal moment she cannot grasp the horror of the truth. Too quickly, her moment of innocence is shattered by an explosion of pain and terror as she is torn with impossible speed, back and forth, through the flickering moonlit water. She screams for help, for rescue, for mercy from the nightmare that devours her. Her confidence in the natural order has been obliterated by the horror of *life gone wrong.* No hope, no help, and no mercy will penetrate the hell that consumes her. There is only bottomless agony, bottomless terror, and bottomless despair. She screams from the center of her soul, pleading for a reprieve from her anguish, but there is only more agony, terror, and despair.

The predator does not hear her pleas. The predator does not perceive her soul. The predator can only perceive its need. Even if the predator had a soul that could resonate with the young woman's anguish, it is of no matter now—whatever soul it might have had has been savaged by the ferocity of its hunger. The predator can only smell and devour her life; it cannot be moved to pity the terrified girl nor to show her any mercy.

On the most elemental level, the essence of the vampire is the essence of a shark who feeds on human beings. The horror of the vampire, however, is that it is not simply a primitive fish with a minimal brain. Like us, the vampire is a human being, and like us, it has known the fear of death and the yearning for love. But the vampire's soul has been savaged by its hunger. It cannot be moved to mercy by the agony of its victims. The human beings who fall prey to the vampire are stripped of their humanity and reduced to lumps of life in the vampire's maw. They are not the targets of its love or wrath, any more than the swimmer is adored or hated by the shark. The vampire's hunger is heartless as well as soulless, and its victims must perish in a cold pit where they scream without echo or answer into the blackest inhuman void.

The vampire's hunger obliterates its heart and its soul, but it does no harm to its mind. This means that although the vampire is indifferent to the anguish of its victims, it knows that they will become creatures like itself.* It realizes that they too will become stealthy hunters who subsist in the shadowy twilight of the void, parasites who cling to their parody of life by feeding on the energy of other people, all of whom will perish in the same spasm of

---

*Although the Dracula myth has led us to believe that a victim will not become a vampire unless forced to drink the vampire's blood, in most of the world's vampire myths, the victim is automatically transformed into a vampire as a result of having been vampirized.

despair. Practitioners of the occult say that the vampire is the most evil of creatures. I cannot claim to grasp fully the nature of what we call "evil," but if one is inclined to call the vampire an entity of evil, this description of its essence seems more than sufficient cause.

My portrayal of the vampire's essential nature will probably be offensive to those who are enamored of the charismatic vampires that proliferate in modern literature, most notably Anne Rice's Lestat and Chelsea Quinn Yarbro's Comte de Saint-Germain. Certainly, these literary vampires are like the real people in whom the vampire archetype is active: they are capable of periods in which they display compassion, altruism, and a social conscience. There comes a time, however, when even the most endearing vampire must revert to its essence. Its fangs must be bared to puncture innocent necks, it must suck the precious lifeblood out of its enchanted victims, and then it must either kill its lovestruck paramours or transform them into undead predators like itself. The predatory essence of the vampire is as inarguable as its capacity for charisma.

The vampire's charisma is important to note because the beast has a special ability to captivate our imagination with its hollow charm:

> The vampire appears empty, like a shadow, and we, the human observers, may project whatever form will grip our imagination most, truly believing that *this* is the vampire. In this complex and disturbing fashion the process of depletion begins, and through this balance of fantasy and reality the vampire sucks not only blood, but the psychic energy which controls our mental and physical functions, slowly but surely becoming a perfect projection of our desires. (Maschetti 1992, 46)

The vampire, like many predators in nature, is capable of appearing in a variety of alluring aspects, some of which we obligingly invent by means of our projected desires. We must, however, look beyond the beast's appearances and allures to its essential truth: the vampire is, at its core, a feeding thing. No matter how comfortable it may be to deny that truth, we must remember that when faced with a psychic vampire, we will pay for every comfy little denial with the blood of our life force.

RECOGNIZING THE PSYCHIC VAMPIRE

Even when we are not the benumbed prisoners of our own denial, we usually don't recognize that we have been victimized by a vampire until we are out of the mesmerizing sphere of its influence. Only after the vampire has departed do we notice that something is wrong—and even then, we are rarely able to identify the source of the wrongness. There are two ways to tell that we have been in the presence of a vampire. The first is a feeling of shameful insufficiency. Remember how worthless and drab Joan felt after every encounter with her vampiric acquaintance? We should look around for a psychic vampire whenever we feel that we are somehow flawed—not because of what we've done, but because of who we inherently *are* (or are not). In this state, we feel that our flaws make us unworthy of life, love, and simple human respect. We feel we are not good enough, or thin or smart or sexy enough. We feel, broadly or specifically and always inescapably, *less than*.

Our feeling of insufficiency is valid, not because we are inherently insufficient, but because some of our life force—the stuff that enables us to perceive our own beauty, talent, and worth—has been bled out of us by the vampire, and we now have an insufficient amount to maintain a healthy self-perception. Sometimes the vampire who has drained us is activated in an external person, and sometimes it is the vampire we carry around in our own psyches. We may experience our insufficiency as a physical fatigue or a psychic depletion, but what we do *not* experience is the subjective feeling of ourselves as "green and juicy," full of vital, abundant, flowing psychic health. The vampire's ravenous sucking transforms our green juiciness into gray dessication—which is simply another way of describing *less than*. Whenever we experience this feeling of shameful insufficiency, we have been the victim of a psychic vampire.

Anyone who has experienced this state of psychic bloodlessness knows that it is extremely unpleasant. When we are in it, we frantically seek to replenish what we have lost. But if we are not clear about what exactly we have lost, then we are likely to go about replenishing ourselves in any old way that occurs to us. The yearning for replenishment is the second symptom of having encountered a psychic vampire, and it usually is experienced as a hunger for *more*. This aspect of the vampiric ordeal is captured explicitly in Paul Monette's novel *Nosferatu* (1979), a modern retelling of the Dracula myth. Monette sets his story in the town of Wismar, where everything is plentiful and perfect. One of the first inklings we have of Dracula's arrival is the emergence among Wismar's inhabitants of the hunger for *more*:

> [Jonathan] gave [his wife] a long kiss, then held her head on his shoulder . . . as if he had all the time in the world. He looked through the solid rooms of his solid house . . . and thought: *I don't need anything else*. . . . Passing jauntily through the busy streets, Jonathan . . . stopped at a market vendor . . . gave the man a friendly greeting and chose a pastry layered with cream and frosted with chocolate. . . . He finished the pastry, smacked his lips, and straightened his tie in the window of the bank. . . . And he had a sudden pang in the region of his heart . . . that left him with the strangest feeling. He put a hand to his billfold, in the inside pocket of his coat, and thought with an anxious shiver: *I have to have more*. (11–13)

More. No matter how much we have, it's never enough. Since we've been bled of what really counts, our hunger for everything else is bottomless. We feel driven to consume goods, experiences, and people as if we were starving, as if those substitutes for life force would somehow fill the void. Madonna, a consumer of cele-brated rapacity, sings a song on precisely this subject in the 1990 film *Dick Tracy*. In the song, the Material Girl tells us how she has risen from simple poverty to self-indulgent excess. As she enu-merates her myriad possessions, Madonna muses that her audi-ence probably assumes she is content with her riches. But we assume wrong, it appears, and Madonna corrects our foolish as-sumption by proclaiming her insatiable craving for additional wealth, love, and power. In a veritable ode to vampirism, Ma-donna punctuates each stanza of her voracious aria with its ex-plicit title: *"MORE!"*

There's certainly nothing wrong with having ambition and set-ting goals, but the yearning for *more* in Monette's novel and Ma-donna's song is distinctly different from simple human aspiration. It is not born of finite ambition, but of the bottomless, shame-driven hunger that alerts us to the vampire's presence. When we feel we must fill our pit of shameful inadequacy and cannot articu-late what will constitute *enough* to fill it, when the only quantity that seems capable of redeeming us is the indefinite *more*, then we have been victimized by a psychic vampire.

BECOMING A PSYCHIC VAMPIRE

As you contemplate the psychic vampires you have met in your life, you may wonder how those people came to be bloodsuckers in the first place. Were they born as vampires, or was their appe-tite for stolen life force an acquired taste? The answer to this ques-tion requires another brief detour into Jungian psychology.

In a 1992 workshop based on her book *The Ring of Power*, Jean Bolen made this observation: "I am convinced that we enter the world seeking love, and when we don't find love, we settle for power." Bolen's assertion works best when we define love as a relationship in which we honor and cherish the sacredness of any being (including ourselves) without any hidden agendas. Whenever we relate in this way, we are savoring the true sustenance of our souls, which we experience in this plane of existence as love.

As we journey through life, we seek love passionately, but not invincibly. If we are met with lovelessness too often, we begin to fear that we will perish emotionally. The prospect of emotional annihilation is terrifying to all human beings, and in order to escape it, we grasp at any lifeline that presents itself, no matter how deceitful its redemptive promise may be. As Bolen suggests, when we sense our impending emotional death, the lifeline to which we most often cling is *power,* or more precisely, *exploitation*—the pursuit of self-enhancement at another's expense. Sometimes we exploit others by coercing them with our demonstrations of unassailable dominance, sometimes by manipulating them with our displays of submissive vulnerability. Either way, we are engaging in exploitation, a profane relationship to the life force in others and ourselves in which both parties are dehumanized and objectified. In contrast, love is a relationship wherein we cherish the sacred humanity of another person while simultaneously cherishing the sacred humanity in ourselves.

The difference between love and exploitation is often obscured, and it is easy to understand how we might be duped into seeking the power of exploitation when we can't find the potency of love. Exploitation is only an imitation of love, however, just as some nonnutritive chemicals are imitations of real food. They may look and taste like food, but they provide no sustaining nourishment. Likewise, the power of exploitation may initially feel like the potency of love, but it cannot provide love's nourishing, self-renewing energy. What's more, although the life force stolen in the process of exploitation appears to empower the exploiter, it inevitably does so at a cost to both the exploiter and the victim. Because stolen goods decay quickly in matters of personal energy, exploiters must constantly embezzle more energy from others in order to sustain their illusion of empowerment—a crusade that is doomed to endless expansion, since stolen power can never satisfy the exploiter's hunger for love.

Most people resort to exploitation only in situations where they are met with lovelessness. A person who seeks love, only to be rebuffed again and again, eventually slides toward the terrifying pit of emotional starvation. Undergoing an emotional death is like being the swimmer in *Jaws*—all of existence is reduced to a scream, without echo or answer, into a black, inhuman void. Every unloved person slides to the brink of this awful pit and teeters there, writhing in terror on the precipice of emotional oblivion. The loneliness of this place seems absolute, but then a new entity slithers up alongside. The newcomer whispers to the despairing soul about a way of life in which love will no longer be needed. It swirls the dark cape of exploitation and weaves for the unloved person a tantalizing yarn of triumph over agony and annihilation. The person takes hold of the glittering bait and embarks on the pursuit of exploitive power, rather than elusive love.

Just as the mythical vampire is a creature who exploits the life force of others as a means of evading its own demise, so too is the psychic vampire the dark newcomer who tries to seduce every love-starved person on the brink of emotional death. Only after the seduction is complete and the vampire has infected the unloved person's psyche does the tragic truth become apparent; a life of psychic vampirism will merely exacerbate the person's loveless solitude. Too late now for the truth—from here on, whenever the vampire archetype is active, the person will feel compelled to pursue the psychic exploitation of others, driven by the vampire's demonic assistants, fear and contempt.

Fear and contempt are the hallmarks of the vampire. Psychic vampires in particular are distinguished by their fear of their own mortality and by their contempt for other lives. In a terrified effort to conquer their human limits, psychic vampires plunder the life force of others and attempt to minimize (and even justify) their horrific predation by displaying contempt for their victims. A perfect everyday example of vampiric fear and contempt is provided by Alice Miller in her landmark work *The Drama of the Gifted Child* (1981). Miller describes two parents who happily lap at their ice cream bars while denying their small child a bar of his own (65–66). The parents hold out their ice creams to the child and offer him a taste, but when the child insists on a whole bar and not just a taste, they quickly grab back the treats and ostentatiously linger over them while making light of his frustration. In the end, the child is handed a "treat" of his own—the stick remaining from his father's ice cream.

These parents are indulging in "the more or less conscious, uncontrolled, and secret exercise of power over the child by the adult." This, Miller believes, is the "fountainhead of all contempt," which is "the best defense against a breakthrough of one's own feelings of helplessness" (67, 69). The fear/contempt dynamic is contagious; it spreads like a disease across cultures and generations. And any person who remains desperately defended against the pain and despair of being unloved (that is, any person whose vampire archetype is activated) is likely to be unkind and cold. Looking down from the dispassionate castle of her contempt, the vampiric person gloats over the energy she has exploited from life lumps below in an effort to avoid her own terrifying mortality.

The exploited life force of others is usually depicted in the vampire legend as blood, but it also can appear as flesh, physical vitality, or psychic energy. Of the four kinds of theft, psychic vampirism is considered to be the worst. This opinion is held not only by vampirologists but also by self-proclaimed vampires themselves, such as the members of the Temple of Set (a vampiric suborder in the Church of Satan):

> Ironically, the Temple of Set deplores other kinds of vampires, called psychic vampires. This idea is based upon a passage in Anton LeVey's *The Satanic Bible,* which describes psychic

vampires as persons who make you feel guilty if you don't do favors for them—those who, like leeches, drain others of their energy and emotions. (Dresser 1989, 35)

Psychic vampirism is not only the worst form of vampirism but also the most common, since it can erupt every time a love-starved person pursues exploitation in order to elude emotional death. In myth, the vampire's evasion of death is essentially a failure; the vampire cannot renew its own blood supply and thus is not truly alive. Instead, it enters the twilit world of the "undead," where it engages in a perpetual frenzy of bloodsucking. Similarly, the person in whose psyche the vampire archetype prevails is not engaged in a self-renewing psychic life. Instead, he enters a frenzied limbo state in which he must endlessly exploit others in order to feed his unholy hunger.

WHY WE ALLOW THE VAMPIRE TO FEED ON US

Myths tell us that the vampire is most likely to attack at night, while we drift in a dreamy unconsciousness. This implies that we yield to the vampire because we don't fully realize what's happening. Specifically, we are most susceptible to the psychic vampire when we are unconscious or dreamily yearning—states in which the vampire can successfully disguise itself as a lover or friend. This makes sense, for which of us would acquiesce to the vampire if we could see, in the bright daylight of consciousness, the cold void behind its eyes and the bloodless pallor of its heart? Obviously, the cloak of night is a necessary part of the vampire's seduction.

Seduction is essential to the vampire's success, for the myth also tells us that a vampire may enter its victim's domain only if the victim can be persuaded to invite the vampire across the threshold of her door (or, in the prevailing Western myth, her window). In other words, something in us must cooperate and invite the vampire into our lives. Of course, this implies that we have the option to refuse the vampire's advances. But for the moment, let's speculate on the reasons why we open the window and allow the vampire to feed on our life force. First, as I just noted, the vampire usually slides in beside us during the night, when we are sleepily unaware of its lethal purpose. Nighttime is not only the classic symbol of unconsciousness but also the time when we are most subject to fearful despair, when we undergo our "dark nights of the soul." The psychic vampire chooses these moments to approach us with its offer of exploitation as a substitute for love because it knows that its "protection" will seem to be our only means of surviving in the dark, loveless place. This is the guiding principle of every con artist—he pitches redemptive bliss in exchange for cash only when his targeted victims are weak with pain or desperation. The psychic vampire uses the same con artistry. And sure enough, we who are frightened and hurting leap straight into its jaws. We are desperate, and we don't know (or can't remember) the grim consequences of the vampire's seductive deal, so why should we refuse it?

Even with such willing victims as we, the vampire proceeds gently—promising us immortality and eternal love, sighing over its solitude, and yearning for a true companion. We hear the vampire's sweet words in the midst of our anguish, and we are reborn with hope. We offer warmth, companionship, and most of all, love, love, love to this beacon of rescue in our black despair. Love and more love for the vampire, who lures us ever closer with gestures of affection, words of respect, and other such baubles as desperate souls crave. Many of us spend a lifetime caught in this dance. We gush with love, and the psychic vampire tosses us bait for more loving. Like homeless dogs, we roll at the vampire's feet, tails wagging, tongues lolling, necks bared in blind rapture at our great good fortune in the quest for love. The vampire stands over us, stroking our fur and lulling us with its caresses. Patiently, it waits for the moment when we will close our eyes in bliss, blinding ourselves to the sight of the fangs, the scent of stale blood, the stab and the draining before the next lure.

This sad dance is well described in the vampire lore. Not all victims of the mythic vampire become vampires themselves. A second kind of monster is the *revenant*, French for "one who returns." Revenants are victims whom the vampire has not transformed into vampires themselves. Instead, they function as servants to a vampire, existing in a state that the vampire maintains

> at a perfect balance between life and death. . . . The servant pledges his will to his lord and acts as if he were perpetually hypnotized . . . keeping curious visitors . . . at bay and providing a constant supply of . . . fresh blood, barring all doors and access to the master's place of rest, and making sure that when away from home, the conditions necessary to the life of his master are maintained. This servant has probably the only close relationship with the vampire, for he is permitted to witness the whole truth of his master's life. (Maschetti 1992, 96)

Thus, the revenant serves as a mesmerized accomplice to the vampire, whom he or she resembles and supports, but does not imitate in predation. The revenant recalls the original notion of codependence, in which friends and relatives enable an abuser (of substances or people) to persist in the abusive behavior, while abandoning themselves to a state of stupefied misery and self-negating unconsciousness.

The second reason that we are likely to open the window to the vampire is that, even in the twilit world of unconsciousness, the vampire cloaks its bleak truth in a dazzling array of disguises, most of which are animals and the most famous of which is the bat. Although the only bloodsucking bat is the rare family of Desmontidae, and despite the many other bloodsucking creatures (such as the mosquito) whose range and population are infinitely greater, the bat is the only creature to whom we have given the name "vampire." This suggests that the nature of the bat is connected in our psyches with the nature of the vampire. Perhaps the bat's nocturnal habits and inverted resting position, along with its ill-deserved reputation for carrying disease, snarling itself in our hair, and sucking our blood, are evocative of the psychic vampire, with its unconscious invasion, its inverted ethic of exploitation, and its contagious capacity for snarling our thoughts and sucking out our life force.

Of course, even the most virulent psychic vampire must appear to us in the physical shape of a human, not a bat. But there is a way in which even a psychic vampire can be a shape shifter. Its physical form may remain human, but its energy can flicker instantly from wolf to mist to cat to spider to bat and *poof!* to invisibility. With all these energetic shapes, it is hard for even the most conscious victim to perceive the vampire that lurks behind the masks. The vampire's mask of invisibility is particularly intriguing, since it suggests our complicity in the vampire's success. As the Dracula scholar Leonard Wolf observes, "we cannot see vampires because . . . we choose not to see those aspects of *ourselves* that are most like those of the vampire" (1975, 27). Thus, our reluctance to see our own vampiric qualities can blind us to the vampiric energies in others. This may be why so many aspiring vampires eventually find that they themselves have been drained of life force. Think, for example, of the stereotypic "trophy wife" who may (unconsciously) hope to parlay her husband's wealth to her own benefit, only to find herself depleted and discarded when her beauty starts to fade. Our reluctance to see our own vampiric potential is understandable but dangerous, since it increases the likelihood that we will be victimized by a psychic vampire.

While collaborative invisibility serves the vampire's ends, the most deceptive disguise in the vampire's repertoire is undoubtedly its charismatic mixture of sexuality and power:

> Although the vampire takes from his victim to feed his hunger,
> it is as if he is satisfying a hunger in his audience—a hunger

for sexuality and sensuality, a desire to live forever, a yearning to be both empowered and powerless and thus completely without any responsibility for one's own actions. (Dresser 1989, 168)

[The vampire is] our eidolon. . . . He is huge, and we admire size; strong, and we admire strength. He moves with the confidence of a creature that has energy, power, and will. Granted that he has energy without grace, power without responsibility, and that his will is an exercise in death. We need only to look a little to one side to see how tempting is the choice he makes: available immortality. He has collected on the devil's bargain: the infinitely stopped moment. (Wolf 1975, xviii)

In our moments of weakness, self-doubt, and desperation, which of us could resist the invitation of such a godly creature? And as if godliness were not alluring enough, we find that this superhuman entity is *lonely:* lonely for a special companion—somebody *just like us.* We are wooed by the vampire's enchanting disguise of loneliness that yearns for transcendent union.

The vampire's mastery of disguise is related to the third reason that we allow it to enter our lives. All too frequently, we admit the psychic vampire out of simple courtesy and compassion. We assume the psychic vampire to be one of us—a person with an empathic soul that resonates with other souls and wishes them well. So we answer the vampire's little questions and indulge its little needs. We may experience a flicker of uneasy suspicion when its questions feel a bit too probing or its needs feel insatiable, but we are usually too busy politely accommodating the vampire to investigate our suspicions. This part of the vampire's tale reminds me of a woman I used to know, someone who always began our conversations with a detailed inquiry about my current state of affairs. At the beginning of our acquaintance, I thought her questions indicated a sincere interest in my life. Eventually, however, her inquiries came to seem impersonal and mechanistic. It was as if she were conducting an in-depth interview with an important stranger. Moreover, my answers seemed to be like loot to her, a treasure to be used later for purposes that were unclear (to me, anyway) at the moment of questioning. The obscurity of the interview's purpose was, in fact, why I continued to comply with the woman's questions, even after I became uncomfortable with them—I was too puzzled and polite to withhold the answers.

Finally, I realized that this woman's careful interviews were always followed by a litany of her woes and usually by a favor she was requesting of me. After responding to her many "concerned" questions about my well-being and needs, how could I refuse to listen and comply with hers? In truth, the whole duet was a double whammy. Not only did the woman receive my sympathy and favors, but she also received information (another tactic of exploitation, because the more you know about someone, the more power you have over them). I, on the other hand, received only the empty calories of my illusion that we were friends.

The fourth reason that we invite the vampire to enter is that its earliest attacks typically occur in early childhood, when we are too physically and psychically dependent on the vampires to refuse their advances. Another piece of common vampire lore states that "the draining of another's energy is particularly likely to happen in a marriage, family, or other close emotional relationship—traditionally the vampire's favorite feeding ground" (Farson 1976, 37). In other words, the first vampire archetypes we meet are likely to be active in our parents' psyches. Later in our lives, we will probably encounter these energies again in the people who most resemble our parents on the psychic level. For most of us, these new bearers of the vampire archetype will be our friends, our colleagues, and our mates.

Before you fall back in revulsion and denial, remember that the psychic vampire is an archetype, which means that it is one of *many* forms of energy that are active in a given individual's psyche. Persons who are vampiric in one situation will usually have many nonvampiric energetic fields in their psyches as well. Consider the ancient notion of vampirism as a kind of infection. There are many ways in which an infection can invade the body. Some infections are localized in one part of the body, while others are systemic and affect the entire body equally. Some are severe and require drastic measures to combat them, while others are mild and can be deactivated by the body's normal immune mechanisms. Some require a form of treatment that will not permanently damage the body, while others require treatment so severe that the body will be destroyed by whatever it takes to kill the infection.

In most people, the vampire archetype operates like a mild or moderate infection. It may compromise the healthy aspects of the person's psyche, but it does not overwhelm them, and the method for deactivating the vampiric energy is rarely severe. Moreover, just as an infection can remain relatively localized, so the vampire archetype in most people is active only in certain situations and with certain people. This is why a parent may feel great love for his children when he is experiencing professional success, but abuses them unmercifully when he fears professional failure or disgrace. And it is why he may abuse his children, but never his co-workers, friends, or spouse. The vampire archetype, like any archetype, can be activated and deactivated in a very localized way.

The abrupt speed with which a vampire archetype may be activated and deactivated can surprise us to the point of disbelief. We cannot believe that the serial murderer Ted Bundy was a successful suicide prevention counselor. We cannot fathom how the officers in Nazi death camps could, after a day filled with torture and genocide, be loving fathers and devoted husbands when they returned to their families at night. We can't believe that such things could be true because, as the great social psychologist Else Frenkl-Brunswick discovered, we are highly intolerant of ambiguity, particularly when the ambiguity occurs in other people. We like to keep our people neatly categorized: right and wrong, good and bad. We love to hate heinous criminals because they permit us to put the bad "out there" in another person. Once all of the bad has been projected onto the Really Bad Person, we can reassure ourselves that there is no bad in ourselves. Nonetheless, the truth is that our inner lives are far more complex than we realize. "Good" people do inhuman things, and "bad" people do humane things—it just depends on the circumstances. Even a person who is severely infected with vampiric energy can be capable of compassion, and even a person with the best of intentions can be driven by the vampire if the situation evokes the beast.

Of course, the person in whom the vampire archetype is activated is unlikely to be aware of the change, since vampires cannot see themselves in a mirror. The psychic vampire may think nothing of her vampiric behavior, or may even label it as "love." Indeed, one of the most frightening aspects of psychic vampirism is that it often travels, even in the mind of the vampire, under the name of love. A vampire's "love" is usually based on a conditional approval that masks its ethic of exploitation. Think of the parent who "loves" us only when we are clean, obedient, or apt. This kind of "love," which is the only kind a psychic vampire can offer, masks a profound emotional hunger, which makes the vampire incapable of offering to our love-seeking heart anything more than a sucking hole of need disguised as the solicitude of love. It is as if some deep part of the vampire cries, "I will *not* feed another unless I am fed first! Now . . . who will be willing to feed me? Ah! Here is a tasty morsel! And since it looks to me for love, it will be happy to be exploited if I promise it 'love' in return!"

"It" is the operative word in the last sentence, for when the vampire archetype awakens in a psyche, we are no longer human in that person's eyes. No matter how much the person may otherwise care for us, we are reduced to a lump of life when his vampire archetype is activated. Of course, sometimes we must be wooed and cajoled by the vampire so that we will open the window and never tell what happened afterward. The sexual predator's promise of ice cream and love is only a protective ruse. As long as the vampire archetype is activated, the victim's soul ceases to exist for the exploiter, just as the swimmer's soul does not exist for the shark. What's more, it may seem as if the vampiric person's soul has also ceased to exist, in order for the vampire to be capable of exploiting the victim's life force. It is as if the soul of the exploiter were dead.

Yet the myth tells us that vampiric infection does not destroy a person's soul. When a mythic vampire is killed, the true soul of the infected victim is usually released to pursue its proper sacred destiny (such as going to heaven). This part of the myth suggests that once a love-starved person has made room for the vampire archetype, the love-seeking part of the person's psyche goes into hiding whenever the archetype is activated. Later, when the vampire is dormant, the loving part of the person's psyche is reactivated, if only to weep over the gory aftermath of the vampire's predation.

The most chilling example of this dynamic can be found in Westley Allan Dodd, the serial molester, torturer, and murderer of children who was recently executed in Washington state. Dodd's vile crimes are not unique in our society, but his response to them was. Unlike most serial murders, Dodd did not deny his guilt, nor did he work to regain his freedom. Instead, he insisted that he be executed, vowing that "if you release me, I'll do it again." Some people felt that Dodd was only trying to woo the media, and if so, he was moderately successful in his attempt. What Dodd accomplished most successfully, however, was to accelerate his execution. I don't know what should have been done with Westley Dodd, nor is it my purpose to debate the relative efficacy of rehabilitation and capital punishment in cases like his. What strikes me about Dodd is that, despite the virulent sadism of his psychic vampire, there was still some part of his psyche that, when the vampire was asleep, could resonate with some semblance of a human soul.* If not, why should he care if he molested and murdered again?

So where was Dodd's soul when he tortured and killed? We can ask the vampire myth where to find the souls of those whom the vampire has contaminated, but it does not give us the answer. It only suggests that when the vampiric infection is active, the loving part of the person undergoes a kind of anesthesia. It may or may not be conscious of the vampire's deeds, but it can do little about them. Then, when the vampiric energy becomes inactive, the loving part of the vampiric person is reanimated and left to face the consequences of the vampiric parasite's reign.

In *Schindler's List,* Schindler reawakens the humanity of a brutal Nazi commandant. The officer's newfound compassion initially makes him more humane, but as his self-awareness reveals to him the anguishing extent of his former vampirism, he reverts into a rampage of even greater predation. Similarly, when our loving souls see the carnage we have wrought under the vampire's spell, we often yearn anew for an escape from our excruciating shame, even if the escape is into another siege of vampirism. Our wish for escape only broadens the portal through which the vampire may reenter at will, and eventually we come to yield mindlessly to the vampire. Just as the myth informs us:

> The hypnotic power of the vampire is also of great use to the creature in getting at victims who are adequately guarded indoors; the vampire can summon its victim by sheer power of will and this, combined with the baleful hypnotic glow of its

---

*I am not suggesting that the existence of Dodd's soul excuses his vile crimes. As Alice Miller argues so cogently in her book *For Your Own Good,* the quest to understand the roots of heinous acts is in no way an effort to excuse them. Rather, it is the only approach to these nightmarish deeds that may result in the prevention of similar acts by others. Punishing the perpetrators of heinous acts, without comprehending their origins, will only give us a temporary sense of retribution that will vanish when we encounter the next offender—when, once again, we must indulge in the transitory palliative of punishment without comprehension.

eyes, can lure the victim from his household to destruction. (Cooper 1974, 39)

Maschetti eloquently describes this vicious cycle, in which people wishing for escape from their painful humanity seek shelter under the inhuman cape of the vampire:

> The longing for oblivion . . . must surely be the door through which the victim is invited into the potential victim's life; to take it, annihilate it, and transform it into something supernatural, into a strange sort of existence that runs parallel to human life and yet is irredeemably separate from it, since it feeds on it as its main purpose. In a sense, therefore, the wish for eternal life endowed with superhuman power becomes the greatest sin of the ego. And vampirism then, the punishment of such sin. (1992, 58)

And now it is time to leave this discussion of abstract theory and global myth. It is time to listen to the stories that speak to our personal relationships with the psychic vampire—the stories that describe the vampiric duets we have danced. We must search in the night (and the mirror as well) for the light of awareness that can guide and protect us. Let us learn what we must do to save ourselves from the hungry eyes and needle-sharp fangs of the ravenous ancient undead. Onward, into the night.

MASCULINE VAMPIRES AND FEMININE VICTIMS

THE TRUTH is in the stories. No matter how intellectually agile or wise we may be, all of our elegant theories and persuasive arguments will have a dull, empty feel if we do not ground them in the stories that captivate our cultural mind. This and the following chapters present four sets of stories that describe our most common vampiric experiences in one-on-one relationships: (1) masculine vampire with feminine victim, (2) feminine vampire with feminine victim, (3) feminine vampire with masculine victim, and (4) masculine vampire with masculine victim. The emphasis on gender may be surprising, since my preceding discussion of the vampire archetype did not have a gendered focus. Our socialization as male or female has a profound influence on our psyches, however, which means that psychic vampires and their victims are likely to assume either masculine or feminine forms. Still, what I describe as a masculine psychic vampire or masculine victim might just as easily be activated in a woman, just as a feminine psychic vampire or victim might be activated in a man. These gendered labels act simply as a kind of conceptual shorthand.

Social psychology tells us that the trait which our culture associates most closely with masculinity is dominance. Males and females who exhibit dominance in our society are often seen as being "masculine," while males and females who are (or seem to be) dominated are seen as being "feminine." Accordingly, "masculine" vampires exploit others while disguised by the cloak of

invincibility and domination, while "feminine" vampires exploit others while disguised by the veil of vulnerability and submission. Similarly, "masculine" victims respond to vampiric attack from positions of empowerment, while "feminine" victims respond from positions of disempowerment. (Remember that vampires are empowered only in the sense that the culture empowers them by its system of patriarchal values. They are not empowered in the psychic sense, for if they were, they would not need to bleed others of their psychic energy.)

The masculine form of the vampire is easily recognized in the familiar shape of Dracula, and the feminine form of the victim in his hapless prey. The feminine vampire and masculine victim may initially seem less familiar. The stories will clarify all four types soon enough. But before I begin to tell my stories, let me offer a serious warning about their interpretation. As I discuss the potential for vampirism in each story's central relationship, I may seem to be implying that *all* personal relationships are pathological and vampiric. Although the last chapter attempts to dispel this impression by describing how certain kinds of relationship can, in fact, destroy the vampire, I am not able to devote as much discussion to nonvampiric relationships as to the vampiric ones, and it may eventually seem to you that all relationships are hopelessly vampiric. Therefore, let me try to inoculate you against becoming pessimistic about relationships per se.

Remember that the mythic vampire can exist only by exploiting others—it is a parasitic beast that dies in isolation. The vampire archetype is essentially the shape we give to a dark potential in all human relations, an ominous shade that creeps over us when we feel (or imagine) the absence of love and settle for exploitation. The dark potential of a relationship, like the dark potential of a person, may or may not be lived out. Jung believed that any dark potential, which he called the *shadow,* is less likely to be lived out in its destructive form if it is brought into consciousness, just as the vampire dies if it is brought into the light of day. If this book

can bring the vampiric shadow of relationships into the healing light of your consciousness, you may not have to live out the vampire's destructive energy in a personal relationship of your own.

DRACULA

Only one of the stories I have selected—*Dracula*—is explicitly about a vampire. The other, "nonvampiric" stories have a vampiric core, and reading them will accustom you to the task of feeling around for the vampiric core in your actual relationships—relationships that probably do not feature human beings whose fangs are prominent and whose mouths drip with blood. We will begin, however, with the explicitly vampiric story of Dracula, since it is the charismatic Count who has brought the vampire myth most clearly into the consciousness of our culture.

Perched on the merciless rock of the Transylvanian mountains, the towers of Castle Dracula stab at the clouds with their insolent grandeur and soar above the rude hovels of the simple folk who dwell below. Who dares to raise these cruel spires against the heavens? Who denies his own humanity and sets himself as a god upon this jagged Olympus? His name in history was Vlad III, and he was the son of a fifteenth-century warlord who fought in the Order of the Dragon for the Holy Roman emperor. When his country was suffering under the cruel hand of the Turks, it was young Vlad who drove the enemy out of his land. Vlad's ferocity in battle sent terror through the hearts of his enemies, and his decisive victories initially earned him the respect of his people.

It eventually became apparent, however, that Vlad possessed a bloodlust that surpassed the bounds of righteousness, even in the eyes of his grateful subjects. In 1461 Vlad trapped hundreds of Turkish men and women on the borders of Walachia. He marched them to the capital, ordered them stripped, and then impaled them on tall spikes. There his victims remained for months, until

their decomposed bodies had been dismembered by scavengers and the elements. Vlad justified his act as a warning to his enemies, but his subjects must have wondered why the enemies would not have been better warned by a field of corpses along the disputed border, rather than in the midst of their capital. Indeed, this massive act of brutality seems to have corrupted Vlad's image among his people. They responded to his sadistic gesture by assigning him a surname, which left him to remain throughout history as Vlad Tepes—Vlad the Impaler.

What force gave birth to Vlad's devouring fury, only part of which is explained by his wartime experiences with the merciless Turkish armies? The full answer is lost in the belly of time. Perhaps Vlad was born with an appetite for power that surpassed his human dimensions. Or perhaps, as Francis Ford Coppola suggested in his 1992 film *Bram Stoker's Dracula,* the great warrior was dealt a profound injustice by fate, an injustice that ignited his excessive predation as a gesture of defiance and revenge against the gods. Whatever the cause, Vlad Tepes vanquished the restraining force of his soul and unleashed the vampire in himself. Like Lucifer, he rebelled against the natural order and declared war on everything sacred. His bloody savagery worked in the minds of his people, transforming Vlad into a terrifying incarnation of the dragon, whose symbol (from the Order of the Dragon) was mounted on his family crest. The word for *dragon* in the Walachian tongue is *dracul,* which is also the word for *devil.* This coincidence made *dragon* an appropriate name for Vlad, since it seemed to his people that he had come to serve both evil forces. So it was that Vlad Tepes became Vlad, son of the Dragon, son of the Devil, son of Dracul. In the tongue of his people, the warlord became Vlad Dracula.

Though it takes its name from Vlad Tepes, the 1897 novel *Dracula* tells a very different tale. It begins with the journal of Jonathan Harker, a junior clerk from England, who obeys the command of his employer to travel deep into the Carpathian mountains on an errand of real estate business. Jonathan is a determined young man whose youth much resembles the youth of the man whose pen gave him life—an aspiring young stage manager and writer named Bram Stoker. Like the naïve Jonathan, Stoker wandered into the shadows of Transylvania at the command of his lively imagination, his considerable ambition, and a fortuitous dollop of synchronicity. Earlier in his life, Stoker had been captivated by Sheridan Le Fanu's popular vampire tale *Carmilla*. Later, he stumbled into an extemporaneous conversation with a professor of Oriental languages named Arminius Vámbery, who recounted the tale of a bloodthirsty medieval nobleman named Vlad Dracula. At some darkly magical moment, the stories of Le Fanu and Vámbery coalesced in Stoker's mind, and he conceived of a book in which he would tell the tale of "a vampire king rising from the tomb to go about his ghastly business" (Wolf 1975, xiii).

We can suppose that Stoker's understanding of the vampire must have evolved slowly, much as Jonathan Harker's does in the book. Although Jonathan's initial focus is on the exotic Transylvanian countryside, his attention is inexorably drawn to the peculiarities of the man with whom he is to conduct business—the mysterious Count Dracula. Of course, Jonathan does not immediately acknowledge Dracula's eccentricities. Instead, he shuns the oblique warnings of the local inhabitants and ignores his own sense of dread until he has, quite voluntarily, crossed the Count's shadowy threshold. Even when the iron doors grind shut behind him, and Jonathan finds himself face to face with the daunting figure of the Count, he perseveres in his demeanor of businesslike courtesy, and he firmly shakes the icy hand of his host.

It is not widely remembered that Stoker's original Dracula had all the physical appeal of a wharf rat. Over the intervening decades, as we have nestled into our fantasies of Dracula and his nocturnal ravishments, we have rejected and replaced Stoker's revolting image for our dark lover. Our denial of Stoker's vision is

most evident in the commercial failure of such films as the 1922 and 1979 versions of *Nosferatu,* in which Dracula is portrayed as the repulsive predator that Stoker described. Our preferred image of the Count is clearly indicated by the commercial success of the 1931 and 1979 film versions of *Dracula,* in which the monster is portrayed (by Bela Lugosi and Frank Langella, respectively) with seductive sophistication and exquisite sensuality.

The seductive appearance that our culture has assigned to Dracula is far better suited to our cultural values, our personal tastes, and, by the way, to the vampire's purpose. In our psyches, the Count is dark as night, tall as trees, and elegant as a cat. His chiseled features denote the bone-deep quality of his power. His eyes are deep pools of promise, and his mouth is a sensuous pairing of full, soft lips over probing white teeth. Our minds are enchanted and our bodies awakened by the assured cadence of his velvety voice. We fidget uneasily in our mundane rags as we stand before this magnificent aristocrat, draped in the ebony of formal attire. But our insecurities are softened by his soothing charm, and we allow him to penetrate through our fear into the pulsing depths of our hearts.

Unfortunately, the novel's Jonathan Harker does not have the benefit of Bela Lugosi's hypnotic gaze and Frank Langella's sensuous lips to sooth his doubts and bolster his denial of the truth. Instead, Jonathan must initially weave his fantasies of transcendence around "a lofty domed forehead and hair growing scantily round the temples but profusely elsewhere. . . . The mouth . . . was fixed and rather cruel-looking. . . . his ears were pale, and at the tops extremely pointed. . . . His breath was rank . . . and [as] his hands touched me, I could not repress a shudder" (Stoker 1897, 26). Jonathan's decision to enter the Count's domain has less to do with sensuality than with other motives, including ambition, pride, and perhaps (in a kinder light) compassion for the lonely aristocrat.

For a while, Jonathan fiercely clings to his stubborn innocence,

even in the face of the Count's disquieting habits. Dracula appears only at night and leaves Jonathan abruptly at the cock's crow. What's more, there are no mirrors in the castle, and when Dracula catches sight of Jonathan's small shaving mirror, he smashes it and snarls that the mirror is "the foul bauble of man's vanity!" (34). As trivial as this incident seems, it serves to provide Jonathan with some more disturbing information. Before the Count destroys his little mirror, Jonathan accidentally cuts himself shaving because he has been startled by Dracula's approach from behind. After the mirror has been smashed, Jonathan realizes that he was startled because the Count cast no reflection in the mirror as he approached. Unfortunately, Jonathan has no time to consider the importance of this news, because when Dracula catches sight of the blood that trickles from Jonathan's cut, "his eyes blazed up with a sort of demoniac fury" (33), and he attempts to grab Jonathan by the throat. This critical event is also driven from Jonathan's mind by the startling effect that his crucifix, a gift from his fiancée, Mina, has upon Dracula's ferocity: the Count instantly withdraws into a cold reserve.

Not long after this encounter with Dracula, Jonathan realizes that all the doors in the castle are locked against him, and that an exit by any window would deliver him to a precipice of more than a thousand feet. Jonathan, who so recently entered the castle's door with carefree assurance, realizes that he has become its prisoner. The young clerk abandons his falteringly cheerful whistle and enters the obscene graveyard of the castle's truth. One night, as he gazes in despair from his window, Jonathan sees the shadowy form of Dracula emerge from the window of his chambers. "My very feelings changed to repulsion and terror when I saw the whole man slowly emerge from the window and begin to crawl down the castle wall over that dreadful abyss, *face down* with his cloak spreading out around him like great wings. . . . I saw the fingers and the toes grasp the corners of the stones . . . and by

thus using every projection and inequality move downwards with considerable speed, just as a lizard moves along a wall" (41).

Now terrified, Jonathan redoubles his efforts to find an avenue of escape. In the course of his search, he comes upon a room that is adorned in a woman's fashion and falls asleep on a couch he finds there. He is awakened by the presence of three beautiful women, whose allure leads Jonathan to confide to his journal that "I felt in my heart a wicked, burning desire that they would kiss me with those red lips" (44). Here at last, Jonathan is permitted to join us in our deluding reveries about the ecstasy of vampiric ravishment. The youngest woman, she of the "great wavy masses of golden hair" (44), begins to kiss Harker with "a deliberate voluptuousness which was both thrilling and repulsive . . . as she arched her neck she actually licked her lips like an animal" (44). Suddenly, the spell is broken by the arrival of Dracula, who explodes into a rage at his consorts' presumption. Yanking one girl from Jonathan's throat, he berates all the women for touching Jonathan, who, he asserts, belongs to him. When the women chidingly ask if they are to have nothing that night, Dracula replies that they may avail themselves of the contents of a bag he has thrown upon the floor. Jonathan faints soon thereafter, when he sees the women pounce on the bag, from which emerges "a low wail, as of a half-smothered child" (46).

Jonathan finally confronts the truth in his journal, where he describes his room as a frail sanctuary from the women who wait to suck his blood. His despair is deepened when he learns that the Count is planning to leave the castle, having promised Jonathan as a reward to his female consorts. In desperation, Jonathan crawls along the outer wall to the Count's room, from which he descends to the old chapel. Among the many crates of dirt he finds there, he discovers a pile of moldy earth bearing the body of Dracula. The vampire's eyes are open and sightless as the dead, and he is without a pulse or a heartbeat, but his cheeks are warm and his lips are red. Jonathan is tempted to search the inert body for

the castle keys, but he is stopped by the Count's inescapable eyes, which despite their lifelessness are filled with such hate that Jonathan is forced to flee.

Jonathan later returns to the chapel, this time intending to kill Dracula by striking at his head with a shovel. He finds the Count markedly younger, a development that seems to be related to his being "gorged with blood . . . like a filthy leech, exhausted with his repletion." Jonathan raises his shovel, but before he can strike, "the head turned, and the eyes fell full upon me, with all their blaze of basilisk horror. The sight seemed to paralyze me. . . . The shovel fell from my hand. . . . The last glimpse I had was of the bloated face, blood-stained and fixed with a grin of malice which would have held its own in the nethermost hell" (57). Jonathan takes flight once more and vows to descend the castle walls after Dracula's departure. He contemplates risking death on the merciless rocks at the base of the castle, in order to escape a more horrible demise in the jaws of Dracula's women. We leave Jonathan's journal, imagining that we have probably heard the last from this forlorn young man whose naïveté has died in the Castle Dracula, and whose body and soul seem doomed to perish there as well.

The story shifts to Whitby, England, where another innocent, Jonathan's fiancée, Mina, awaits her beloved's return with increasing unease. Mina is occasionally distracted from her growing concern by the love tales of her close friend, Lucy Westenra. Lucy counts among her numerous suitors the brash young Quincy Morris from Texas, Dr. John Seward (in whose mental hospital the perplexing patient R. M. Renfield resides), and the wealthy aristocrat Arthur Holmwood, whom Lucy eventually decides to marry. We are given just enough time to care for this convivial group before the tranquillity of their lives is exploded by the arrival of the *Demeter,* a ghost ship bound from the Black Sea of eastern Europe.

The mystery of the *Demeter* seems initially to be an empty one. Her tiller rests in the hand of a dead captain as she slams onto the

beach during a violent storm, and she is found to hold nothing more than fifty boxes of earth and a mysterious dog, who leaps to the beach as the ship runs aground. The *Demeter* has just delivered a cargo of lethal corruption, however, and the stench of death slips over Mina and her friends as soon as the ship's hull crashes onto the Whitby shore. Lucy begins to wander about, apparently in a trance, during the chillest hours of the English night. When she awakens, she retains little of her experience, other than two small marks on her neck and a growing fatigue that is depleting her life force. Lucy regains some of her former vigor only after Mina insists on staying with her every night, preventing her from leaving the room or opening her windows to the cold night air.

Unfortunately, Lucy's convalescence is interrupted when Mina is suddenly called away to Budapest. A group of nuns has written to inform Mina that they have in their care a certain Jonathan Harker, whom they have treated ever since he was found wandering through the Transylvanian forest, sick and disoriented. In a whirl of fear and relief, Mina flies to Jonathan's side, and the couple is married in Budapest. After the wedding, Mina writes to Lucy, expressing her joy about her marriage and her deep concern about Jonathan's nightmarish experience.

Mina's letter is never opened, for Lucy's condition has deteriorated badly since Mina's departure. Alarmed, Dr. Seward calls for his mentor, Dr. Abraham Van Helsing, to come from Amsterdam. But even Van Helsing cannot bind Lucy to the world of the living, as she glides into death as twilight slips into night. Lucy Westenra is buried in the family tomb, and her grieving friends hope that her death will, at least, herald a new peace from the barrage of distressing events. But that is not to be. Soon after Lucy is buried, small children begin disappearing after sunset, only to be found hours later. Weak, disoriented, and wounded in the throat, the children tell a story of a "bloofer lady" who accosted them. With growing suspicion, Van Helsing travels to Exeter to visit Mina, who has recently returned with Jonathan from Budapest.

The Harkers' fortunes initially seem to have improved. As a reward for Jonathan's loyalty during his personal travails and professional success in eastern Europe, his recently deceased employer has bequeathed to Jonathan and Mina his real estate firm and manor house. At first blush, it appears that Jonathan has indeed achieved the goals that spurred him across Dracula's threshold. However, the cost to Jonathan and Mina has been enormous. Mina gives Van Helsing a detailed accounting, relating the contents of Jonathan's diary and his various illnesses since his escape from the Castle Dracula. Armed with this information, the Harkers and Van Helsing reunite with Morris, Holmwood, and Seward in Whitby, where Van Helsing reveals the putrid core of the mystery. He tells Lucy's friends that she has become a vampire, a *nosferatu,* an undead—a bloodsucking parasite that maintains its parody of life by stealing true life from others. Worse still, Van Helsing warns his horrified listeners, Lucy has been contaminated by another *nosferatu,* a vampire of enormous power and sophisticated cunning, a monster whose name is Dracula.

Van Helsing tells the group of friends, now allied against Dracula's depravity, that they must first kill the Lucy vampire and set Lucy's soul to rest. That night, the men slip into the graveyard and find Lucy absent from her tomb. Van Helsing now reveals all that he has been able to glean from the ancient texts with regard to the ways of vampires, speculating that the vampire's most powerful weapons may be its insidious charm and its absolute mercilessness. Van Helsing reminds the allies that the vampire is the most evil of creatures, for it preys with conscious intent upon its victims, knowing that it will transform these innocent beings into monsters that are as soulless and evil as the vampire itself. This news is bleak, but not hopeless, for it seems that the monster is not invincible. Van Helsing has learned that because the vampire is the antithesis of all that is sacred, it detests any sacred thing or place. It also abhors the buds and flowers of garlic, and as Jonathan Harker observed, it holds a special hatred for mirrors and

the light of day. Virile in the night, the vampire must seek shelter at the first glimmer of dawn, shrouding itself in the earth of its burial home, for its unholy feasting is destroyed by the sun. Furthermore, a vampire will die if it is stabbed through the heart by a stake of living wood, or if its heart is cut out of its body, or if its head is chopped off, or if it is burned to ash in a white-hot fire.

The allies begin their vampire hunt by chasing to ground Lucy's vampiric incarnation. As they corner the Lucy vampire near her tomb, her behavior corroborates Van Helsing's research—she recoils from sacred objects and garlic flowers, and as dawn nears, she evinces an animal-like desperation to return to the tomb, even to the point of casting to the ground a small child she had taken as her next victim. When the Lucy vampire is blocked from her goal by Van Helsing, her cold beauty is transformed into seething malice:

> The beautiful colour became livid, the eyes seemed to throw out sparks of hell-fire, the brows were wrinkled as though the folds of the flesh were the coils of Medusa's snakes, and the lovely, blood-stained mouth grew to an open square, as in the passion masks of the Greeks and Japanese. If ever a face meant death—if looks could kill—we saw it at that moment. (200)

Having exposed the Lucy vampire's hideous truth, Van Helsing removes from the tomb's doorsill the holy wafers that have blocked her progress, and the would-be vampire killers are witness to the vampire's transmutational power: "We all looked on in horrified amazement as we saw . . . the woman, with a corporeal body as real at that moment as our own, pass in through the interstice where scarce a knife-blade could have gone" (200). Once the Lucy vampire is locked within her tomb, her destruction becomes the responsibility of her fiancé, Arthur Holmwood, who quickly learns that while a vampire may be killed, this one will not give up without a fight:

> The Thing in the coffin writhed; and a hideous, bloodcurdling screech came from the opened red lips. The body shook and

quivered and twisted in wild contortions; the sharp white teeth champed together till the lips were cut, and the mouth was smeared with a crimson foam. But Arthur never faltered. He looked like a figure of Thor as his untrembling arm rose and fell, driving deeper and deeper the mercy-bearing stake, whilst the blood from the pierced heart welled and spurted up around it. (203–204)

Once the vampire has been destroyed, it becomes clear that something of the real Lucy remained untouched by its contamination. Her sweet beauty returns, freed from the infection that usurped her as a vehicle for its hunger. Lucy Westenra is still dead, but she is no longer undead. On whatever plane she now inhabits, Lucy is once again in possession of her soul.

With Lucy's soul safely departed on its natural journey, the allies turn with optimistic ferocity to the destruction of their nemesis, Dracula. They are knowledgeable and dedicated to their purpose, but the vampire possesses an ancient cunning that befuddles his pursuers. He first attacks Renfield, the madman in Seward's hospital, who seems telepathically connected to the vampire. Before Renfield dies, the poor man warns the allies that Dracula has chosen Mina as his next victim. And a very special victim she is to be. While the men are dashing about the countryside destroying the fifty crates of Transylvanian earth, Dracula enters Mina's room at night, shrouded in mist and dream. He first drinks her blood and then reveals his plan for her: "You, their best beloved one, are now to me, flesh of my flesh; blood of my blood . . . and shall be later on my companion and helper" (269). Dracula then takes the step that will transform Mina into his unholy mate—he cuts his chest and induces her to drink his blood.

Mina is now in Dracula's thrall and begins a descent into her own vampiric hell. Unless Dracula is destroyed, nothing can prevent her total corruption. Every night she finds her psychic bond with the vampire has intensified, and it imposes an increasing servitude on her soul with every dawn. The men can no longer con-

fide in Mina, for she is now, however unwillingly, as much Dracula's ally as theirs. Nonetheless, she can and does provide them with important clues to the vampire's whereabouts. Guided by Mina, the group embarks on a transcontinental pursuit of Count Dracula from the ports of England to the peaks of the Carpathian mountains. After a frantic chase, the allies' vampire hunt reaches its conclusion on the steps of the Castle Dracula. Since Van Helsing and Mina arrive first, the old doctor enters the castle during the day and destroys the three female vampires. Van Helsing finishes just in time to see Arthur Holmwood, Jonathan Harker, John Seward, and Quincy Morris storm up the mountain on the heels of the Gypsy cart that bears Dracula in his coffin of moldy earth. Jonathan and Quincy jump on the cart, knocking the coffin to the ground, but Mina fears it may be too late:

> [Dracula's] eyes saw the sinking sun, and the look of hate in them turned to triumph. But, on the instant, came the sweep and flash of Jonathan's great knife. I shrieked as I saw it shear through the throat, whilst at the same moment Mr. Morris' bowie knife plunged into the heart . . . almost in the drawing of a breath, the whole body crumbled into dust. (350–351)

In the next passage, Mina tells us something that may surprise those who have not actually read Bram Stoker's tale: "in that moment of final dissolution, there was in the face a look of peace, such as I never could have imagined might have rested there" (351). Even Dracula, the most formidable and ancient of vampires, apparently regains his soul when the vampiric usurper is destroyed. Dracula the vampire is killed, but it is the body of Vlad III that will be buried in the Transylvanian soil.

THE SILENCE OF THE LAMBS

It takes no great leap of induction to observe that Dracula epitomizes the empowered masculine vampire. Yet Dracula's story can mislead us when we seek the masculine psychic vampires in our lives, since their wardrobe extends far beyond the sensuous ebony of Dracula's satin cape. Examining several different kinds of relationship between masculine vampires and their feminine victims can clarify the variety of forms this duet can assume. Although these relationships are all present in *Dracula*, they are more explicitly depicted in another story of psychic vampirism—Jonathan Demme's film based on Thomas Harris's novel *The Silence of the Lambs*.

At the beginning of Demme's film we meet Clarice Starling, a courageous young FBI student who is determined to follow in the footsteps of her deceased policeman father. In the first scenes of the film, Clarice is sent by her revered FBI mentor, Jack Crawford, to interview an imprisoned serial murderer, a man who may help the FBI identify another serial murderer who is killing and skinning young women. The imprisoned murderer is Hannibal Lecter, a brilliant psychiatrist who has been nicknamed "Hannibal the Cannibal" because his preferred means for disposing of his victims was to eat them.

The distastefulness of dealing with Lecter is increased by the requirement that in order to gain access to his cell, Clarice must face off with Dr. Frederick Chilton, the lecherous, sadistic, and egomaniacal superintendent of the prison where Lecter is incarcerated. Once Clarice maneuvers past Chilton, she is confronted with Lecter, and she must marshall all her resources to avoid being physically and psychically vampirized by the predatory doctor. With her earnest innocence and incisive intuition, Clarice earns the respect of the contemptuous Lecter, with whom she cuts a dangerous deal: she will share with him some important pieces of her inner reality if he will share with her the identity of the woman-mutilating murderer who is still on the loose. The deal culminates in an intensely pressured dialogue in which Lecter provides Clarice with vital clues to the identity of the murderer, a misogynistic transvestite named Jame Gumb.

In exchange for this information, Clarice shares with Lecter

her memories of the nightmarish period following her father's death, when she was sent to live on a relative's farm at the moment when the farmer was slaughtering his lambs. Horrified by the screams of the dying lambs, the recently orphaned Clarice had opened the pen to let them out, but her efforts were futile. The condemned lambs would not leave the open pen, and little Clarice was not strong enough to carry even one of the lambs to safety. Clarice admits to Lecter that she still awakens in the night hearing the crying of the slaughtered lambs. Indeed, Clarice still yearns inside (and works in her external life) to achieve the silent peace of rescued innocents. Lecter has forced Clarice into the realm of her darkest hours, and she has stood firm throughout the ravaging experience. In return, Lecter gives her the final clues to Gumb's identity, and at a dangerously close proximity: his finger slides along Clarice's finger as he hands her the information, and we suspect that Clarice is one of the few people whom Lecter has ever touched without a subsequent bloody feast.

Although Clarice must relinquish to Crawford the final pursuit of Gumb, the FBI boss sends her to obtain some incidental evidence from the neighbors of Gumb's first victim. On this assignment, Clarice unknowingly enters the house in which Gumb is actually holding his latest victim. After being stalked by Gumb in the lightless basement of the house, Clarice succeeds in killing the murderer, thereby securing her future in Crawford's division of the FBI. In the final scenes of the film, Clarice is graduating from the FBI academy. At the reception afterward, she is congratulated by Crawford, who takes her hand—the same hand that was so recently caressed by Lecter. Then Clarice excuses herself to receive a phone call—a call that leaves her standing motionless and wide-eyed. The caller is Hannibal Lecter, who has engineered a dazzling, blood-soaked escape from custody. Lecter tells Clarice that he has decided to show her a unique mercy from his predation, since "the world is more interesting with you in it." But this does not mean that Lecter has abandoned his ghoulish ways. Even as

he grants Clarice a reprieve from his voraciousness, Lecter is stalking the sadistic Dr. Chilton, and he tells Clarice that he must hang up because he is "having an old friend for dinner."

THE CHARISMATIC MASCULINE VAMPIRE

The Silence of the Lambs contains at least four forms of the masculine psychic vampire, all of which are reminiscent of the male-female vampirism in *Dracula*. Let's discuss each of these vampiric duets, along with some ways in which these kinds of psychic vampires can be deactivated.

First, there is the obvious vampire of Demme's film, Hannibal Lecter. It is easy to see a modern incarnation of Dracula in Lecter's superhuman power, sexual magnetism, feline grace, blinding genius, cosmopolitan tastes, and of course, taste for human flesh and blood. It is interesting to note that for all his unbridled bloodlust and psychological rapacity, Hannibal Lecter's allure was sufficient to transform a middle-aged Anthony Hopkins into an international sex symbol. How we love the sensual, overwhelming power of the vampiric dominator! We will risk everything to bask in his glow and earn his acceptance (even as prey), as we seek to share in his omnipotence. From this kind of empowered vampire, Clarice Starling seeks a murderer's name and a springboard into a successful career, just as Jonathan Harker seeks from Dracula professional success and Mina Harker (I would suggest) unconsciously seeks transcendent union.

The Draculan vampire seduces us with an implicit promise of protection. Under his omnipotent wing, who would dare challenge us? I have heard many people say that as they shivered through the scene in which Clarice is trapped in the basement with Jame Gumb, they half expected Hannibal Lecter to suddenly appear and rescue her. We dream of a benefactor with Lecter's enormous power, a Draculan vampire who will protect us from the vicissitudes of life and share with us his immortal potency.

This, in fact, is what Dracula promises Mina in his pledge of matrimony and what Lecter promises Clarice in his pledge of mercy. Mina's belief in the promise is almost her undoing, but Clarice is not so vulnerable to this form of the vampire. When we last see the young FBI agent, she is huddled against the wall, looking about in fear and calling with increasing agitation into the now-dead phone, "Dr. Lecter? *Dr. Lecter? DR. LECTER?*" She is smart, our brave Clarice. She knows that "mercy" is only a relative term with a vampire like Lecter. What if he becomes bored someday and decides to find that special someone who is interesting enough to spice up his diet of blandly normal victims?

In this scene, and indeed throughout the film, Clarice keeps a death grip on her awareness of Lecter's extremely dangerous potential. Similarly, it is essential to our survival to maintain our awareness of the psychic vampire's predatory core. Mina's failure to maintain this awareness about Dracula nearly leads to her demise. The notion of maintaining one's consciousness as a means of deactivating the psychic vampire has a parallel in vampire lore: one instrument of death to the vampire, who operates at night, in our moments of unconscious oblivion, is the radiant light of day. What does daylight look like in psychological reality? When you first see the word *vampire,* the dawn of consciousness glimmers on the horizon of your mind. When you read about the vampire's essence and tactics, your consciousness ignites and sunlight pierces the morning mist. As you look to your life and recognize the vampire in yourself and others, your consciousness is blazing bright as the midday sun. It penetrates into the darkest corners of your psychic reality, shriveling the creatures of the night that feed on your life force. The more you become aware of the vampire's presence in your life, the brighter the sun of your consciousness will shine, and the safer you will be from the vampire.

Of course, it is easy to see how we might fail to remain conscious of the vampiric core in men like Lecter and Dracula, for such vampires are creatures of mesmerizing charisma and sophis-

tication. The sheen of refinement that veils their bloodlust lends power to Shakespeare's observation that "the prince of darkness is a gentleman." Nor are Lecter and Dracula simply fictional monsters—both characters were based on real men. Indeed, charismatic vampires are disturbingly common in the world, and their superhuman allure is matched only by their superhuman potential for destruction. As Maschetti has observed, the vampire

> is often an intellectual. His extremely long life, after all, permits him a considerable knowledge of the world around him, of culture, literature, art, and even music. . . . having trespassed the curtain of death, the vampire is endowed with a heightened sense of reality. This would make sense, for the vampire is also more "animal" than an ordinary human being; he is predator, he must kill in order to survive, and therefore he must listen and eye everything around him keenly and attentively in order to fulfill his purpose. He has become, furthermore, a supernatural being, and as such he possesses powers that go far beyond the human capacities we rely on for survival. (1992, 62, 92)

Maschetti makes another observation that is particularly appropriate to the depiction of Lecter, Dracula, and their psychic counterparts in the external world:

> Some vampires gloat in the limelight and in high society—their game of hide-and-seek with victims and vampire hunters providing a pleasant diversion to their eternity. The titillation and excitement of being swifter in movement, governed by laws outside those of the human world . . . [the] hypnotic powers that paralyze victims, the power to become invisible, to be, in other words, quite different from us mortals, all this must be an amusing distraction when moving amid human circles. . . . Evil is perhaps still more terrifying when met in a recognizable world. (153)

Whenever I see a man or woman of extraordinary power—be it financial, sexual, political, intellectual, or spiritual—I feel

around for the vampiric potential in that person's psyche. Certainly, there are many gifted people who are not predominantly ruled by the vampire archetype. It is difficult, however, to wield exceptional power without being subjected to the requests and manipulations of power-hungry supplicants. A charismatic person who is drained too low (even as a result of voluntary generosity) will be tempted to activate the vampire archetype in order to retrieve the lost power. Thus, many powerful people resort to vampirism in order to survive. And of course, some exceptionally powerful people, such as the psychic vampire I described in the first chapter, clearly owe their empowerment to vampirism. At the very least, every person who achieves a position of power in our narcissistic society risks activating the vampire archetype in order to survive.

We who serve as food for such charismatic psychic vampires contribute to the problem, for we are inclined to rationalize and even revere their behavior. Both Lecter and Dracula are explicitly identified in their tales as empowered persons of extreme danger, and yet both of them have become cultural sex symbols. Each of their adoring fans seems to float along in the belief that, should she encounter such a demigod, she would woo him out of his predatory ways and inspire him to pursue with her a life filled with love and transcendent fulfillment. What a rich resource these worshipers offer the vampire! What a plethora of prey! And the greatest irony of this game is that it is often the noblest of victims, like Mina, who fall most definitively into the charismatic vampire's jaws. It may be that the charismatic vampire, with his apparently godlike power, seems to the noble victim to be someone who can finally match her larger-than-average psychic force.

The chilling irony of this deception reminds me of a woman I knew who married a charismatic vampire because "he was the first man who could stand up to my personal power and meet it with his own." She did not realize that the charismatic vampire had embezzled his impressive life force from less exploitive creatures, and that she would be plundered in her turn. She only perceived in him a mate whose force could match hers, and thus she believed she had found true love. After she had bled her life into the charismatic vampire's jaws, after she had descended from a dream of self-actualization into a reality of self-loathing, after she had sacrificed her every resource in the vain hope of obtaining the loving protection of her "mate," the woman awakened from her illusion into a depleted despair. I imagine this to be the dark fate of every smart, ambitious sorority woman who marries a wealthy barracuda, no less than it is the fate of every smart, ambitious gang girl who dons her boyfriend's colors. Enchanted, aspiring, and noble, they all rush optimistically into the swirl of the vampire's cape. There they remain, cherished and protected as all food resources must be, until they no longer have the energy to qualify as food.

Of course, in order to be a vampire with the drawing power of Lecter and Dracula, one must be a person of unusual force and charisma. Unusual, yes, but it is all too easy to cite real-life examples. Think for a moment of the infamous gurus of our time. Bhagwan Shree Rajneesh, Jim Jones, David Koresh of the Branch Davidians—these are all men who held their victims captive with personal charisma and promises of transcendence over pain and death. And these are only the vampires whose plans have gone awry, the ones whose abortive predation has swept the headlines. For every one of these deposed vampires, there are many more who continue to feed on the energy of their adoring flocks. Their messages may differ, but their strategies are the same. They all offer their followers morsels of divine dispensation, in exchange for the followers' gushingly reverential attitude toward the vampiric guru.

How can we spot this kind of vampire? Charismatic vampirism is operating any time a leader or teacher sets himself up to be a conduit of wisdom, truth, or divinity that is not directly available to lesser mortals. I am thinking of a particular example in which

the teacher of an "enlightened" community shared with his clus-
ter of followers his personal version of truth, which, he assured
them, was the core of Truth itself. And perhaps he was correct.
But it seemed as if the teacher also bestowed his wisdom upon his
flock as a kind of reward for their acknowledgment of his specialness (while bestowing on certain female followers some additional
blessings of a sexual nature). Eventually, the teacher implied that
his followers' membership in his flock had exalted them to a
status above other, less "enlightened" mortals. Thus, the teacher
secured his followers' devotion by appealing to their honest desire
for transcendence, their personal sense of insufficiency, and their
human yen for specialness. And just as the teacher fed off his followers' subordinate status on the pyramid of "enlightenment," so
his followers fed off the subordinate status of those who (they had
learned) were less "enlightened" than they.

The teacher in this story displays most of the symptoms of
charismatic vampirism. But beyond these, there is one sure way
to know whether someone we admire is acting as a charismatic
vampire or simply a wise soul. When we approach the person,
how does he respond to us? If the object of our esteem is acting
nonvampirically, he will greet our admiration by holding up a
double-sided mirror. The mirror shows us that the power we perceive in the teacher is actually a projection of our own power, and
it also invites us to look for the blemishes that attest to our own
humanity. Similarly, the teacher's side of the mirror will render an
honest reflection that shows the teacher, every time he teaches, to
be a human blend of implicit power and explicit weakness. The
vampiric guru, on the other hand, will greet our admiration by
holding up a magnifying glass, with the glass positioned such that
it both magnifies (or more precisely, inflates) our perception of the
vampire's glory, while it diminishes the vampire's perception of
us. This mirror-or-magnifying-glass test is, in fact, a good way to
spot many kinds of psychic vampire, since all vampires will want

to magnify their power in our regard, while simultaneously diminishing our power in theirs.

The mirror-or-magnifying-glass test is also consistent with the lore that vampires cast no reflection in a mirror and, in fact, that they detest all reflective surfaces. In Stoker's novel, Dracula snatches up a little shaving mirror and smashes it in a frenzy of rage. This scene tells us that we can break through the poised assurance of most psychic vampires by confronting them with a mirror of their vampiric behavior. Although the myth doesn't say so, however, it is only a certain type of mirroring that the vampire detests. Vampires seek to exploit others, and anything that feeds their sense of power, particularly in comparison to others, will be perceived as a good thing. A mirror full of compliments is ambrosia to most vampires.

What charismatic vampires loathe is a mirror that casts a true reflection, one that includes both strength and weakness, both light and shadow. The nonvampiric teacher, in contrast, knows what Heraclitus knew: the mirror is essential to true teaching, because the real teacher is truth itself, both dark and light, and truth is always hidden in our midst and in ourselves. Thus, the nonvampiric teacher will want all students to look in the mirror for their inner truth, both dark and light, so they won't project it outward onto the teacher. This is the only way that true teaching can occur, because the teacher is not burdened with inflationary projections, and the students are not disabled or deluded by projecting away their own power. What's more, when the students refrain from viewing the teacher as a source of truth, the teacher's vampire archetype is less likely to be activated by the students' projection of superhumanity.

A charismatic vampire can don the guru mantle in many settings, not necessarily religious. He can work his "guru whammy" in any corporation where he has accumulated sufficient power to set himself up as a demideity. And charismatic vampires have historically plagued the political arena; Caesar, Napoleon, Hitler,

and Joe McCarthy were all leaders whose psyches were driven by the charismatic vampire. And the field of fine arts has been rife with charismatic vampires, such as Rodin and Picasso, who fueled their work with the creative energy of their families, lovers, and protégés.

But beyond these notorious examples, some of the most nefarious cases of charismatic vampirism occur in the healing professions—particularly in my own field of psychology. As the Jungian analyst Adolf Guggenbühl-Craig has observed in his landmark book *Power in the Helping Professions,* we who are in the business of healing the psyche are haunted by the vampiric shadows of our quasi-medical, quasi-spiritual profession. Specifically, because we can easily be misled by the projections of our clients or by our ignorance of ourselves, we are in constant danger of becoming charlatans who peddle spurious treatments for purely personal gain or false prophets who spout facetious dogma for purely personal aggrandizement. This is why we who achieve some expertise in matters of the psyche should pay close attention to the story of Darth Vader in the *Star Wars* movies. Darth is a powerful leader whose darkness is all the more dangerous for his having been a Jedi knight. In a similar way, any healer or teacher of the psyche can become all the more vampiric for being knowledgeable about psychic processes.

THE MEDIOCRE MASCULINE VAMPIRE

Regardless of the field in which they operate, charismatic vampires are extremely seductive and therefore extremely dangerous. But a lack of charisma does not prevent less powerful folks from becoming vampires. For example, in *The Silence of the Lambs* and *Dracula* we find examples of a noncharismatic masculine vampire that preys on others quite successfully, despite his mediocre empowerment; the two asylum wardens, Dr. Frederick Chilton in *The Silence of the Lambs* and Dr. John Seward in *Dracula,*

both medical men of mediocre talent that is insufficient to support their ambitions.

Mediocre vampires like Chilton and Seward cannot compete with vampires like Lecter and Dracula (who can prey on the choicest of victims), so they must settle for whatever prey they can subdue. They frequently appear in the external reality at the level of drill sergeants, prison guards, social service managers, bureaucratic administrators, and medical care supervisors. (The Big Nurse who supervises the psychiatric ward in Ken Kesey's *One Flew Over the Cuckoo's Nest* is a superb example of a mediocre masculine vampire in a female body.) The victims of mediocre masculine vampires are often the incarcerated, the sick, the poor, and the insane, but they can also be people who are simply less empowered than the vampire. In *Dracula,* for example, Seward politely lusts after Lucy, who as a woman in a patriarchy wields less power than he. Chilton, much less politely, lusts after Clarice. Lucy rebuffs Seward's advances by marrying a more powerful man, while Clarice rebuffs Chilton by taking refuge in the power of her FBI boss.

Lucy's and Clarice's rebuffing suggests another means of destroying the vampire, one that is implied but never explored in the vampire legend. The beast avoids its demise by stealing the life force of others; consequently, in the absence of stolen power it would starve to death. Given the abundance of willing victims in our vampire-smitten society, death by starvation does not seem to be the greatest threat to the vampire, and I have not found any lore in which a vampire dies from starvation. But such a possibility is an obvious corollary to its ravenous hunger. The vampire is a parasite, lacking in substance or sustenance when it can't find a nourishing host. Without a victim, I imagine that the vampire would revert to its essence—a cold, sucking, lightless void, and under the force of its remorseless hunger, the starving vampire would shrivel and fall in on itself, until it imploded into death.

I once met a woman who seemed to incarnate this awful

image. She was a woman of mediocre charms, but she seemed magnificent when compared to her daughter, who was a vacuous blob at her side. The daughter eventually died of an elusive illness in which her vital organs shut down, one by one, like embers going cold in the night. When I saw the mother about a year later, her charm had hardened into a litany of stylized grimaces and affections. At first I thought that she was suffering from her grief, but her face in repose showed no sadness, only depletion. When I saw the woman again a year later, she had become a grinning, agitated mannequin—a windmill that continued to spin long after the well had gone dry. I realized that while some survivors are folding inward with grief, others are actually dwindling from starvation.

When we contemplate starving a vampire, we enter a danger zone, for the act cries out to our soulful compassion. Clarice does not appear to suffer any pangs of conscience about her refusal of Chilton, but Lucy rattles on at length about the difficulty of saying no to Seward. This dangerous form of altruism reminds me of a woman I once knew who admitted, with much anguish, that she would rather jeopardize her own mental well-being than confront her father about his continual attempts (often successful) to dominate her life. When we falter at the prospect of saying no to the vampire, we must remember that we are starving only the vampiric invader that infects the psyche of its human host—a person who might discover real love if only the vampire were to die.

In *Dracula* and *The Silence of the Lambs,* the frustrations of the rebuffed asylum lords are not targeted directly at the women who have denied them access to their life force. Instead, these mediocre vampires sink their scientific teeth into their straitjacketed charges—Renfield in Seward's case and Lecter in Chilton's. Seward sees Renfield as his ticket to scientific renown, much as Chilton attempts to build his reputation by parlaying Lecter into a political showstopper. Mediocre psychic vampires prowl the external reality in much the same way. When they fail at luring the choicest prey, they stalk whatever prey they can catch. We see the victims of mediocre vampires in every childhood abuse survivor who marries an insecure abuser, in every desperate employee who trusts an exploitive boss, and in every prostitute who accepts the "protection" of a pimp. Mediocre vampires such as Chilton and Seward are the henchmen of history; they prey on whomever they can subdue—usually those on the bottom rungs of the societal ladder.

THE OPPRESSED MASCULINE VAMPIRE

And what about the people on society's bottom rungs? Are there no masculine vampires among them? Are they too disempowered to find weaker victims on whom to prey?

Even among the abused, the insane, the impoverished, the sick, and the rejected there is room for a certain kind of oppressed but desperate vampire. In *The Silence of the Lambs* and *Dracula,* this kind of vampire is manifested in the characters of Jame Gumb and R. M. Renfield. Gumb and Renfield occupy the lowest rungs of their respective social ladders. Renfield is psychotic in a time when the mentally ill were regarded as little more than animals, while Gumb incarnates several demons in our contemporary collective mind: he is poor, he is psychotic, and worst of all in our homophobic culture, he is a man of alternative gender identity. Not that Renfield and Gumb are benign—in truth, they are both very dangerous. Both have deliberately given themselves over to the dark side of the psyche, and both explicitly serve the forces that lurk in those unsavory depths.*

Gumb and Renfield both take their victims by force, although the victims are lured by these vampires' pretended weakness. Renfield uses the compassion of his asylum caretakers to facilitate

---

*In the film, Gumb is devoted to his brood of *Acherontia atropos,* the death's head moth, which is the same moth that Dracula sends for Renfield to eat—a delicacy among his many nonhuman conquests.

their victimization by Dracula, while Gumb exploits his victims' sympathy for his pain, as he pretends to move a large chair into his van with one arm in a cast. When his targeted victim tries to help him, he maneuvers her into the van and clubs her with the fake cast. Renfield and Gumb incarnate the form of the vampire that we probably fear the most—the Ted Bundy or Jeffrey Dahmer who ferments in his psychic hell, then pops up unpredictably to snatch innocent victims from the womb of their insulated society. It seems from the work of therapists such as Alice Miller that oppressed vampires are seeking from their victims a little chunk of the power they lost to an unnamed vampire in their past. The only power they have left for this task of retribution is their superior strength and cunning, which are sometimes sufficient to ensnare an innocent victim.

Although we greatly fear oppressed vampires like Gumb and Renfield, they actually may be the hardest to spot. Since the oppressed vampire is so desperately and explicitly vampiric, he must hide his vampirism under a cape of acceptability until the moment of his attack. He must stalk and strike and flee, then stuff the evidence of his predation into some dark hole of his psyche, until hunger drives him back into the dangerous open spaces where an outraged society awaits, bent on revenge. Oppressed vampires are dangerous because they have been placed (and so place themselves) outside society's rules. They cannot consistently maintain the guise of innocuous solicitude that empowers mediocre vampires like Seward and Chilton, and they lack any Draculan charisma. Still, the oppressed vampire can masquerade for short periods as a safe or even pitiable soul, particularly if we are gullible to his disguises of pathos and infirmity.

Once we are in the clutches of an oppressed vampire, we are usually in extreme peril, but this does not mean that we have no defenses at our disposal. The stories of *Dracula* and *The Silence of the Lambs* indicate that one way, and perhaps the only way, to protect oneself from an oppressed vampire is to employ the most famous method for killing a vampire—piercing its heart with a sharp stake of living wood. The vampire lore tells us that our stake should be between two and three feet long and made of strong wood that can withstand a heavy blow without shattering. The blow must be forceful enough to kill the monster with a single stroke. If the vampire's heart is not pierced with the first impact of the mallet, the monster will simply reanimate in its fury to wreak a bloody revenge. The most desirable woods from which to fashion the stake are hawthorn and ash. Hawthorn's early spring bloom signals the beginning of spring's rebirth from winter's death—a regenerative moment that would be odious to the vampire. Ash is the wood of Yggdrasil, the tree of Norse mythology from which all life was created.

What does the vampire-killing stake look like in human relations? In the story of *Dracula*, Mina's compassion for Renfield penetrates his heart long enough to deactivate his psychic vampire, thereby allowing him to warn her of Dracula's plans. In *The Silence of the Lambs*, the stake takes quite a different form: The latest of Gumb's victims, Catherine, manages to psychically impale Gumb's vampire by abducting and holding hostage his pampered little poodle, Precious. Catherine realizes that Precious is the only stake she can drive into Gumb's heart, and although it takes the arrival of Clarice to break the stalemate, Catherine's dognapping does serve to stymie the vampiric Gumb long enough to keep her alive for her rescue.

THE NOBLE MASCULINE VAMPIRE

Each of the masculine vampires I have described—the Lecters and Draculas, the Chiltons and Sewards, the Renfields and Gumbs—is dangerous in his own way, and each tends to endanger a particular kind of feminine victim. Far more dangerous than all of these, however, (particularly for the most conscious of feminine victims), are the noble vampires, who operate under the cloak of

valor, integrity, and social approbation. In *The Silence of the Lambs* and *Dracula,* this kind of vampire is manifested in the characters of Clarice's FBI boss, Jack Crawford, and the distinguished Dr. Abraham Van Helsing.

Crawford is a man of strength, courage, and incisive intelligence who replaces Clarice's adored father, a town marshal who was killed in the line of duty. Clarice relishes Crawford's special attention to her, a mere candidate in the FBI training school. When Crawford calls upon Clarice to interview Lecter and pursue the case of Gumb's serial killing, Clarice is deeply flattered. He is her hero, her champion, her king and her protector . . . or is he? It is Crawford who sends the loyal Clarice to interact with a man who has repeatedly savaged others both physically and psychologically. Lecter's power is such that he has talked a man in the next cell into killing himself by swallowing his tongue. Nonetheless, Crawford sends Clarice back to Lecter again and again, and he even uses her to present Lecter with a dangerously false offer of better quarters in exchange for information. Crawford repeatedly uses Clarice to further his own ends, once by withholding important information from her, and once by disparaging her as a woman in a room full of men. In the film's climactic scenes, it is Crawford who sends Clarice to the house where Gumb nearly kills her, and at the end of the story, Crawford takes Clarice's hand with a deliberate possessiveness that mirrors the attitude that Lecter displayed when he stroked the same fingers. We sense that Clarice, who is so careful to avoid Lecter's dangerous enticements, would fall on her sword for Crawford. Indeed, she nearly dies in the pursuit of his wishes.

The peril in which Crawford places Clarice is similar to the danger in which Mina is placed by Van Helsing. Like Crawford, Van Helsing's ostensible motivation is to protect a special woman by eliminating a threatening vampire. The truth of the matter, however, is that Van Helsing, with his secretive machinations and his vengeful fanaticism, repeatedly organizes the group's actions

such that Mina is nearly destroyed by Dracula. Certainly, Van Helsing and Crawford value the profound strength and level-headed intelligence of Mina and Clarice. But for all the respect and appreciation that Van Helsing and Crawford grant their young female protégées, they do not fulfill the obligation implied by the word *protégée,* which in French means "the protected one." In other words, they do not protect Mina and Clarice. In fact, the gravest dangers the young women face are brought about by the actions of their mentors, who use the women to achieve their personal goal as bait to lure and entrap their foes.

To be sure, Crawford and Van Helsing give every indication that their conscious purpose is to ensure the well-being of Clarice and Mina. But a solicitous demeanor does not preclude a capacity for vampirism. Indeed, most vampires display some level of concern for their victims' well-being—doesn't one feed and shelter the lamb up to the moment of slaughter? Even Gumb and Renfield make efforts to husband their captive prey: Gumb commands his victims to moisten their precious skins with lotions, and Renfield sacrifices juicy little flies in order to nourish a treasured spider he plans to consume later. Lecter and Dracula are also solicitous of Clarice and Mina, since they wish to hoard the women's life force for their sole enjoyment. Lecter springs to Clarice's aid when she is attacked by the man in an adjoining cell, thereby ensuring her return. Later he feeds her morsels of information about Gumb's identity, in exchange for her traumatic memories that fuel his famished soul. Similarly, Dracula feeds Mina his own blood after depleting hers, so that she will enter the immortal state of vampirism, rendering her life force available to him for all eternity. Similarly, Crawford and Van Helsing make efforts to protect their female aides, even as they are exploiting their power and endangering their lives.

True, most of these men are more conscious of their protective efforts toward the women than they are of their exploitation. The person who slaughters the lambs gives more attention to feeding

his charges than to the ax in his hand. And who is to say that the wife-battering husband doesn't focus on the lovely income he provides to his human whipping post? Who is to say that the vampiric boss doesn't focus on the bounty of opportunity he extends to his exploited subordinate? Who is to say that the pimp doesn't focus on the roof he puts over the heads of the women whom he bleeds of money and self-esteem? In each of these cases, the vampire may experience actual feelings of care for his victim, as well he should if he is to maximize her nutritional value. Although the vampire is a predator, his actions are not unilaterally predatory; often he behaves with genuine concern for the victim he is about to exploit. And why not? His survival is dependent on the lamb he is fattening for slaughter.

Vampirism and the Father-Daughter Relationship

The most alarming aspect of this fattening-the-lamb scenario is that the victims of attentive vampires usually respond to the vampire's gift of exploitive solicitude with return gifts of loyalty and love. In *Dracula* and *The Silence of the Lambs,* Mina and Clarice acquiesce gratefully to Van Helsing and Crawford. They willingly place their lives and souls in the balance, and they count themselves fortunate for the opportunity to do so. Like good little girls who ache to earn the love of a kingly father, Mina and Clarice throw themselves into the fray, pledging their gifts to the cause of a mentor who can appreciate them like no other. And here we come to an important root of the tangled vine that binds female victims to masculine vampires: the relationship between daughters and their vampiric fathers. Among the very good books about the intricate dance of exploitation between fathers and daughters in our patriarchal culture, two—Marion Woodman's *Leaving My Father's House* and Linda Leonard's *The Wounded Woman*—are most pertinent to this discussion. Woodman and Leonard observe that many men seek their empowerment in the loyal adoration of

a stalwart, loving female, and that the prime candidate for this role frequently falls to their daughters. Let's revisit the vampires in *The Silence of the Lambs* and *Dracula* to see how various vampiric fathers might feed on their daughters' love.

For the oppressed vampiric fathers, the Renfields and the Gumbs, daughters are usually taken by violence and forced to succumb in whatever manner is possible. Sexual and physical assault are common forms of vampirism among this kind of predator, but there are subtler methods as well, such as psychological harassment, emotional torment, societal degradation, and financial extortion. For the mediocre vampiric fathers, the Chiltons and Sewards, the more indirect methods of feeding on a daughter's power are innuendo, manipulation, bribery, and derision. The lure of charismatically vampiric fathers, the Lecters and Draculas, is their excessive giftedness. Although some daughters are conscious and strong enough to avoid the power bait of a Draculan father, every charismatic father-vampire knows that there will come a moment of weakness in his daughter's life when, at the promise of shared empowerment, she will leap into his jaws. As for the nobly vampiric fathers, such as Crawford and Van Helsing, the game is the simplest and the most nefarious, since it can be played with minimal consciousness by both father-vampire and daughter-victim. The game is based on a subtle dance in which the father exalts the daughter, who reveres him in return, giving her blood as the proof of her love.

The vampirism of daughters by their fathers is bleak but not surprising, since the patriarchy despises anything feminine, particularly the feminine energy that lives in all men. An example is the story about a man who, like so many men, was afraid of displaying or even acknowledging his feminine side. His fear was understandable, given the virulence of gynophobia and homophobia in the patriarchy. But since this man did not live out his inner feminine energy, which the Jungians call the *anima,* he was forced to seek her on the outside by projecting her (unconsciously, of

course) onto a variety of mortal women. Because the man did not perceive a distinction between his feminine projection and the human screens onto which he projected it, he would suck up the women's energy as if it were his own—which it seemed to him, in his muddled state, to be. His mother initially made a good target for his projection of anima, but because society mocks the man who is oedipally attached to his mother he shifted his projection to his wife. Yet his wife was not a satisfactory idol, because after the first few years of marriage, she wouldn't maintain her unconditional adoration for the man. Instead, she tended to sink into adamant assertiveness or realistic appraisal, which made her a lousy projection screen for the man's beloved anima.

But then the man found the perfect candidate for his projection. She was full of life force, anxious to serve, and best of all, a woman of his own blood—his daughter. She loved him and sought to please him in any way he would let her. And so the man was fed, and his daughter was happy to feed him. She feed him for as long as her blood and ideals held out, which wasn't forever, since her father had discovered that there were many ways she could feed him—intellectual stimulation, professional accomplishment, sexual favors. All were within her power and, he believed, within her pleasure as well. At least, that's what she told her beloved father. So the man was reassured that the game was a good one, that the pleasure was his daughter's to give and his to receive. And so they went, until the daughter had no more to give.

Since the daughter in this vampiric relationship was well socialized, her final depletion looked like an event of her own making, for it was manifested as addiction, depression, and self-destructive behavior. The father grieved over his daughter's misery, and his pain was real, for his life source was threatened. Without her to animate him, to give life to the rest of his soul by incarnating his feminine side, the man felt he would surely die (without understanding the root of his feelings, of course).

This man's concern for his feminine life source is mirrored in

the climax of *Dracula,* when the male heroes slay the vampire in Mina's defense: "At this point . . . the men are seen as chivalric knights pledged to heroic deeds for the sake of Mina's salvation. Here, perhaps more than in any other place, Mina's name may have emblematic meaning. Spelled backwards, it almost achieves the Latin *anima,* or soul" (Wolf 1975, 264). It seems these men were fighting to save their own animas, as much as (or more than) the soul of Mina Harker.

DEACTIVATING THE MASCULINE VAMPIRE

Of the several mythological examples of vampirism in the father-daughter relationship, two from Greek mythology—the stories of Athena and Aphrodite—show how such a relationship can come into being, and how it can be deactivated.

The goddess Athena sprang at birth from the head of her sky-god father, Zeus, and so she felt she was a daughter without a mother. Athena went on to become a true father's daughter, relying on her head—that is, her reason and intellect—to guide her actions, and ignoring the softer, more compassionate voices of her intuition and feeling. In her worst moments, Athena is the intellectual minion of her father's patriarchy, a heartless engine of logic and law whose implacable anger is the shadow side of her potential for profound feeling. If Zeus commands, Athena complies, thus earning the cherished praise of her father, even though she must occasionally sacrifice the truth of her own feminine soul in the process. Athena's energy is often an influential force in the woman who succeeds in male-dominated arenas. In the psyche of this kind of woman, the masculine (father) is often revered, while the softer energy of the receptive, carnal feminine (mother) is often reviled. At her worst moments, the Athenian woman can deteriorate into a merciless harpy, and over the course of her tenure in the patriarchy, she will often find that her clarity and reason have well served her father (as he is incarnated in her masculine mentors), but at the cost of her feminine heart.

Aphrodite is the daughter of Uranus, a sky god who was a cultural ancestor to the sky god Zeus. Before Aphrodite was born, Uranus had several children by his earth-goddess wife, Gaia. Uranus was disgusted by earthy Gaia and their earthbound children, just as the modern patriarchy is disgusted by the earthiness of women's body matters. Uranus tried to incarcerate his brood out of his sight and under the earth, but one of his sons, Cronus, escaped to wreak revenge on his father. He managed to cut off Uranus's genitals, which fell into Gaia's sea and mingled with the sea foam, giving birth to Aphrodite. Like Athena, Aphrodite believes herself to be a motherless daughter of her sky-god father. Born of Uranus's genitals, Aphrodite becomes the essence of sexual union and carnal empowerment, relying on her body and her seductiveness to shape her life, and often ignoring the clearer voices of knowledge and discipline. In the worst case, Aphrodite becomes the sexual minion of her father's patriarchy, a shameless harlot whose libidinous self-indulgence brings pain to her consorts and ridicule to herself. Aphrodite serves the sexual needs of the patriarchy, as well as her own carnal lust, which earns her the approving wink of the male gods, even though she must sacrifice her feminine dignity in the process.

Aphrodite's energy is an influential force in the psyche of the woman who succeeds by means of her passionate sexual allure. A close look at the psyche of an Aphrodisian woman will often reveal a framework in which the masculine is revered, though in a more sexual way than the intellectual respect offered by Athena-driven women. Similarly, the Aphrodisian woman will often dismiss or distrust her potential for independence, and at her worst moments, the woman deteriorates into a de-selfed trollop. These women often find themselves after several years in a situation where the father (incarnated in her masculine consorts) has been served by the woman's intimate sexuality, but at the cost of her independence and dignity.

Although Athena-inspired women tend to dismiss as simpering

whores the women inspired by Aphrodite, and although Aphrodite-inspired women tend to dismiss as heartless viragos the women inspired by Athena, the myths of these two goddesses and the energy fields they represent are really quite similar. Similar, too, are the means for healing the father-daughter vampirism evident in these goddesses's stories and in the women inspired by them.

Both Athena and Aphrodite are born of authoritarian sky-god fathers, and both initially seem to be without mothers. In fact, they both have mothers who were victims of the sky gods' tyranny. Athena's true mother, the ancient goddess Metis, was swallowed by Zeus. When Athena springs from Zeus's head, she has actually been born of Metis. Similarly, Aphrodite's true mother, the earthy Gaia, was disowned by Uranus in a futile attempt to disempower her and her children. While Aphrodite may not acknowledge the feminine half of her ancestry, it was in Gaia's sea cradle that she was born. Thus, in both stories, a sky father's vain attempt to maintain his absolute power results in the birth of a daughter who perceives herself to be motherless and who focuses her attention on placating the masculine. In their shadow aspects, both Athena and Aphrodite turn on their sisters and pander to the masculine, thereby compromising themselves (intellectually in Athena's case and sexually in Aphrodite's) in order to curry the patriarch's favor. They feed on the empty calories of the father's reflected glory and bleed out their souls in the process.

For Athena to heal the wound from her intellectual servitude to the patriarchy, she must reclaim her feminine ground by rediscovering the passionate power of her mother, Metis, independent of her oppressive wounding by Zeus. And for Aphrodite to heal the wound from her sexual servitude to the patriarchy, she must reclaim her feminine ground (or more precisely, ocean) by rediscovering the spiritual power of her mother, Gaia, independent of her oppressive wounding by Uranus. In both myths, the daughter who is born of her father's head (the literal one in Athena's case

and the phallic one in Aphrodite's) can cut herself loose from her patriarchal birthplace only by reclaiming her feminine ground— the bodily matter (and *mater*) of her soul. This coincidental imagery is reminiscent of the vampire lore that states that beheading a vampire will result in its death. Both Athena and Aphrodite must cut themselves off from their patriarchal "heads" and reestablish themselves in their bodies in order to break the dynamic of father-daughter vampirism.

The vampire is heartless and soulless, but not without mind, and the mind one of the psychic vampire's most loyal defenders. How quick we are to justify our behavior, no matter how vampiric! To quote Jeff Goldblum's character from the 1984 film *The Big Chill*, "Rationalization is more important than sex. You don't believe me? Try going for a week without one good rationalization." The mind's propensity for rationalization is dangerous when the psychic vampire is activated, for it promotes the illusion that logic and thought constitute the entirety of the psyche, which renders feeling and intuition into a meaningless mirage. In order for the psychic vampire to be killed, the mind must be briefly unplugged; that is, the rationalizing psyche must be beheaded.

In myth, the weapon of choice for beheading a vampire is a clergyman's ax or a silver sword, both of which must be wielded like the stake-pounding mallet—with a single deadly blow. A one-strike decapitation is quickly accomplished in the reductionist imagery of myth, but as Monsieur Guillotine observed long ago, the actual truth is that we are not so easily separated from our heads. The psychic truth is identical: the tyranny of reason is pervasive in the psyches of most human beings, and we are remarkably inept at beheading ourselves and unplugging our minds. (Perhaps this is why the legend tells us to place the severed head of the vampire far from its former position at the neck—under the arm or at the feet—so the head won't reattach itself and enable the vampire to reanimate.) This is not to imply that our minds are evil or destructive per se. The mind is an invaluable servant whose brilliant logic is simply corrupted by its delusion that it is the master. It is actually the soul—that which we profoundly feel, intuitively know, and innately are—that is designed to reign supreme in the psyche. The soul needs its logical servant to incarnate its essence, but the soul is meant to be the Why behind the logic. When the mind does its work in the service of the soul, the result is psychic art.

Unfortunately, our minds more often operate in a vacuum, revving themselves like manic hamsters in a cage: goals, plans, reasons, and facts, all whirling around until the little dynamo is stopped by death. Sometimes death stops our minds with a direct blow of its scythe, but more often our frenzied logic is halted by the deathly chill we feel in depression. In these icy moments, our minds must pause and shiver in the awareness of their own hollow mortality. The meaningless solitude of this place is intolerable, and most of the time our minds try to flee the painful truth by resuming their frenetic spin. But occasionally, in a moment of desperate grace, we dangle in the void long enough to ask, "Why? Why die? Why live? Oh, *why*?" And in that moment, the mind acknowledges its sovereign, the soul—the source of all Why. When the mind releases its iron grip on the psyche, feeling and instinct are permitted a fleeting chance to prevail. Broadly speaking, we are most likely to get out of our heads when we get into our bodies—when we take a hot bath (with bubbles and music and candles, as all baths should be taken), when we get a massage, when we let our bodies feel and move with joy, and when we are physically injured or sick. At these times, we have the opportunity to slip free from the collar of linear reason and the iron rule of our will. The mind is benumbed, and the feeling/dreaming/knowing body prevails. Whenever we are in a state that places the mind in service to the body and the soul, then we are truly beheaded, and the vampire within us may die in that moment.

What does this feel like in external reality? My best example is a personal one. Once when I was visiting friends in France, I

strained my back and then became ill just before my scheduled departure. Although I am very comfortable in my friends' home, I wanted—or more exactly, I felt that my *body* wanted—quite unreasonably and quite desperately, to return home on schedule. Against all reason and will, I acquiesced to my body's yearning for home, and thus began our most memorable journey together. The place where my friends live is a thirty-six-hour trip (involving planes, trains, and automobiles, plus a lot of waiting) from the place where I live. As I lay in their guest room, I wondered how I would ever make the long journey with a congested head, an aching back, and infuriated intestines. In an apparently impossible act of negotiation, I—that is to say, my mind—made a deal with my body. "I will do all the planning, caretaking, and problem solving. But I can only do superficial things to open your ears, ease your muscles, and calm your intestines long enough to endure this journey. I will do my best for you in order to get you home, and I will trust you to do the rest." Thus, for the next forty-eight hours, I was beheaded—my mind placed itself at the feet of my body, in its proper role as the devoted servant to my soul.

What I remember most from that journey is a deep feeling of calm. "I" knew my role; "I" served the Why. The Why was something deeper and greater that wanted to go home. I trusted and served its needs, and it, in turn, entrusted itself to my service and did its part to help. My ears unplugged when the plane took off. My back did not pursue its threat to spasm. My intestines were quiet and still. My mind and my body were gentle and calm. No yearning, no trembling, no anger or angst. For those forty-eight hours, the vampire was dead. And indeed, I felt that I was living the epitaph on the grave of Nikos Kazantzakis, which says, "I desire nothing . . . I fear nothing . . . I am free." I would happily spend the remainder of my life in that state. But as Linda Leonard has observed, in order to kill the vampire, we must "fight this battle, not just once but daily" (1986, 107).

Although I'm never sure I understand what Carl Jung wrote, I

think that he might have called my journey home from France an exercise in "consciousness." Jung postulated that if we are lucky, we reach a point where we recognize that *the mind is not alone in the psyche.* We learn that some of our psychological experiences are not accessible to linear thought and logical analysis, and we grant our internal reality the same respect and attention as our external reality. We entertain the possibility that our dreams are more than meaningless pictures in our sleep, and that there is a symbolic language relating body and soul. These are the moments when, in Jung's view, we have embarked on the journey of consciousness. In order to begin this journey, it seems, we must chop off our heads in order to escape the mind's tyranny and explore the rest of our psyches. As the heart and body and soul find their voices, the psyche is brought into health. This is the task of every Athena and Aphrodite: to cut off the tyrannical "head" of her patriarchal mind-set and reclaim the feminine ground of her soul.

Now let's bring the myths of Athena and Aphrodite back to the stories of *Dracula* and *The Silence of the Lambs.* A woman must be in a healthy relationship with all of her feminine power—mind, heart, and body—or she is likely to bleed out her life for a patriarch's love. The vampiric exploitation of the formidable Mina and Clarice tells us, however, that a healthy relationship with one's feminine matter and *mater* is not sufficient to defend us against the temptation of a noble vampire. In the Dracula myth, Mina's rescue and redemption is actually accomplished by the efforts of the men around her, which we might interpret as a rescue of the woman by the positive masculine energy in her personality. Similarly, Clarice survives her encounter with Jame Gumb by dint of her masculine FBI training. These stories suggest that we must be in a healthy relationship to our positive masculine side, as well as our feminine ground, in order to survive vampiric attack.

In chapters 4 and 5 I will talk more about the use of masculine energy to defend against the vampire. For the moment, I'll just

observe that a strong relationship with *all* of our positive energies, both masculine and feminine, is integral to our safety when vampires are skulking nearby. This is true in our struggles with the masculine vampire, but it is just as applicable in our struggles with a kind of vampire we seldom see in Western lore: the vampire who operates under the feminine veil of vulnerability. The masculine vampire is dangerously seductive to his compassionate feminine victims, but the allure of the feminine vampire can be even deadlier bait. That is the moral of our next set of tales—stories of feminine vampires who prey on feminine victims. Onward into the darkness, for we have only begun our journey.

FEMININE VAMPIRES AND FEMININE VICTIMS

In Asian folklore the vampire bears little resemblance to Bram Stoker's powerful lord of the undead. Instead, the Asian vampire appears to its victims as a sweet mist that wafts alluringly by the side of the nighttime road. The unwary passerby, sensing in the mist an inviting vulnerability, enters the soft cloud with the dream of enjoying its gentle caress. Once the ethereal vapor has enveloped its victim, it coalesces into a suffocating fog, and the victim wanders around in circles, gagging on the syrupy air. The victim senses the sharp, clear relief of the air outside, but her liberation seems to portend a cold solitude, so she recoils back into the vapor's cloying embrace. Despite her distrust of the outside world, however, the victim occasionally breaks free of the smothering cloud and stumbles into the crisp night air. She glances back at the mist, which is sadly huddled once more by the side of the road, wishing only for someone on whom it can bestow its sweet, gentle affection. The victim falters and slows to a halt, then turns around and tentatively approaches the inviting mist. The night is cold, the road is isolated, and no one is in sight—save the mist. The victim runs her hand through the vapor, which swirls enticingly in response. The victim relents, reenters, and begins anew her dance with the feminine vampire.

The Asian vampire's veil of sweet vulnerability is as effective as a Draculan cloak of power when it comes to baiting the hook. This "vulnerable" vampire I call feminine because the role of vul-

nerability has generally fallen to women in our patriarchy. Yet this archetype is not only active in the psyches of women but also available to men who can don the veil of disempowerment. A feminine vampire is stalking you whenever you feel beholden to a helpless waif who promises loving gratitude in exchange for your life force—a waif who implies that the guilt will be all yours if she should suffer from your refusal to comply with her request.

The myth of the feminine vampire is not well known in the West, but it is high time we brought it into the clear light of our consciousness, for the archetype it describes has permeated our psyches as deeply as that of the Draculan vampire. More deeply, perhaps, since our unconsciousness about the feminine vampire grants her free access to our psychic depths, where she can feed on us at her soft, cloying will. She preys upon the strong as well as the weak, but I will first address the ways she feeds on vulnerable feminine victims, the better to compare her predatory tactics with those of the masculine vampire of the previous chapter. Listen now to a story that haunted your childhood—both as you heard it, and as you may have lived it. This is not the sugary fluff of a Disney confection, but the tale of a most insidious vampire. Listen now to the truth of the vampire who stalks the maiden.

SNOW WHITE

Once upon a time, there was a beautiful queen who mourned the fact that she had no child. One day, the queen pricked her finger on her embroidery needle, and three drops of blood fell onto her new linen cloth. "Oh!" cried the queen, "if only I could have a child as white as my snowy linen, as red as my blood, and as black as the wood of my embroidery frame!" There must have been a fairy listening to her plea, for soon the queen gave birth to a beautiful daughter with skin as white as snow, lips as red as blood, and hair as black as ebony. Unfortunately, the poor queen died soon after she named her daughter—Snow White.

A year later, the king found a new queen of surpassing beauty, which she prized above everything else. Hour after hour, she would stand before her magic mirror and ask of it: "Looking glass upon the wall,/Who is fairest of us all?"

And the mirror would reply, "Queen, I answer to your call,/You are fairest of them all."

So the years passed, and Snow White became lovelier with every dawn. Life was perfect for the princess until the dark day when the magical mirror gave the queen an awful new reply: "Queen, you are lovely, it is true,/But Snow White is lovelier still than you."

As soon as the queen heard these words, a terrible change came over her face. Her clear eyes narrowed into slits of cold fury, her charming smile dragged downward into a gaping grimace of rage, and she pulled at her shining hair until it stood on end like a nest of snarling vipers. If anyone had seen the queen in this state, that hapless viewer would surely have turned to stone. In her rage, the queen ordered a rough woodsman to take Snow White into the woods, cut out her heart, and bring it back to the queen as a token. Reluctantly, the woodsman consented, but when he drew his long knife, Snow White fell to her knees and begged for his mercy, promising that she would vanish into the forest and never return to the kingdom. The woodsman agreed to release Snow White, and instead he killed a huge bear, whose heart he cut out and took to the queen. With enormous relish, the queen cooked and ate the heart, then sat back on her throne to savor the satisfaction of having finally consumed the object of her envy and resentment.

As the queen gloated over her full stomach, the heart that she thought she had eaten was in fact pounding in the breast of Snow White, who fled through the forest in terror. Just as the princess felt she must lie down to die from exhaustion, she spotted a little house nestled in a clearing. Snow White could not resist entering the cottage, where she found a table piled high with food on seven plates. She nibbled a bit from each plate, so as not to be detected, and then she curled up near the fire, where she hoped to sleep a little before the owners came home. But Snow White was so exhausted that she was still sleeping when the owners returned. They were the seven dwarves who searched for gold under the Great Mountain, and they were not home long before they found Snow White nestled in a fur rug near the hearth. "Oh, how lovely she is!" cried the dwarves. This awakened Snow White, who shook with fear at the sight of the seven odd little men. But the dwarves assured her, "We would love to have you stay here, if only you will care for us!" Since Snow White loved to care for others, this seemed to be a perfect arrangement. And since the dwarves had come to care for Snow White in return, they went on to warn her, "Your stepmother will soon learn where you are, so do not roam in the forest nor let anyone into the house!" This warning seemed wise to Snow White, so she vowed to obey it.

Now, you can imagine the queen's surprise that night when her magic mirror told her:

> *Queen, thou art a woman fair,*
> *But Snow White's beauty is more rare,*
> *Living by the Great Mountain*
> *With her seven little men.*

The queen's mouth drew down into a grimace of rage and her locks stood on end like vipers.

> *That damned Snow White! That heartless wretch!*
> *She tortures me and plots my death!*
> *She takes from me that which is mine,*
> *And so she has done since the dawn of time!*

Suddenly, the queen realized that if Snow White were to die, the queen would have to see to it herself. So she opened a black coffer in the corner of her room and removed a shining object.

The next day, a knock sounded at the door of the dwarves' cottage. When Snow White peeked out the window, she beheld an

old woman who leaned on a cane as gnarled as her bones. "Fine wares to sell!" called the old woman in her cracked voice, as she held up a shimmering bodice of gold and silver bands, "Wouldn't you enjoy these pretty laces?" Snow White yearned for the bodice, so she said, "I may not let you in, but perhaps you could pass it across the sill?"

"With pleasure, my girl," the old woman cried, "and what's more, I'll lace you up myself!" So Snow White turned her back to the old woman, who laced the bodice so fast and tight that it took the princess's breath away, and she fell down as if she were dead. You see, the old woman was the queen in disguise, and she cackled with glee at the sight of the lifeless body.

That evening, the dwarves grieved over the crumpled figure of the Snow White. But then they saw how tightly the bodice was laced, so they cut it away and watched as Snow White returned to life. The dwarves asked her what had happened, but she could remember nothing except the glint of gold and silver.

That night, the queen's mirror told her, "Queen, thou art a woman fair,/But Snow White's beauty is more rare"—at which the queen ran crazily around her room and howled till the blood ran from her eyes. Finally, she stumbled over the black coffer, from which she removed a glowing object.

When Snow White looked out the window the next morning, she beheld at the door a young woman of her own age who spoke in a friendly voice: "Good wares to sell! Perhaps a comb for your black hair?" Snow White felt a sisterly kinship with the young woman, and she was enchanted by the comb of pearl. So she opened the cottage door and said, "I may not let you in, fair miss, but perhaps you could pass me the thing across the sill?"

"With pleasure, my lady," the young woman cried, "and what's more, I will place it in your hair myself, for we young women should aid each other in adorning ourselves for love!" Snow White bowed her head to the young woman, who fastened the comb with a deft gesture. But the young woman's collabora-

tive friendliness was just another disguise of the queen, and the comb that she held had been poisoned. When the pearly bauble had been in Snow White's hair for an instant, the poison began to work and she fell down as if she were dead.

That evening, the dwarves sorrowfully lifted up the motionless Snow White, and as they did, the comb fell from her hair, permitting her to slowly return to life. So it was only natural that when the queen interrogated her mirror that evening, it replied as before: "Queen, thou art a woman fair,/But Snow White's beauty is more rare."

This time, the Queen did not waste time with curses and shrieks, but ran immediately to her coffer and lifted from it an object that shone dull red in the flickering light.

The next morning, a knock sounded tentatively at the door of the cottage. Snow White crept to the window, where she beheld the forlorn shape of a little child, which touched her warm heart as no other sight could have done. Snow White opened the door and the child cried with delight, "Mama! Appo fo Mama!" And there, in her tiny hands, she clutched a large red apple.

"But I'm not your mama," Snow White said gently to the child. The baby's lower lip started to tremble, and her adoring eyes filled with tears. "Mama . . ." she hiccuped in her distress, ". . . appo fo Mama . . ." It seemed to Snow White that she was being cruel to refuse the child, so she accepted the apple. The little girl beamed up at her and cried, "Mama eat appo!" Again, the child's request seemed such a small thing that Snow White could not refuse. She took a bite of the bright red apple and fell down as if dead. The child's face now seethed with cold triumph, for she was, once again, the queen in disguise, and the apple had been poisoned. "No one can save you now!" she spat as she ran off into the woods.

That evening, the dwarves found Snow White's cold body on the doorsill, but try as they might, they could not revive the princess. Since they could not bring themselves to put their beloved

Snow White in the cold ground, they placed her in a beautiful glass coffin with her story inscribed in its golden frame, and they set her high upon the Great Mountain. And of course, that night the mirror gave the queen the answer for which she hungered: "Queen, I answer to your call,/You are the fairest now of all."

As for Snow White, her body lay for a long time in the glass coffin on the mountaintop. It seemed as if she were asleep rather than dead, for her skin remained as white as snow, her lips remained as red as blood, and her hair remained as black as ebony. In fact, when a prince rode by one day, he immediately fell in love with her, and he decided to take her back to his father's castle. The prince carefully lifted Snow White's body onto his great black warhorse, and he mounted behind her for the long ride home. The warhorse started off at a gentle walk, but suddenly, the great beast thought he saw something in the shadows, and he jigged to the side (as even the nicest horses will do), sharply bumping his two riders. The prince pulled the horse up short, but not before the bump had jostled a bit of apple out of Snow White's mouth. The prince did not notice the apple bit, so he nearly fell off his horse when Snow White stirred in front of him.

"Where am I?" she cried in her confusion, "and who are *you*?"

"I am the one who loves you and wishes to marry you," the astonished prince replied.

Snow White loved the prince at once, so she accepted his proposal with the greatest joy. Then they continued to his father's castle, where a huge wedding feast was prepared. Hundreds of noble folk cheered when the prince and Snow White entered the castle's hall. A fire blazed in the great hearth, and all the neighboring kings and queens were in attendance. Then, as the prince and his bride drew closer to the guests, Snow White suddenly froze and went pale as death.

"What is it, my love?" the Prince asked anxiously.

"My stepmother!" gasped Snow White, pointing to a beautiful lady at the table of honor. And so it was, for the queen was one

of the honored guests. "Please, my love!" cried Snow White, "Protect me! Kill her! For she has tried to kill me so many times!"

The prince stepped away from Snow White in horror. He still loved her deeply, but he had never seen her in this murderous state. He did not know her full story (for indeed, she did not fully comprehend it herself), so all he could see was that his beloved bride was asking him to murder one of the most prominent guests at their marriage. Moreover, this queen was Snow White's own stepmother, and he felt as if this mother's murder would be a murder of mothers in general, including his own. At the same time, the prince had never loved anyone as much as he loved Snow White, and she was crying for his aid as if her life depended on it. The prince felt that the eyes of all the guests were upon him, judging him before he had even moved, and he felt himself sinking into a familiar soft fog . . . sinking away from the painful decision before him.

"Please, my love!" screamed Snow White, "Choose to be a *man*!"

In the pause after Snow White's cry, the prince felt clearly the fork in his path. On the branch of the path in which the queen's life was spared, the prince saw his life as it had always been—structured, familiar, and blind to his unique essence. On the other branch of the path, in which he defended Snow White, the prince felt his life as it was meant to be—thrilling, revolutionary, and deeply fulfilling. The prince looked longingly to the known path and then, with a shift as subtle as a sigh, he moved toward Snow White.

Up came the shining steel of the prince's sword, flashing high in the air. The queen turned toward the prince, and her face underwent a chilling metamorphosis. The silken curls, liquid eyes, and honeyed lips seemed to melt away, and in their place grew a mane of twisting vipers over two empty pits and a gaping maw of darkness. The prince put his full strength behind the sword and drove it into the queen's heart. Or was it a heart? An object

popped out of the wound and fell to the floor with an icy metallic clang. This was the queen's heart—a cold lead box around a sucking black hole. Everyone in the hall recoiled as the box turned its gaping mouth toward Snow White.

Fighting the rising sickness in her stomach, Snow White reached for the foul little cube. With a lunge, she grabbed it and tossed it into the roaring marriage fire. A thin wail, like the cry of a dying babe, shivered through the great hall, and everyone wept at its black despair. When the guests could look finally through their tears, they saw that the body of the queen had vanished, leaving only a dark stain on the floor. Then a cool breeze blew through the hall, and it was clear that the land had been purged. Snow White and her prince knew that their love could now shine in safety and peace. And so they were joined, and so they remained for the rest of their lives ever after.

THE VAMPIRIC VEIL OF FEMININE DISEMPOWERMENT

In the fairy tale of Snow White, a witch-queen-mother vampirizes an innocent princess-daughter by exploiting her victim's naïve compassion. Whether she is disguised as a beautiful queen, a solicitous crone, a collaborative girlfriend, or a forlorn child, the feminine vampire appears to her victim like a sweet, helpless mist who promises love in exchange for a simple act of compassion. The princess-daughter complies, for she sees in the mist the divine femininity she yearns for. Her vision is only a projection of the feminine energies that she carries inside, but she does not realize this, so she gives whatever is asked in order to bask in the reflected brilliance of her projection. And thus she bleeds out her energy into the mouth of the feminine vampire.

The princess's plight in these stories reflects that of many innocent people who gush out their life force in the hope of winning a feminine vampire's unconditional love. Of course, the kind of love for which we yearn and bleed will never be granted by the vam-

pire from whom we seek it. The person in whose psyche the feminine vampire is activated can only dole out the fragile shelter of a ginger cake house—a superficial confection of shared confidences, honeyed words, and syrupy sympathy. The taste is sweet, but the calories are empty, and the cost to the victim is her life. In the external reality, this tactic is manifested in the feminine vampire's frosting of solicitous concern: "Here, let me make that decision for you—you were always uncomfortable with hard decisions," or "He never had enough ambition, and he wasn't respectful to me, either. You're really better off without him," or "Don't you think that the red dress would be more slenderizing? I know you never take my opinion, but I only want what's best for you." How many women are bled dry by a feminine vampire's subtle derision, cunning manipulation, and insidious induction of guilt!

And what is it that the feminine vampire really wants of her victims? In one sense, the answer is simple. The feminine vampire wants what every vampire wants—power at the expense of anyone but herself. But in another sense, the answer is more complex, for her tactics and targets differ from those of the masculine vampire, in accordance with her feminine role.

For example: The most notorious feminine vampire in recorded history is surely the "Bloody Countess" Erzsebet Báthory of Hungary. Erzsebet was born in 1560 to a prominent noble family whose crest, ironically, bore the symbol of the same Order of the Dragon under which Vlad Dracula had fought a century earlier. Erzsebet was betrothed in an arranged marriage to the Count Ferenc Nádasdy, who, like Vlad Dracula, spent most of his time away from home as a warrior fighting the Turkish invaders. In the long months while her husband was absent, Erzsebet roamed around in his gloomy Castle Csejthe, which was located in the same shadowy Carpathian mountains where Bram Stoker was to lodge Count Dracula.

Although Erzsebet's story seems in many ways to be linked to the story of Dracula, there is an important difference between the two vampires. Dracula, in both history and fiction, had the cultural empowerment necessary to exercise his will in the world. By contrast, Erzsebet lived a woman's life under a repressive patriarchal regime. Forced to live with her aging mother-in-law in her husband's isolated castle, Erzsebet's only means of feeding her ambition was to exploit her beauty and sexual allure, although even this tactic was limited by her married state. So Erzsebet tried to content herself with seducing her naïve serving girls and feeding on their shattered innocence. Later, as she became trapped in the vampiric dilemma of devouring that which cannot satisfy, the countess began to physically abuse the young women after she had seduced them, adding their pain to her vampiric repasts. But even this pursuit could not appease Erzsebet's hunger for power, especially when she realized that her precious beauty was starting to decay. Finally, she became convinced that the blood of her innocent victims was the antidote to her aging, and Erzsebet Báthory launched a gory campaign in which she drank and bathed in her serving girls' blood. Protected by her regal manner, her enormous wealth, and the political clout of her family, Erzsebet's vampiric spree spanned two decades and claimed over six hundred victims. When her predation had spread to the point where her family could no longer protect her, she was walled up in her room at the Castle Csejthe until she died, four years later, at the age of fifty-four.

The social inequalities of Erzsebet's culture permitted her to victimize hundreds of other women who were less powerful than she. The shape of today's culture makes it harder for a feminine vampire to manifest her bloodlust in the manner of Erzsebet, but innumerable feminine vampires have emulated Erzsebet's predation on the psychic plane. The beautiful socialite in chapter 2 who withered after the death of her unremarkable daughter might have been a metaphorical descendent of Erzsebet Báthory, as are all those who slice manipulatively at the psychic jugulars of others in order to enhance their status in the collective. Erzsebet died in

1614, but her legacy lives on in every woman who feeds off less powerful people by exploiting her victims' innocent sense of shame, guilt, and compassion.

A MODERN STORY OF FEMININE VAMPIRISM

The feminine vampire's capacity for guilt-inducing martyrdom is described with excruciating precision in Tennessee Williams's play *The Glass Menagerie* (1945). The vampire in Williams's autobiographical work is Amanda Wingfield, a fading Southern belle whose husband has left her alone to raise their two children—the discontented dreamer, Tom, and Laura, his crippled, reclusive sister. Although Amanda devotes most of her energy to feeding on the resistant Tom, she achieves her greatest vampiric success with Laura. Bled to the point of transparency by her mother, Laura drifts through each day by playing with her glass menagerie, the little crystal animals that are as fragile and as translucent as Laura has become in the grip of Amanda's vampiric "love."

Amanda clearly operates under her vampiric veil of vulnerability when she confronts Laura with her truancy from the secretarial school in which Amanda has forcibly enrolled her:

[*Amanda leans against the shut door and stares at Laura with a martyred look.*]

AMANDA: Deception? Deception? [*She slowly removes her hat and gloves, continuing the sweet suffering stare. She lets the hat and gloves fall on the floor—a bit of acting.*]

LAURA: [*shakily*] How was the D.A.R. meeting? [*Amanda slowly opens her purse and removes a dainty white handkerchief which she shakes out delicately and touches to her lips.*] Didn't you go to the D.A.R. meeting, Mother?

AMANDA: [*faintly, almost inaudibly*] No. No. I did not have the strength—to go to the D.A.R. In fact, I did not have the courage! I wanted to find a hole in the ground and hide myself in it forever! [*She crosses slowly to the wall and removes the diagram of the typewriter keyboard. She holds it in front of her for a second, staring at it sweetly and sorrowfully—then bites her lips and tears it in two pieces.]* . . . What are we going to do, what is going to become of us, what is the future?

LAURA: Has something happened, Mother? [*Amanda draws a long breath, takes out the handkerchief again, goes through the dabbing process.*] (29–31)

Amanda describes how she has gone to the secretarial college, only to find that Laura has dropped out after the first test, during which she threw up on the floor and had to be carried out of the room. Laura confesses that since then, she has spent every day walking in the park, in order to avoid telling Amanda about her disgrace at the school. Then, noticing Amanda's martyred expression, she blurts out:

LAURA: Mother, when you're disappointed, you get that awful suffering look on your face, like the picture of Jesus' mother in the museum!

AMANDA: Hush! . . . [*hopelessly fingering the huge pocketbook*] So what are we going to do the rest of our lives? . . . Amuse ourselves with the glass menagerie, darling? . . . We won't have a business career—we've given that up because it gave us nervous indigestion! . . . What is there left but dependency all our lives? (33–34)

The martyred looks, the despairing words, the air of tragic suffering—these are all powerful weapons in the hands of feminine vampires such as Amanda. When Laura holds up the mirror to Amanda's tactics, comparing her expression to "that awful suffering look . . . like the picture of Jesus' mother," Amanda silences her. Then she further alarms Laura by demolishing the boundaries between them, using "we" and "our" in her final flood of pathos. Against these weapons, Laura has no defense, and she crumbles before her mother in a spasm of culpability and remorse—both of which are ambrosia to the power-seeking Amanda vampire.

From the depths of her shame and guilt, Laura acquiesces to

another of Amanda's schemes—the invitation of a "gentleman caller" to dine with the Wingfield family. Laura is soon appalled to find that the caller, Tom's friend Jim, is someone on whom she had a crush in high school. It initially seems that Laura will not be able to interact with Jim at all, but they eventually have an innocently romantic conversation while Amanda and Tom wash the dinner dishes. Unfortunately, it soon becomes clear that although Jim appreciates Laura's delicate charm, he is already engaged to be married. After Jim has departed, Amanda explodes in fury at Tom for not having alerted her to Jim's engagement. Her abuse finally drives Tom to leave, even though it means abandoning Laura to their mother's predation. As the play ends, Tom speaks retrospectively of his departure, while the vampiric duet between Laura and her mother continues in silence along its tragic path:

> [*We see, as though through a soundproof glass, that Amanda appears to be making a comforting speech to Laura, who is huddled upon the sofa. . . . Laura's hair hides her face until, at the end of the speech, she lifts her head to smile at her mother. Amanda's gestures are slow and graceful, almost dancelike, as she comforts her daughter. . . . At the close of Tom's speech, Laura blows out the candles, ending the play.*] (114)

So it is that the feminine vampire shepherds her enfeebled prey, driving her with spurs of guilt, soothing her with sugary appeasements, penetrating her psyche with fangs of shame, and draining as much life force as she can without destroying the precious resource. Laura, for her part, drifts along in the customary torpor of a vampire's victim, yearning and despairing in the smothering fog of her mother's embrace. And although we can sense the frustration that simmers in the depths of Laura's psyche, it is clear that she will bleed out her life into her mother's psychic maw. Indeed, Laura seems to curl up voluntarily in that bloody cavern, possibly because its truth is obscured by Amanda's pathos and by

Laura's desperate need to believe in her projection of the Great Feminine. But there is something else, too. Laura accommodates the feminine vampire because she knows that the penalty for refusing will be the paralyzing force of Amanda's righteous rejection and the guilt that she will be forced to bear for having "abused" her martyred mother.

In a lighter example of this vampiric guilt game, the hilarious book *How to Be a Jewish Mother* (1964), Dan Greenburg informs us that neither Jewish heritage nor maternal status nor even female gender are required to be a Jewish Mother. All that is required is the capacity to manipulate one's victims by the use of martyrdom and guilt induction. The same is true of all feminine vampires—their primary tactic is the use of vulnerability and guilt induction to bleed their victims dry.

The Jewish Mother's strategies, as Greenburg describes them, bear a striking resemblance to the machinations of Amanda Wingfield and her fellow feminine vampires: Underlying all techniques of Jewish Motherhood is the ability to plant, cultivate, and harvest

> guilt. Control guilt and you control the child. . . . Let your child hear you sigh every day; if you don't know what he's done to make you suffer, *he* will. . . . your power, authority and credibility as a Jewish Mother are directly proportional to how much you are perceived to be suffering at any given moment. If you are not actively suffering, how can you expect anyone in your family to do what you want them to? . . . [As a practice drill,] give your son Marvin two sport shirts as a present. The first time he wears one of them, look at him sadly and say . . . "The other one you didn't like?" (15, 18)

This passage reminds me of a woman I once knew (a mother, but not Jewish) who merely had to sigh and quiver helplessly like the Asian mist in front of her well-meaning daughter. The daughter would unfailingly inquire about her mother's pain, only to

learn that she herself was the cause. In essence, the daughter would regularly become convinced that she was the vampire and her mother the victim. Desperate to atone, the daughter would offer her life force to her mother as compensation. The mother would graciously allow the daughter to purchase her pardon with blood, usually in the form of her acquiescence to the mother's will. Mollified, the mother would then reward the daughter by bestowing upon her a dollop of forgiveness. The daughter would bask briefly in her reprieve from guilt hell and, encouraged by the opportunity to absolve herself, would vow to do all she could to avoid inflicting any further pain on her mother. Of course, all the daughter's efforts to fulfill this goal were doomed, and she was accused of endless crimes against the mother, just as falsely and just as effectively as she was accused of the first. The daughter never woke up to the predatory game, and she continues to bleed out her life force trying to unload her maternal vampire's countless burdens of guilt.

Feminine vampirism, for all its fragile appearance, is as tenacious as it is virulent. The feminine vampire can be separated from her victims by years, continents, even death, and still the victims will bleed for her. One woman I know swears that she can hear her mother's eyelid narrow at a distance of three thousand miles. Indeed, many of us have been astonished to find that we still cower before the internal images of our pathetic, martyred vampires, long after we thought we had freed ourselves from their jaws. And this is just how it was for Tom Wingfield as well:

> I didn't go to the moon, I went much further—for time is the longest distance between two places. . . . I descended the steps of this fire escape for the last time and followed, from then on, in my father's footsteps, attempting to find in motion what was lost in space. . . . The cities swept about me like dead leaves, leaves that were brightly colored but torn away from the branches. I would have stopped, but I was pursued by

something. It always came upon me unawares, taking me altogether by surprise. (Williams 1945, 114–115)

Although we may cringe at the thought of Amanda's continuing predation beyond the end of the play, it is not surprising that her children remain powerless to stop her. For Tom and Laura, and for most of us as well, the work entailed in deactivating a pathetic feminine vampire makes us feel as if we were strangling a bunny, and the distastefulness of the task often dissuades us from pursuing it. Even if we manage to stick to our guns (or stakes), we should understand the factors that lead us to be her victims in the first place—which is also what encourages us to remain in her thrall. In addition to capitalizing on their victims' compassion with the induction of guilt, how exactly do such feminine vampires as the wicked queen and Amanda Wingfield exploit their feminine victims?

First, both Snow White and Laura Wingfield have been distanced, through no fault of their own, from the positive energies of the Great Feminine. This separation occurs in the stories because of fateful accidents (the death of Snow White's mother and Laura's physical incapacitation). Most of us have also been separated from our positive feminine energy by four thousand years of patriarchal socialization and, in some cases, the wiles of a feminine vampire. Feminine vampires like to convince us that we must fight alone to survive in a ruthless world where our sacredness will never be honored. Of course, life and love usually entail risk and hardship. But many of us have been trained to feel a profound distrust for life and love, period, much as Amanda trains Laura to withhold her trust from the outside world and to give it instead to Amanda, the very vampire who threatens her safety. Laura is like many women who have been convinced by a vampiric mother that there is no protective, positive feminine force in the world, and that they are safe and loved only when they are huddled under the vampire's wing.

Once Laura has been cowed by her mother's fallacious world-view, Amanda lulls her into a dreamy semiconsciousness that makes her even easier prey. Amanda spoons down Laura's throat her antebellum confections of fantasy and nostalgia, creating a lovely dream world that Laura can retrieve for herself only by repetitiously contemplating the melodies of her old records and the luminescence of her fragile glass animals. In this sense, Laura is like many feminine victims who spin out their dreams in a lethargic limbo that prevents them from bringing those dreams to life. Using food, fantasies, and a variety of other drugs, these feminine victims numb their pain and frustration as they drift off to elaborate endlessly the fantasyland that a feminine vampire has designed for them. Snow White suspended in her glass coffin and Laura dawdling among her little crystal animals call to mind the millions of people (most of them women) who dawdle their days away in the glass coffins of romance novels and soap opera sagas. These drugs, though not lethal (particularly when compared to alcohol, nicotine, and Valium), become psychically dangerous when they are a substitute for life.

Amanda and the wicked queen also use their vampiric mastery of shape shifting to prey upon Laura and Snow White. In one instant, the feminine vampire may appear to us as a concerned wise woman who dispenses valuable advice. In another instant, she may don the seductive garb of a feminine soulmate who pretends to help us realize our romantic or professional aspirations. In yet another instant, the feminine vampire may adopt the appearance of a helpless, adoring child who wants only our love and attention. Or she may appear in the disguise of a maternal protector who stands between us and a host of ostensible predators, all of whom are vividly described to us by the vampire. With each mask, the feminine psychic vampire appeals to a different aspect of our psyche, switching disguises frequently so we do not become wise to the game.

The most effective of the feminine vampire's disguises, how-

ever, is the mask she dons for those outside the vampire-victim dyad. Like Amanda and the wicked queen, the feminine vampire frequently appears to the outside world as a model of solicitude and goodwill. This may be the most devastating of the vampire's disguises, because it leads us to doubt our own sense of reality when we are confronted with the disbelief of the duped onlookers. "What do you mean, your mother is a guilt-inducing blood-sucker? She's so nice and innocuous!" "How can you say that your mate is a wheedling manipulator? She's so accommodating and good natured!" "Aren't you being ungrateful to refer to your boss as a vampire? She's so sweet tempered and vulnerable!" In the face of public response like this, it is no wonder that we may decide to slump back into the sweet, suffocating fog. It takes a fierce conviction regarding our endangerment, such as Snow White possesses at the end of her story, for us to deactivate a sugar-coated vampire.

The final ploy of the feminine vampire in both these stories is to separate her intended victim from the powerful forces of masculine energy and her own instincts, particularly her potent sexuality. In the story of Snow White, the queen's poisoned apple threatens to separate her victim from the masculine energies of the dwarves and any potential suitors, and from the instinctive power of the great warhorse who will eventually save her. In *The Glass Menagerie,* Amanda subtly tries to sabotage Laura's connection with Jim by flirting with him and denigrating Laura. The maternal vampire compounds her daughter's sense of powerlessness by attempting to either seduce or suppress any male energy (including the daughter's own masculinity) that might free her daughter from her clutches. As long as the mother can control the masculine energies in and around her daughter (energies that Jung would call the *animus*), the daughter is gravely endangered. Her mother will never permit her to attract external masculine energies by embodying her own feminine sexuality, nor is the daughter allowed to reclaim her own masculine energies, and she certainly

cannot attack the maternal vampire who holds her animus hostage. Instead, the daughter is obliged to serve as a masculine champion to her vampiric mother, while simultaneously remaining in a subordinate feminine position. Sadly, this story is lived out in the life of every woman who serves her mother's masculine aspirations by excelling professionally, but who abandons her personal assertiveness and her feminine sexuality in the face of her mother's envy and resentment.

Given the feminine vampire's insidious power, it is essential that we find a model for her deactivation. But first, we must remember not to become too dogmatic in our interpretations of these stories. Not all relationships are permeated with vampiric energy. The difference between normal loving and vampiric exploitation has to do with the nature of the energy that underlies the behavior. The vampiric person does not simply feel that "I don't know what to do when my beloved is gone." Rather, she feels that "I *cease to exist* when my beloved is gone." The feminine vampire attempts to neutralize this feeling by manipulating her victim with the guilt-inducing tactics of martyrdom and conditional gratitude. This may be why feminine vampirism is so insidious: in order to extricate ourselves from its embrace, we must deactivate the vampiric energy in an apparently vulnerable person who seems to profoundly, indeed desperately, appreciate us. That is a very difficult strategy to resist. If we don't refuse these pathetic vampires, however, we are likely to follow in Laura Wingfield's tragic footsteps.

GYPSY

The next story, like that of Snow White, gives us a model for deactivating our feminine vampires, particularly if one of those vampires is active in the psyche of our mother. The biography of the burlesque queen Gypsy Rose Lee is a rather unlikely but, I hope to persuade you, uncannily suitable choice for our purposes.

I have taken the story from the 1962 Mervyn LeRoy film of the Jule Styne–Stephen Sondheim musical *Gypsy* (1959), which in turn is based on Lee's autobiography of the same name (1957).* Lee's story serves as a rare modern myth in which a feminine victim comes to terms with her vampiric mother and nobody dies in the process.

Once upon a time, there was a shy young tomboy named Louise who had a little sister named June and a mother named Rose. Louise's mother, Rose, thought the world of her daughters, particularly little June, who could sing and dance like a star. This delighted Rose, who had always loved the theatrical world of vaudeville. In fact, Rose loved vaudeville so much that she devoted her life to promoting her daughters as an act on the vaudeville circuit. The life of a vaudeville performer was very hard: living in hotel rooms, cooking on hot plates, scraping together money for cheap hotels and food and trains. Louise and June often felt that they were living the lives of gypsies. Worse, perhaps, because gypsy girls didn't have to reckon with the fanatic ambition of their mother. Rose's ambition easily surpassed that of most mortals, and she knew it:

> *Some people can get a thrill*
> *Knitting sweaters and sitting still.*
> *That's okay for some people who don't know they're alive.*
> *Some people can thrive and bloom*
> *Livin' life in a livin' room—*
> *That's perfect for some people of one hundred and five!*
>
> *But I*
> *At least gotta try,*
> *when I think of all the sights that I gotta see yet,*

---

*A 1993 television remake features Bette Midler in the mother role, which Rosalind Russell originally played, and Cynthia Gibb in the title role, which Natalie Wood originally played. Although the remake is more faithful to the stage musical, the first film's compelling portrayal of their relationship is more suitable to my discussion.

All the places I gotta play,
All things I gotta be yet—
Come on, Poppa, whadya say?

Some people sit on their butts,
Got the dream—yeah, but not the guts!
That's living for some people
For some humdrum people,
I suppose.
Well, they can stay and rot—
But not
Rose!

Rose was too old to be a vaudeville performer, so she treated Louise and June as the living extensions of her body and her dreams, doing everything in her power to live out her aspirations through them. By conniving, cajoling, and manipulating, Rose grabbed every opportunity she could to promote the careers of her daughters, whom she referred to as her "babies." And when Rose called Louise and June her "babies," she meant it completely, for her denial of her daughters' budding womanhood was as extreme as her aspirations for them. Even when Louise and June were well into their adolescence, Rose insisted that they continue to perform as child characters. And although she faithfully celebrated their birthdays every year, she never let them know how old they were. As far as Rose was concerned, Louise and June would always be twelve and ten years old, respectively. Suspended in this eternal childhood, "Dainty" June continued to sing falsetto in her baby-doll attire, while the untalented Louise faithfully held up the front end of the cow costume, long after she had developed the unmistakable curves of a woman.

Despite their peculiar life, Louise and June loved their indomitable mother. If only she would fall in love and marry a wonderful man, they thought, everyone would be happy. But Rose had already been married three times, and she was opposed to letting any man penetrate that far into their lives again. Eventually, how-

ever, Rose was persuaded to accept a man named Herbie as the troupe's booking agent. Rose loved Herbie, but she refused to marry him, and she made it clear that he would be booted out the minute his presence did not serve her daughters' success. In fact, Herbie and the boys in the chorus were the only males that Rose allowed near her daughters, and they were tolerated only because they enhanced the careers of her "babies."

Rose's blind ambition for her daughters also blinded her to their realities. When a big producer offered June a career in the movies, Rose turned him down because her own heart belonged to vaudeville and she could not comprehend that June might feel otherwise. Furious that her mother had jeopardized her chance at stardom, June eloped with one of the chorus dancers, a departure that left the act without any trace of talent whatsoever. June's elopement might have forced Rose to acknowledge her daughters' womanhood, but she would not permit that shaft of enlightenment to penetrate into the tunnel of her fanatical vision. She viewed June's decision as the betrayal of an ingrate, and even though the rest of the chorus boys departed the same day, Rose immediately began to plan a new act in which Louise would take over June's starring role. Louise and Herbie were deeply pessimistic about this plan, but Rose promoted her dream with the finesse of a star performer, describing for Louise what her future could be:

> *You'll be swell, you'll be great,*
> *Gonna have the whole world on a plate!*
> *Starting here, starting now,*
> *Honey, everything's coming up roses!*
> *Clear the decks, clear the tracks,*
> *You got nothing to do but relax,*
> *Blow a kiss, take a bow—*
> *Honey, everything's coming up roses!*

Then Rose made a subtle shift in her framing of the dream:

> *You can do it,*
> *All you need is a hand!*

We *can do it,*
Momma is gonna see to it!
Curtain up, light the lights!
We got nothing to hit but the heights!
I can tell,
Wait and see!
There's the bell,
Follow me,
And nothing's gonna stop us till we're through!
Honey, everything's coming up roses . . . for me and for you!

Reluctantly, Louise agreed to play the lead, on the condition that she have star billing. Since Herbie had insisted that the new chorus of girls should be blondes in order to set off Louise's dark hair, Rose agreed to a compromise name for the new act, dubbing it "Rose Louise and Her Hollywood Blondes." Of course, a new act was no assurance of new bookings, and sure enough, Herbie had little luck in finding a place for the dreadful troupe to perform. Finally, he was able to book the act into the Wichita Opera House. Rose was thrilled to return to performing, particularly since they were flat broke. When the troupe arrived at the "Opera House," however, they found that it was, in fact, a house of burlesque, and their act was the "legit" billing that would keep the cops from shutting down the strip show. Rose was horrified. Not only did she hold the vaudevillian's terrified disdain for burlesque (since playing in burlesque meant that a vaudeville act was finished), but she saw the world of burlesque as a place of disgusting contamination for ladies like herself and the innocent "babies" in her charge. Rose wanted to leave immediately, but Louise convinced her to let them stay, reminding her that they needed the money and time in order to find another booking. Rose finally relented, permitting "Rose Louise and Her Hollywood Blondes" to play the two-week gig.

The burlesque show introduced Louise to a completely new side of life. The strippers with whom she shared a dressing room were warmly gracious to the girl-woman they called "Gypsy,"

and they responded to her innocent questions with a full account of their professional philosophies ("Ya gotta have a gimmick") and theatrical skills ("To be a stripper, all ya need is no talent"). Louise listened in wide-eyed wonder, for her only experiences of womanhood had been her girlish crushes on the chorus boys. This, on the other hand, was a world of full-blown female sexuality.

On the last night of the booking, while Louise sat in her dressing room, Rose heard that the head stripper has been busted for prostitution, and the management was seeking a replacement. Rose immediately offered to have Louise take her place, on the condition that she be paid star salary. Herbie stomped out, disgusted by Rose's scheme, but Louise was rooted to the spot in horror at the prospect of stripping in front of all those men. "Don't be silly, Louise," Rose assured her, "You aren't gonna strip! You're only gonna go out, sashay around, then drop a shoulder strap and leave 'em beggin' for more!" Accustomed as Louise was to obeying her mother, she numbly complied, putting up her hair and donning an evening gown and long gloves. Then she plodded behind the curtain to center stage, almost as if she were sleepwalking, and stood there trembling, while one of the strippers wrapped her in a fake fur stole. The emcee cobbled an impromptu rendition of Louise's name and announced, "We now present our newest star, Miss *Gypsy Rose Lee!*" The band struck up, the curtain parted, and the bump-and-grind music pulled Louise down the runway, almost into the laps of the catcalling men.

Until now, Louise had been an innocent tomboy who obeyed her mother and dreamed of upcoming roses. Now, suddenly, she found herself yanked into the life of "Gypsy Rose Lee," a woman who performed as a kind of visual prostitute before a crowd of leering men. At first, Louise was so terrified that she could hardly sing above a whisper, and she clutched the fake stole around her. Then, slowly, she looked at the men who gaped at her, and she realized with amazement that they wanted her. In fact, for reasons

that neither she nor they could have fully articulated, they *needed* her. Suddenly, Louise understood that she possessed a kind of power in her new role, and if she used that power wisely, she could serve herself as well as these men. Moving very slowly, she began to saunter along the stage. "Let me entertain you," she sang with increasing volume,

> *Let me make you smile.*
> *Let me do a few tricks,*
> *Some old and then some new tricks.*
> *I'm very versatile . . .*

With exquisite care, she peeled off one of her long white evening gloves.

> *And if you're* real *good,*
> *I'll make you feel good—*
> *I want your spirits to cliiiiiimb.*

She paused and threw the glove at the cheering men. "So let me entertain you,/And we'll have a real good time—yessir . . ." Louise walked to the edge of the curtain, looked at the men over her shoulder and drawled, "We'll . . . have . . ." then she paused, dropped a shoulder strap, and promised, *"A reeeeeeal good time!"* and walked off the stage. The men in the audience hooted and cheered with joyous abandon. And so it was that Louise, the no-talent tomboy, became Gypsy Rose Lee, the Queen of Burlesque.

Gypsy's rise to fame was meteoric. Her dances were less explicit and more suggestive than any other stripper's, and yet thousands of people, women as well as men, paid top dollar to watch her perform. She wore fabulous gowns, which she removed with slow, deliberate gestures, and she flirted with the audience throughout, spicing her conversation with her saucy wit. She became famous and rich, and her friendship was sought by a variety of celebrities, many of whom she eventually lured onto her television talk show. Although Gypsy had little formal schooling (thanks to Rose's overprotectiveness), she became "the book-worm of burlesque," reading all of Proust in French and eventually writing her autobiography and several mystery novels. With intelligence, humor, and a clear sense of her strengths and limitations, Gypsy Rose Lee reigned supreme in the life that she had created for herself.

And what about Rose? At the end of the film, we meet up with Rose after Gypsy has risen to stardom. Rose accosts Gypsy in her lavish dressing room and tries to run her daughter's life as she did for so many years. At first, Gypsy responds with a patience born of her deep love for her mother. But when Rose persists in her meddling, Gypsy stands her ground, saying, "I'm not a baby, Mother! You have to let go of me!"

Furious at Gypsy's rebuff, Rose's eyes narrow and her mouth compresses into a sharp line. Then she attacks. "Who do you think you are, Miss Gypsy Rose Lee? . . . They're all laughin' at you, the burlesque queen who speaks lousy French and reads book reviews like they was books! . . . You know what you are to them? A circus freak—this year's novelty act!"

Finally, Gypsy snaps. "Turn it off, Mother!" she screams. "Nobody laughs at me, because I laugh first! . . . Momma, look at me now! I'm a star! Look how I live . . . Look where I'm going—I'm not staying in burlesque. I'm *moving* . . . maybe up, maybe down, but wherever it is, I'm enjoying it. I'm having the time of my life. And this time, it *is* my life. And I love it! I love every second of it. And I'll be damned if you're going to take it away from me! I am *Gypsy Rose Lee*! And I *love* her. And if you don't, you can just clear out now!"

"All right, miss," seethes Rose, "but just one thing I wanna know—all the scrimpin' and the savin' and the schemin' . . . what did I do it for?"

Gypsy looks at her mother sadly and replies, "I thought you did it for me, Momma."

Rose stares wide-eyed at Gypsy and then rushes out of the

dressing room onto the empty stage. "'I thought you did it for me, Momma!" she fumes to herself. "Well, miss, I made you! And ya wanna know why? Because I was born too soon and started too late. . . . What I got in me . . . if I'd ever let it go, there wouldn't have been signs big enough, there wouldn't have been lights bright enough." And then, as Rose's powerful vision fills the theater with life, she sings:

> *Here she is, boys! Here she is, world! Here's* Rose! . . .
> *You either got it,*
> *Or you ain't.*
> *And, boys, I got it!*
> *You like it?*
> *Well, I got it! . . .*
> *Ready or not, here comes Momma!*
> *Momma's talking loud,*
> *Momma's doin' fine . . .*
> *Momma's got the stuff,*
> *Momma's lettin' go. . . .*

Rose falters in her performance to the empty theater and mutters in sudden comprehension, *"Momma's gotta let go!"* Then, confused and uncertain, she murmurs, "Why did I do it? . . . They're takin' bows and I'm battin' zero."

> *Well, someone tell me, when is it my turn?*
> *Don't I get a dream for myself?*
> *Startin' now it's gonna by my turn. . . .*
> *This time, boys, I'm takin' the bows and*
> *Everything's coming up* ROSE—
> *Everything's coming up roses*
> *This time for* me!

Rose finishes in triumph, and in the hush that follows, she hears the applause of a single pair of hands—Gypsy's. Rose turns to her daughter and stammers with embarrassment, but Gypsy smiles and says, "So why *did* you do it all, Momma?"

"Aw," replies Rose, "I guess I did it for myself."

"Why, Mother?" asks Gypsy.

"Guess I just wanted to be noticed," admits Rose.

"Like I wanted you to notice me," Gypsy says gently, "and I still do, Momma." Then she takes her mother in her arms, saying, "OK, Momma . . . OK, *Rose*."

"You know," Rose says after a moment, while drying her eyes, "I had a dream last night. It was a big poster of a mother and daughter . . . it was you and me wearing exactly the same gown . . . and the headline said *Madame Rose* . . ." Rose's voice pauses as her hand sweeps down and across in front of her, and her eyes glow with her vision. Then looking at Gypsy, Rose smiles and sweeps her hand hugely across the sky as she finishes, "*. . . and her daughter, GYPSY!*"

DEACTIVATING THE FEMININE VAMPIRE

The story that I originally selected for this section was the Greek myth of Persephone, a story about a "nameless maiden" who is abducted from the arms of her enveloping mother by a dark stranger. Persephone manages to transform herself from a rape victim into a Queen, so that by the end of the story, she has created a unique role for herself in the world—one in which she is neither the chattel of her husband nor the minion of her mother, but a woman sufficient unto herself. Wonderful story, huh? Then a wise reader pointed out that I was far from the first person to appreciate the wonderfulness of this myth. In fact, one might say that it's been "done." A *lot*. "Surely," said my wise reader, "there must be a modern version of such a great myth!! Perhaps a film?" "Of course," I replied, "let me just find it." So I looked. and looked. And *looked*. In the end, Gypsy's story was the only one that I could find which provided a modern look at the great myth of Persephone. I don't know whether this puzzling dearth of examples is just more evidence of the extreme patriarchal focus in our culture, or whether we are truly mystified about how one

might live out Persephone's story. What I do know is that Gypsy's story, perhaps even more than Snow White's (or Persephone's), provides feminine victims with a model for deactivating the feminine vampire. Although both Snow White and Gypsy are wrestling with the shadow of the Great Feminine, they both have access to Her positive aspects as well. Snow White has the precious image of a dead mother who cherished her, while Gypsy, who struggles with Rose's shadow, has also known Rose's fierce mother-bear love. Likewise, regardless of the actual mother figures whom we encounter after birth, we all experience the positive Great Feminine whenever we feel at home in the world, whenever we feel ourselves to be completely accepted and safe just as we are right now. We who are threatened by a feminine vampire must hold the shape of the positive Great Feminine close to our hearts. We must allow it to guide our actions, for it will help us to distinguish between healthy feminine love and the duplicitous vampiric version. When we are in the arms of the Great Feminine, the feminine vampire's tactics of yearning vulnerability, importunate requests, and effusive gratitude are shown up for what they really are—empty enticement, cunning manipulation, and contemptuous predation.

The stories of Snow White and Gypsy show us a second way to free ourselves from the feminine vampire that involves a different kind of warmth—the kind generated by our creative spark. Snow White is repeatedly rescued from oblivion by the industrious dwarves. As creatures who dig for wealth in subterranean places and craft wondrous objects with the riches that they find there, dwarves have long been the symbols of manifest creativity, particularly with regard to the sacred work of discovering our true destiny. We connect with the creative energy of the dwarves whenever we manifest our inner visions in external reality, and whenever we work to uncover our personal destiny and bring our dreams to life, independent from the expectations and judgments of others. In these moments, we live the power of our own truth,

and we can burn away the suffocating mist of someone else's vampiric agenda.

We can do the dwarf work of discovering our own true destiny in many ways, but they all seem to involve an interaction between the web of coincidence that Jung called *synchronicity* and our courageous determination to look within ourselves. In *Gypsy,* this conjunction of synchronicity and courageous insight begins at the moment when the sleazy music pulls the terrified girl-woman down the runway toward the hooting men. Gypsy's forced descent into the male audience corresponds to the moment in our lives when our naïve inner child is separated from the Mother and begins a free fall into the mortal fear of annihilation. The pain of this descent can be horrible. In fact, its attendant feelings of terror, helplessness, and despair could have destroyed Gypsy, as they had destroyed thousands of innocents who descended the runway before her. Gypsy's predecessors had disappeared without a trace into burlesque's maw of defilement and exploitation, but Gypsy did not follow them to their fate, nor did she turn and run screaming back into the arms of her vampiric mother. Synchronicity may have dragged Gypsy onto the runway, and fame may have eventually rescued Gypsy from serving either her mother or the leering men. But long before fame arrived, Gypsy Rose Lee had rescued her own sense of self. She had turned within to find her sacred destiny and bring it to life in the external world. What was it that Gypsy found within herself? What was the force that transformed her from Louise the victim into Gypsy the queen, thereby rescuing her from the feminine vampirism of her mother and the masculine vampirism of the audience? And what might Gypsy's transformative act look like in our lives?

Remember that Gypsy was virtually abducted from a childlike innocence in the arms of her vampiric mother and forced to engage the vampiric masculine energy of the burlesque audience. The tragic potential in Gypsy's plight is great. For example, a certain young woman, seeking refuge from her vampiric mother, ran

to the arms of a male "rescuer," only to realize later that she was being embraced by a masculine vampire. The young woman valiantly tried to survive, like so many others in her place, by using her sexual power to exploit some power back from her vampiric "rescuer." She thus became simply a different kind of feminine vampire, one who treated herself and others as objects, and who used her sexuality for exploitation.

When Gypsy was synchronistically caught in a similar trap between her vampiric mother and a vampiric masculine "rescuer" (in the form of the burlesque audience), she also parlayed her sexuality to achieve her own rescue, but she managed the affair with a profound psychic difference. Instead of degenerating into sexual vampirism, Gypsy somehow activated in her psyche an archetype that had once ruled civilization for centuries, until the patriarchy tried to banish Her into the collective shadow. Specifically, when Gypsy became aware of how her audience needed her to embody the mystery of feminine sensuality and sexuality, she began to incarnate the archetype of the sacred prostitute.*

After four thousand years of Judeo-Christian socialization, the words "sacred" and "prostitute" sound utterly antithetical to our ears. But in the millennia before God was necessarily male, there were two kinds of prostitutes. The first were "profane prostitutes," who used sexuality simply as a way to exploit others and (inevitably) themselves. For profane prostitutes, sexuality had no transcendent meaning or reverence; it was simply an act of commerce. Profane prostitutes are the only kind we know about today, since the patriarchy has spent several millennia teaching us that sexuality is, by definition, profane. In the millennia before the patriarchs damned the sexual potency of women, however, there existed a special class of sacred prostitutes. These women

---

*My discussion of the sacred prostitute is largely based on the excellent book *The Sacred Prostitute: Eternal Aspect of the Feminine* by Nancy Qualls-Corbett, which I highly recommend to any reader wishing to know more about this immensely important archetype.

were selected to serve as revered priestesses in magnificent temples dedicated to love, and they devoutly performed a variety of rituals, including ritual lovemaking, whose explicit purpose was to exalt the human spirit through the power of sexuality:

> Her beauty and sensuous body were not used in order to gain security, power or possessions. She did not make love in order to obtain admiration or devotion from the man who came to her. . . . She did not require a man to give her a sense of her own identity; rather this was rooted in her own womanliness. . . . Her *raison d'être* was to worship the goddess in love-making, thereby bringing the goddess' love into the human sphere. In this union—the union of masculine and feminine, spiritual and physical—the personal was transcended and the divine entered in. (Qualls-Corbett 1988, 40)

Where the profane prostitute practices soulless pornography, the sacred prostitute embodies divinely soulful eroticism. She ensures, with exquisite care, that every aspect of her sexuality serves to exalt her spirit and the spirits of those who bask in her provocative radiance.

The sacred prostitute's modern incarnation was ignited in the moment when Gypsy languorously peeled off her evening glove. And she has burst into flame more recently in Maya Angelou's thrilling poem "Phenomenal Woman":

> *Pretty women wonder where my secret lies.*
> *I'm not cute or built to suit a fashion model's size*
> *But when I start to tell them,*
> *They think I'm telling lies.*
> *I say,*
> *It's in the reach of my arms,*
> *The span of my hips,*
> *The stride of my step,*
> *The curl of my lips.*
> *I'm a woman*
> *Phenomenally.*

Phenomenal woman,
That's me.

I walk into a room
Just as cool as you please,
And to a man,
The fellows stand or
Fall down on their knees.
Then they swarm around me,
A hive of honey bees.
I say,
It's in the fire in my eyes,
And the flash of my teeth,
The swing in my waist,
And the joy in my feet.
I'm a woman
Phenomenally.
Phenomenal woman,
That's me.

Men themselves have wondered
What they see in me.
They try so much
But they can't touch
My inner mystery.
When I try to show them,
They say they still can't see.
I say,
It's in the arch of my back,
The sun of my smile,
The ride of my breasts,
The grace of my style.
I'm a woman
Phenomenally.
Phenomenal woman,
That's me.

Now you understand
Just why my head's not bowed.
I don't shout or jump about

Or have to talk real loud.
When you see me passing,
It ought to make you proud.
I say,
It's in the click of my heels,
The bend of my hair,
The palm of my hand,
The need for my care.
'Cause I'm a woman
Phenomenally.
Phenomenal woman,
That's me.

In my opinion, much of the healing of our societal wounds lies in the archetypal energy of the sacred prostitute. To whatever degree we are able, as women and men, to reunite our sensuality with our spirituality, we can ease the deep pain of our body/spirit rift and rejoice in our renewed sacred potency. More specifically to the subject of this book, whenever we activate the archetype of the sacred prostitute in our psyches, we protect ourselves from the syrupy tactics of the feminine vampire and the Draculan tactics of the masculine vampire. The sacred prostitute celebrates the magnificent, mortal flesh that incarnates our souls, while the psychic vampire displays only contempt for the flesh as a means of exploiting the soul. Whenever we accept or indulge in contempt for a body, including our own, we are succumbing to the psychic vampire. When, on the other hand, we celebrate the body, especially in the exaltation of sexuality as a golden path to our divinity, then the vampire's predation is foiled.

Have you ever seen the sculpture of Saint Teresa in the throes of her ecstatic union with God? Have you ever read the words or seen the paintings derived from the visions of the twelfth-century abbess Saint Hildegard von Bingen? Have you ever read the evocative poetry of King David and King Solomon? Religious education usually denies the sexuality inherent in these images, but anyone who has experienced sexual ecstasy must admit that for

these people, touching the face of God seems to have been an orgasmic encounter. The poetry of the Jewish kings also teaches us that the sacred prostitute's energy is not exclusively the province of women. Indeed, it is essential for men to own their sacred sexuality, particularly if they are facing a feminine vampire—otherwise, they will leap straight into her maw when she deceitfully promises to "give" them the sensuality they already possess. Whether we are male or female, when the sacred prostitute connects us to our immortal divinity through our phenomenal bodies, we can easily see through the smoke and mirrors of the vampire's pornographic ploys, and we can cleave instead to the sacred sexuality that leads us home to ourselves.

This was the perilous path that Gypsy traveled between her forcible abduction into the underworld of burlesque and her creation of a life that celebrated her sacred power. Gypsy journeyed far from her ignominious role as the clueless, nameless, eternal daughter, in order to find the place where she could simultaneously relish the vessel of her feminine energy and the penetrating force of the masculine. (Gypsy's deactivation of her mother's feminine vampire also seems to have liberated Rose to experience her own sacred prostitute energy.) From the couch of this union, Gypsy could conceive, gestate, and give birth to her rightful role in life. This is the ultimate act of manifest creativity. The birthing of one's Self is, like most birthings, a painful, frightening journey that requires deep courage, brute endurance, and for most of us, some outside assistance. The assistance may come through therapy, a spiritual practice, or any creative activity that gives form and power to our inner endeavor. For Snow White, that assistance was provided by the dwarves, while Gypsy's "dwarves" were the strippers who introduced her to a world where she eventually ruled as queen.

In addition to the sheer effort it takes to give birth to ourselves, we must also have access to our instinctual power. In the fairy tale of Snow White, this kind of power is embodied primarily in the

form of the prince's warhorse, who saves her life. The warhorse does not contemplate life in a cognitive way; he simply perceives and mulls and feels. Sometimes he does nothing more. But sometimes he is impelled to act instinctively in response to the truth that formulates in his great heart. The warhorse is that in us which sees the truth, feels its shape, hears its voice, knows its essence, and then acts on what we know. He is also that which jogs us out of our victim's lethargy, just as he jogged the poisoned apple out of Snow White's mouth. When we feel we have been brought to our senses, gently or with a jolt, after a period of delusion or inertia, we are experiencing the intuitive power of the warhorse.

It is vital that we know the difference between the clear, honest voice of intuition, and the persuasive, deceptive murmurings of our wounds. The only way I know to master this difficult task is through the disciplines of spiritual, physical, and artistic development (many of which can be experienced in the course of the therapeutic process). A person who engages in these pursuits eventually enters the special place that guides the warhorse and the stake—a place which is called many things, but which I know as the Sacred Ground. We are in the Sacred Ground whenever it feels as if we have only to remain quiet and attentive in order for life to move joyfully through us. It is the place where everything makes sense, regardless of what we desire or fear. It is the place of innocence and wisdom, assertiveness and acceptance, compassion and self-affirmation. When we are living from the Sacred Ground, we feel in the way that the warhorse feels, and know in the way that the warhorse knows. Nonhuman animals like the warhorse live their lives unconsciously in the Sacred Ground of instinctual truth. We human animals are born in the Sacred Ground, but we must leave it so we can later reclaim it with conscious intent and appreciation.

The warhorse, as a nonhuman animal, is also in unconscious possession of his proactive force. As human animals, particularly

as disempowered feminine humans, we are often disconnected from our proactive force. We experience proactivity (which some people refer to as "masculine" energy) when we feel directed and effective in accomplishing our goals, and when we hold views that are precisely articulated and forcefully espoused. In contrast, we experience reactivity (which some people refer to as "feminine" energy) when our perspective is flexible and inclusive, when we are inclined to let matters resolve themselves, and when we aren't bound to a crisp, firm opinion. Both proactive and reactive energies are essential to our health and joy, but their relative importance in a given situation depends on the circumstances.

The stories in this chapter suggest that it is of particular benefit to feminine victims to have close contact with their proactive masculine energies in order to slay their feminine vampires. Indeed, this is one reason why the feminine vampires in myth frequently attempt to alienate the feminine victim from her champion, since the united couple poses a powerful threat to the vampire. This is why Gypsy needed to claim her sexual power in relationship to men in order to free herself from Rose's death grip. Similarly, one has the feeling that the right gentleman caller might have succeeded in wresting Laura free of Amanda's clutches, were he stalwart and conscious enough to recognize the vampiric threat. And Snow White is explicitly reliant on her prince in order to escape from the witch's maw.

Many feminists abhor the moment when Snow White sings, "Someday my prince will come." But my feminist heart does not sink at these words, for I know that in order to fulfill our destinies, all of us need to connect with the archetype of the prince—the energy that is noble, heroic, forceful, and true. Snow White intuitively recognizes the need to destroy her stepmother's vampiric core, but she needs the energy of her prince to wield the sword. When we attempt to behead any vampire, particularly a feminine vampire, our masculine forces must be with us absolutely or the stroke will go astray. When we are lost in the sweet

mist, we need all the energies that produce wholesome bound-aries, healthy autonomy, clear focus, and beneficial goal setting. And when we send our decapitating sword on the great arc of its journey, we must be infused with resolute courage. All these things are in the province of the masculine—which, after all, is only a word that we use to describe the province of these things.

What prevents us from having access to the proactive mascu-line when we face off with a feminine vampire? As noted above, most of us have been alienated from our masculine force during the course of our socialization by the patriarchy and, in many cases, a feminine vampire. We have learned to distrust all mascu-line energy and to render to the feminine vampire any masculine energies that arise in our environment or ourselves. These are the factors that lead us to abdicate to our feminine vampires our im-petus, our effectiveness, and our potency. And yet, if there is so much strength in our proactive masculine energies, why don't they support us in a revolt against the vampire's oppression? For example, Snow White's prince is fully dedicated to his beloved bride, but he suddenly quails at the notion of killing the wicked queen, even though Snow White urgently tells him that she is lethally dangerous. What is it that stops the prince's hand until the moment of action? The problem is that the wicked queen is a mother. Mothers are sacred. The prince's mother is sacred. How can the prince, powerful and noble as he is, kill a *mother*?

And here lies the seed for the next of the vampiric duets we shall visit—the dance between feminine vampires and masculine victims. Snow White's prince awakened in time to kill her femi-nine vampire. Not all princes do. Let's visit a prince who awak-ened too late, a prince who paid with his blood and the blood of his children for his ignorance about the feminine vampire, a prince whose blind ignorance doomed him to a life of perpetual darkness. Onward into the night.

FEMININE VAMPIRES AND MASCULINE VICTIMS

IT MAY SEEM incomprehensible that a powerful person could be victimized by a psychic vampire who seems to be completely disempowered. Yet there are few lures more potent for a powerful champion than rescuing a grateful waif in distress. How exciting it is to save someone from the jaws of tragedy, particularly if the recipient is adoring and appreciative! You, the noble champion, journey alone down the desolate nighttime road, when there appears by the wayside a sweet little mist who is weeping in loneliness and alluring despair. Ah, you think, here is a perfect chance for me to put my sword to its proper use! Here is someone to save! And how charmingly pathetic she is! Perhaps there will be some love for me at the end of the heroic rescue! Your sword flashes up, and you dash to her aid—slaying all foes, fixing all woes, and paying each bill that she hands you. You parry and thrust past the point of exhaustion, for two adoring eyes are watching and their owner must not be let down. Onward you march, beyond fatigue, beyond all means, until your every resource is spent. But still you fight on, despite your depletion, to rescue the sweet, helpless mist, for how could you let down the poor little thing? Whatever would become of the helpless mist without your sword to defend her against the great cruel world?

The dance between an empowered masculine victim and the feminine vampire who hides under the veil of vulnerability may be the most insidious vampiric duet of them all. So many of us

have gone to our physical, financial, and spiritual ends, never realizing that we have been duped, never relenting in the deployment of our swords, never stanching the flow of our blood, and all for the sake of a pitiable feminine vampire. How can we be so powerful and yet so blind? But really, our gullibility is no mystery. When we embark on the path of the Champion, when we don the armor of empowerment, we expect our vampires also to be draped in the cloak of power. We never suspect that a vampire might veil itself in the guise of weakness and vulnerability. What's more, when the Champion is active in our psyches, we strive to serve those less fortunate than ourselves, so when we come upon the sweet mist by the side of the road, is it any wonder that we bleed on its behalf? What a cruel ruse this is, for in fact the mist is a vampire who will feed on us by exploiting the very nobility on which our Championhood is based.

OEDIPUS REX

The myth of Oedipus is a story about a woman and a man. It is essential, however, to move beyond the gendering of the story as you feel around in your life for the shape of this vampiric duet. Gender is not the key element of this dance. With many women now experiencing more empowerment than they have for centuries, and with many men becoming more conscious of their personal disempowerment at the hands of the patriarchy, the gendering of these roles could easily occur today in any combination. The key element is the embezzlement of an empowered victim's blood by a vampire who operates under the veil of vulnerability. The story as told by Sophocles (I use the Dudley Fitts and Robert Fitzgerald translation [1977]) is a familiar one. Because of its somewhat perverse appropriation by Freud, however, we need to make a special effort to hear the myth with new ears. So wipe your mind clean and listen to the story of King Oedipus.

Once upon a time, in the ancient city of Thebes, there lived a mighty king named Oedipus. Oedipus was a noble king, and he nurtured the prosperity of Thebes as if it were his own. So when the people of Thebes grew morbid and diseased and came to him in anguish, Oedipus felt their agony in the depths of his soul:

> *Poor children! You may be sure I know*
> *All that you longed for in your coming here.*
> *I know that you are deathly sick; and yet,*
> *Sick as you are, not one is as sick as I.*
> *Each of you suffers in himself alone*
> *His anguish, not another's; but my spirit*
> *Groans for the city, for myself, for you. (5)*

What a great king was Oedipus! His spirit and compassion were equal to that of a god. In fact, King Oedipus suffered so much the ills of his kingdom that he sent Lord Creon, the brother of his beautiful queen, Jocasta, to the oracle of the sun god, Apollo, at Delphi in order to learn what evil held Thebes in its poisoned jaws. When Lord Creon returned from the Delphic oracle, he reluctantly informed King Oedipus of Apollo's pronouncement:

> *In plain words*
> *The god commands us to expel from the land of Thebes*
> *An old defilement we are sheltering.*
> *It is a deathly thing, beyond cure;*
> *We must not let it feed upon us longer. (7)*

Specifically, the oracle proclaimed, the people of Thebes must find and banish the man who had murdered King Laïos, the Theban king who had preceded King Oedipus. One day, when King Laïos had been out driving in his chariot with a few of his men, he was attacked by a band of outlaws. The outlaws were so fierce that only one of the king's men had escaped, and King Laïos himself had been killed.

The kingdom of Thebes had been grieved and frightened by

the loss of its king. Fortunately, soon after his murder, another kingly man arrived in Thebes—a man of noble bearing, great courage, and sharp intelligence. This last gift served him well in Thebes, because it enabled him to solve the riddle that was posed to all newcomers by the Sphinx, a fantastic creature with the head of woman, the body of a lion, the tail of a serpent, and eagle's wings. The Sphinx had devoured every newcomer to Thebes who could not answer her riddle, which was this: "What being, with only one voice, has sometimes two feet, sometimes three, sometimes four, and is weakest when it has the most?" Up to this point, no newcomer had ever found the answer to the riddle, so the Sphinx had devoured them all. All, that is, until the kingly newcomer arrived before her. "The answer is man," the newcomer replied, "because he crawls on all fours when he is weakest as an infant, stands firmly on his two feet in his youth, and leans upon a staff in his old age." The Sphinx was so enraged by the newcomer's impudent cleverness that she destroyed herself. And thus the newcomer not only survived the test but also freed Thebes from the tyranny of the Sphinx.

Rejoicing at their deliverance, the Thebans took the noble stranger as their new king to replace the murdered King Laïos. The newcomer, who was in fact Oedipus, married King Laïos's widow, Queen Jocasta, and lived with her in King Laïos's palace, where they had four lovely children. In this way, the story seemed to have a happy ending for King Oedipus and his new Theban subjects, who were delighted with this satisfying resolution to the dual crises of their kinglessness and tyranny by the Sphinx. In fact, they were so pleased with the whole affair that they had put behind them the mystery of King Laïos's murder. The murderer was never caught, and the sole survivor of the marauders' attack had gone into retirement in a quiet place far from the city, where he worked as a shepherd tending the flocks.

But now it appeared that, however satisfying this solution may have been to King Oedipus and the Thebans, it was far from satis-

factory to Apollo. Apollo's oracle decreed that Thebes would con-
tinue to wither and die until the man who had murdered King
Laïos, a man who still lived in Thebes, was brought to justice.
When Lord Creon delivered the oracle's words, King Oedipus
rose in righteous fury and issued a command that the murderer of
King Laïos, however high or low his caste, should be brought to
the justice ordained by Apollo:

> *I pray that that man's life be consumed in evil and wretchedness.*
> *And as for me, this curse applies no less*
> *If it should turn out that the culprit is my guest here,*
> *Sharing my hearth.*
> *You have heard the penalty. (13)*

Despite King Oedipus's fierce resolve, however, it seemed it would
be very difficult to determine the identity of the murderer. It had
been years since King Laïos was killed, and there had been only
one witness to the crime. In order to scrape together a few clues
about the murderer's identity, King Oedipus sent to Delphi for the
most famous truthseer of the age, Teiresias.

Teiresias could see the truth, but nothing else. Apollo had given
him the gift of inner sight, but as payment for this gift, had made
Teiresias blind to the outer world. So when the truthseer appeared
before King Oedipus, he had to be led in by a page. And while
you may think that blindness was penalty enough for being a seer
of truth, that was not the case. In his many years as a truthseer,
Teiresias had learned much about the heavy burden borne by all
truthseers, which is that no matter how fiercely people clamor
after the truth, they are often very uncomfortable when it actually
lands in their laps. The discomfort of a truth-hearing client can be
particularly problematic for professional truthseers when the client is a highly placed person with a bad temper.

This is why Teiresias was very unwilling to deliver the information that King Oedipus demanded: he knew that the powerful
king would be distressed by the news. But King Oedipus's com-

mand was not to be denied, and Teiresias had to comply. So he told Oedipus:

> *You yourself are the pollution of this country . . .*
> *I say that you are the murderer whom you seek . . .*
> *I say you live in hideous shame with those*
> *Most dear to you. You cannot see the evil. (18–19)*

Needless to say, King Oedipus was horrified and embarrassed by these words, and like many people who are horrified and embarrassed by bad tidings, he was less than gracious to their bearer. Specifically, he accused Teiresias of lying and of conspiring with Lord Creon to overthrow him. He screamed at Teiresias that he was a "sightless, witless, senseless, mad old man," to which the truthseer replied (out of perversity, resignation, or simply the fulfillment of his duty): "*You* are the madman. There is no one here who will not curse you soon, as you curse me" (20).

King Oedipus, now beside himself with rage, ordered Teiresias to leave at once. But Teiresias had evidently decided that since he was telling the truth, he would tell it all:

> *The man you have been looking for all this time,*
> *The damned man, the murderer of Laïos,*
> *That man is in Thebes. To your mind he is foreign-born,*
> *But it will soon be shown that he is a Theban,*
> *A revelation that will fail to please.*
>   *A blind man,*
> *Who has his eyes now; a penniless man, who is rich now;*
> *And he will go tapping the strange earth with his staff.*
> *To the children with whom he lives now he will be*
> *Brother and father—the very same; to her*
> *Who bore him, son and husband—the very same*
> *Who came to his father's bed, wet with his father's blood. (23–24)*

And with that awful pronouncement, Teiresias the truthseer left.

Some images are so appalling that once they have been brought into awareness, the mind cannot hold them for long. These images are white hot with power and would melt the mind into a puddle

if they remained in consciousness for more than a flicker of time. So the images are pushed away and denied. Whenever possible, we try to push them into a deeply unconscious part of the psyche. But since their power is usually too great to bury completely, they are more frequently banished to the bad-boy corner of abhorrent lies. This is precisely what King Oedipus did with the images conveyed by Teiresias's words; he denounced them as treasonous lies brewed by Lord Creon. Now, Lord Creon was deeply angered by the accusations of King Oedipus, but he was a smart man and a prudent one, so he calmly confronted the king and bade him seek the facts that would refute the seer's words.

At first, King Oedipus refused Lord Creon's reasonable suggestion, but when the Thebans begged him to heal the sickness of the land by pursuing his search for the murderer, he reluctantly agreed to the plan. King Oedipus could always hear the voice of his people, since without them, he was king to no one. He began his search by asking Queen Jocasta for the details of King Laïos's murder. Based on her disquieting account, King Oedipus sent for the shepherd who was the sole survivor of the attack. While they were waiting for the shepherd, King Oedipus explained to Queen Jocasta why her account of the old king's murder had disquieted him. It seems that Oedipus was the son of King Polybos and Queen Meropê in the neighboring land of Corinth. When Oedipus had reached his manhood, the Delphic oracle foretold that he should kill his father and marry his mother. Aghast at the horror of these words, Oedipus had fled the kingdom of Corinth, hoping to outrun the oracle's prediction. On the road between Corinth and Thebes, he had nearly been run down by a group of men at a crossroads, one of whom rode in a chariot and beat Oedipus as he passed. In angry retribution for the attack, Oedipus had assaulted the men and killed them all. King Oedipus explained to his queen that he felt uneasy because the details from his battle at the crossroads bore a strong resemblance to Queen Jocasta's account of King Laïos's murder. But then again, Oedipus remem-

bered, the surviving witness had said that many men, not a lone traveler, had attacked King Laïos and his group, so perhaps there was nothing to fear.

While the king and queen awaited news of the shepherd, a messenger arrived from Corinth bearing the "joyful and grievous" news to King Oedipus that his father, King Polybos of Corinth, had died of old age. Despite his sadness, King Oedipus was much relieved by the messenger's tidings, since they dispelled the hideous Delphic prediction that he would murder his father. When the messenger said that the people of Corinth awaited the return of Oedipus as their new ruler, however, the king refused, saying that he still feared the second half of the oracle's pronouncement, in which he was doomed to marry his mother. For this reason, Oedipus explained, he was adamant in his refusal to return to Corinth. The messenger, for his part, feared to return home without the new Corinthian king in hand. So, in an attempt to assuage Oedipus's fears about returning to Queen Meropê's side, the messenger informed Oedipus that King Polybos and Queen Meropê were not, in fact, his parents.

"What do you mean?" cried the king.

The Corinthian messenger responded by telling King Oedipus that many years ago, when the messenger was a young man in the service of King Polybos and Queen Meropê, he learned that the Corinthian monarchs were heartbroken because they were unable to conceive a child. So when the messenger came upon a shepherd who offered him a beautiful abandoned baby, it occurred to him that he might bring it to the king and queen to raise as their own. That, explained the messenger, is exactly what transpired, and King Oedipus was the baby that he took from the shepherd and gave to the Corinthian monarchs. "So you see, sire," reasoned the messenger, "Queen Meropê is not really your mother, and there is no danger if you return to Corinth."

"Who was this shepherd from whom you took me?" asked King Oedipus, with growing trepidation and rage.

"I think he was said to be one of Laïos's people," replied the messenger tremulously. With a sick horror rising in his stomach, King Oedipus turned and cried to his people:

> Does anyone here
> Know this shepherd that he is talking about?
> If you have, tell me. It is time things were made plain. (54)

And the Thebans replied:

> I think the man he means is that same shepherd
> You have already asked to see. (54)

So King Oedipus and Queen Jocasta, along with the Corinthian messenger and the people of Thebes, awaited even more anxiously the old shepherd's arrival.

When he was finally brought to the palace, the old shepherd was, like Teiresias, very reluctant to speak with the king. But King Oedipus commanded him to speak what he knew and, in terror and grief, the old shepherd told the king his story. Long ago, he said, the oracle at Delphi had foretold to King Laïos and Queen Jocasta that King Laïos would be killed by his own son. To avert this loathsome prediction, at the birth of their first son, Queen Jocasta had bound her baby's feet and then commanded a shepherd, the one who stood before them now, to take the infant into the wilderness to die. But the shepherd was a kindly man, and he could not bring himself to kill the helpless child. As he pointed to the Corinthian messenger, he explained:

> I pitied the baby, my King,
> And I thought that this man would take him far away
> To his own country.
> He saved him—but for what a fate!
> For you are what this man says you are,
> No man living is more wretched than Oedipus. (62)

And so it came to be known to King Oedipus, to Thebes, and to all of horrified history, that Oedipus had murdered his father and married his mother.

The end of this story is as sad as its middle. Queen Jocasta fled from the hall and hanged herself in the room where their marriage bed stood. King Oedipus, when he found her, put out his eyes with the pins of the golden brooches that held her gown, crying

> *"No more shall you look on the misery about me,*
> *The horrors of my own doing! Too long you have known*
> *The faces of those whom I should never have seen,*
> *Too long been blind to those for whom I was searching!*
> *From this hour, go in darkness!"*
> *... And the blood spattered his beard,*
> *Bursting from his ruined sockets like red hail. (67)*

Finally, after bidding his children and his kingdom an anguished farewell, the "great wreck and hell of Oedipus, whom the gods hate" (70) set upon the road of revulsion, banishment, and death.

RECOGNIZING THE FEMININE VAMPIRE

The story of Oedipus is the story of a man who was caught in the vengeful web of the gods and who was condemned to commit two of humanity's most heinous acts—parricide and incest. Traditionally, the myth of Oedipus is interpreted as a lesson about the mortal error of *hubris*—the vain human inclination to take oneself as equal to the gods. The consequences of hubris are generally unpleasant, because the gods tolerate with very poor grace all mortal pretenders to their immortal realm. We experience the consequences of hubris every time we identify with (rather than relating to) the archetypal power that moves through us. Remember from chapter 1 that when we identify with an archetype, we take ourselves to be the incarnation of a god or goddess rather than remembering that we are simply a mortal coil through which the immortal power passes. When we commit hubris and identify with an archetype, we are likely to be perverted or incinerated by the divine power as it possesses, deforms, and finally obliterates our human identities.

Oedipus was certainly guilty of both literal and psychic hubris.

In the literal sense, Oedipus attempted to outwit the Delphic oracle by fleeing Corinth, and he hoped that his cleverness would hoodwink the gods into overlooking his flight from destiny. Once in Thebes, Oedipus indulged in psychic hubris by exercising his kingship as if he were the divine patron of his devoted subjects, to whom he actually owed his inflated position of demidivinity. By believing himself more cunning than the gods and by acting as a god himself, Oedipus marched arrogantly toward his awful fate. In this way, Oedipus's sins of parricide and incest were the direct consequences of his conscious efforts to outrun the edict of the gods and play at being a god himself.

It is important, however, to remember that for all his hubris, Oedipus committed the sins of parricide and incest unconsciously—indeed, he sinned in the very process of trying to avoid them. Thus, Oedipus's intent was noble; his only conscious sin was the hubris involved in trying to avoid the ugly Delphic decree. It is Oedipus's innocence of his parricide and incest that makes his story a tragedy. If he had known that he was murdering his father and marrying his mother, Oedipus's story would have been simply another epic in which a detestable villain is brought to justice. The tragedy is that Oedipus's worst sins were committed in innocence. When the truth of his unconscious parricide and incest began to plague his land, Oedipus sought to learn the truth for the sake of his people, and it was for their sake that he continued to pursue the truth despite his mounting terror. Later, when Oedipus arrived at the root of his nation's cursed state and learned that the criminal was none other than himself, he immediately imposed upon himself an even more severe punishment than the one he had ordained for the murderer of King Laïos.

In light of these facts, it is difficult to see Oedipus as the conscious villain of this tragic story. And yet it is precisely the villainy of Oedipus that Sigmund Freud invoked in his theory of psychic development, when he hypothesized that sons are possessed of an Oedipus complex, in which they wish to kill their fathers and

mate with their mothers. Interestingly, Freud repeated this strategy in his theory of "childhood seduction," in which he postulated the villainy of innocent children by asserting that children seduce adults into incestuous relationships. Many people are now appalled by the inside-out reasoning of Freud's theories about childhood seduction, and Jeffrey Masson (1992) has shown us that Freud himself backpedaled into the childhood seduction theory only after his colleagues ridiculed his original theory of parent-perpetrated incest. Today it is unthinkable to accuse incest victims of being the perpetrators of their own suffering. The same might be said of Oedipus. He, like an abused child, may have been blindly seduced into "sinning." But villainy implies consciousness wrongdoing, and most of Oedipus's wrongdoing was entirely unconscious.

The conscious wrongdoing that is required for villainy is one of the reasons that the vampire is the most villainous of entities. The vampire is not an innocent slave of Satan, nor a mindless minion of hell. On the contrary, the vampire is conscious of its virile contagion but spreads its curse anyway to appease (however momentarily) its infinite hunger. If you want to find a vampire in a tale, look for a conscious villain. When we look for conscious villainy in the story of Oedipus, we find one of mythology's most insidious vampires.

Let's return to a part of the story that we hear about only in retrospect: the moment when the old shepherd had escaped from the murderous attack on King Laïos and returned to Thebes, just in time to find Oedipus ensconced on Laïos's throne and in bed with his widow, Jocasta. Queen Jocasta tells Oedipus that when the shepherd came back

> *And found you enthroned in the place of the dead king,*
> *He came to me, touched my hand with his, and begged*
> *That I would send him away to the frontier district*
> *Where only shepherds go—*
> *As far away from the city as I could send him.*

I granted his prayer; for although the man was a slave,
He had earned more than this favor at my hands. (39)

The shepherd had earned the queen's favor because, as we later learn, it was he who had relieved Jocasta of the baby Oedipus, whom she had condemned because of the Delphic prediction that he would someday kill his father. Thus, when the shepherd asks the gift of oblivion from the queen, Jocasta becomes the only person to possess several pieces of important information. First, she knows that the shepherd, who is aware of the oracle's prophecy, participated in the banishment of the baby Oedipus. Second, Jocasta knows that the shepherd, who witnessed the murder of Laïos and now sees Oedipus on Laïos's throne, is requesting a voluntary exile away from the palace. Third, Jocasta knows (because Oedipus figures it out with her help) that Oedipus is the man who has killed Laïos—a man who was fated to be killed by his son. In the face of this web of circumstance and awareness, it is hard to believe that Jocasta could still be innocent of the fact that her marriage was incestuous. Nonetheless, it is possible that she was in such denial that she was rendered monumentally impervious to these revelations.

Jocasta's presumed innocence is definitively shattered, however, in her response to the Corinthian messenger's account of how he took the infant Oedipus from the old shepherd. When Oedipus hears this news, he asks the people for their help in locating the shepherd. The people quickly reply that the shepherd from whom the messenger received Oedipus is the same shepherd who witnessed Laïos's murder. But when Oedipus asks his mother/wife to explain this extraordinary coincidence (about which she knows a great deal), Jocasta replies,

Why think of him?
Forget this herdsman. Forget it all.
This talk is a waste of time. (54)

Oedipus assumes that Jocasta responds this way because she fears that the shepherd will identify his parents as slaves. He at-

tempts to reassure her that his spirit is not base, no matter who his parents may have been. But Jocasta rebuffs her husband/son, crying:

> *For God's love, let us have no more questioning!*
> *Is your life nothing to you?*
> *My own is pain enough for me to bear. . . .*
> *Listen to me, I beg you: do not do this thing! . . .*
> *Everything I say is for your own good! . . .*
> *You are fatally wrong! May you never learn who you are! (55)*

In her book *Les Enfants de Jocaste* (*The Children of Jocasta*, 1980), the French psychoanalyst Christiane Olivier asks, "Thus, did Jocasta know something of the origin of Oedipus, of the death of his father, and of the crime that she continued to perpetuate with her son? Could Jocasta be more guilty than Oedipus? Could Oedipus be the toy of Jocasta and her desire?" (11). Given the limits of Sophocles' story, it is impossible to ascertain whether Jocasta knew that Oedipus was her son when she married him. What is certain from the words of Sophocles is that Jocasta knew the truth about her marriage long before Oedipus did and that, unlike her noble husband/son, she responded to the truth by attempting to cover it up and preserve her unholy alliance with Oedipus. What's more, once Jocasta had dedicated herself to perpetuating her conscious mother-son incest, she used all of her persuasive power to keep Oedipus at her breast. Perhaps Jocasta told herself that she was only attempting to protect her beloved Oedipus (and herself, by the way). But regardless of her motive, Jocasta depicts in detail the type of woman that Oedipus calls an "unspeakable mother." Jocasta is a disempowered feminine vampire who preys on an empowered masculine victim—her own son.

Let me tell you the story of a real Jocasta. She was born into a middle-class family, where she became a target of negligence and abuse. She might have become another wan girl-victim of the patriarchy, but she was smart and strong and she had the survival instincts of a wildcat. Scratching through school, purring at kind

strangers, slinking in the shadows and strutting in the light, the woman struggled into adulthood. She became a paragon of achievement and an expert at social grace. She was deemed a beauty, which impressed other women, but she chose to enter the professional world of men, where she defied the odds and won a modicum of professional prestige. These triumphs were not enough to give her a sense of her own reality and security, however, so her energies evolved increasingly into a lust for control and a hunger for power. She scanned the horizons for a king who would admire and protect her—a partner whom she could safely manage. When she found a likely candidate for the job, she married him. She felt she was safe, empowered, and in control. She crowned herself queen.

And then something awful happened. It seemed that fate had tricked her cruelly. Her man was no protector—he couldn't even protect himself against the larger world that she had learned to fear and revere. Indeed, her supposed king cowered like a frightened puppy in the face of danger. Horrified, the woman discovered that this whimpering cur was no king at all. The woman felt terrified, desperate, and alone. Her old mate may have adored her, but there was no salvation in the adoration of a worm. (The woman had not learned to experience the simple humanity of herself or others, so for her, men were either kings or worms, and she was either a queen or a victim.) The woman had survived and even thrived in the patriarchy's jaws, but she was growing older, plainer, and weary. She realized that she was pinned under a professional glass ceiling, like a precious but inarguably dead butterfly who is pinned under an entomologist's mounting slide. In this deteriorating state, how could she continue to feed her hunger for professional success and personal gratification, without a championing mate by her side? She lusted for a mate who was worthy of her, and she hunted him with a quiet desperation.

One day, a carefree young man appeared before the woman. He was as strong and smart as she, and he adored her. Thrilled

by this gift of fate, the woman took the young man as her new king. The man could not believe his good fortune—the woman he adored most in the world, a woman of awesome power and allure, had chosen him as her favorite. He was granted access to her chambers and permitted to look upon her treasures, and he was rewarded for his achievements with her glowing praise and encouragement. His triumphs were her glory, his gifts were her gold. She inflated his life to match her dreams and he soared on the wings of her ambition. When he seemed to weary or falter, she gave him a taste of her hunger so that he could feed on others and live on their life force, just as she was living on his.

True, there were moments when the man grew uneasy, when he felt that his life was laid upon the altar of the woman's needs and was therefore unavailable to him. In these moments, the man felt flickers of resentment and anger and, eventually, hate. Of course, he was appalled as soon as he perceived his dark feelings, and he buried them under mountains of guilt and penance. But as the years passed, the man occasionally held onto his anger long enough to struggle against the woman's embrace. He would journey afar, dally with younger women, and speak treasonous words of rebellion. When the woman learned of these betrayals, she raged in private, but to the man's face, she smiled indulgently, allowing that all men must stray and crow. Then, softly caressing the ego she had worked so hard to inflate, she called the man back to her side with her siren's song of ambition, suspicion, and arrogant elitism. Apart from her, he could not appease his overblown hunger; only by her side could he ease his yearning for *more*.

The woman called their profane relationship "love," and the man came to believe in her definition; that is, he came to see "love" as an alliance of inflation, manipulation, and mutual feeding. And so they lived, the woman and the man, in an unholy marriage where they danced their mesmerizing duet of mutual emotional embezzlement. Sometimes the young man's rebellions

would last for years. And sometimes the woman would yearn for a depth of union with him that was unspeakable—unspeakable to him, to herself, or to anyone who ventured near their duet. Her yearning was unspeakable because the mate whom the woman had chosen was her son.

VAMPIRISM AND THE MOTHER-SON RELATIONSHIP

Although we must be cautious not to get too attached to the genders of the characters in the Oedipal drama, I would like to pursue the mother-son version of this vampiric duet for a little while longer, since so much of the Oedipus myth points in that direction. Moreover, the maternal aspect of the myth is important, since the feminine vampire inevitably leads us, in this chapter as in the last, to the shadow of the mother archetype.

The energy of the shadow mother, which Jung refers to as the Terrible Mother, makes two early appearances in Oedipus's life. The first occurs when Jocasta binds her baby's feet and sends him to die in the wilderness, in order to protect the life of her husband-king and, not coincidentally, her queenly status as well. Faced with such a Terrible Mother (in both the archetypal and everyday senses of the term), Oedipus is left to rely on fate and his own fortitude in order to survive. In this case, Oedipus is like many of us who have become champions in our adulthood; we have had to develop our champion strength in order to survive the danger of our childhoods, when we were unprotected or abused by our supposed caretakers. Like young Oedipus, we struggle to survive.

Not only does Oedipus survive, but he even lands a cushy deal as the princeling son to another set of royal parents, who seem to care for him a great deal more than his birth parents did. But the pain of our original parenting can't be neatly swept under the carpet of denial—not in our external lives, not in our internal lives, and not in the life of Oedipus, either. In Oedipus's case, the truth returns in the form of the first Delphic oracle, which serves

both to warn him about his familial fate and to drive him toward it. In an effort to escape the oracle, Oedipus leaves Corinth on the road to Thebes, and there he has his second encounter with the Terrible Mother, this time in the form of the Sphinx.

The Sphinx is well suited to this role—so much so that Jung once referred to her as the *synthesis* of the Terrible Mother.* She is cunning, alluring, enigmatic, devouring, and widely present in global culture. The Sphinx challenges Oedipus to answer her riddle, with the intent of devouring him when he cannot beat her at her own game. But Oedipus is prepared for the Terrible Mother this time, perhaps as a result of his earlier encounters with her energy. He outwits the Sphinx and thereby destroys her. This would imply that Oedipus is well armed against the dark aspect of the Great Feminine, as long as She presents herself in an explicit form, such as the monstrous Sphinx.

Unfortunately, Oedipus is not so well prepared to survive his next encounter with the dark feminine when she appears in the form of Jocasta—a widowed queen who trembles precariously (and prettily) between the throne of a large realm and the next man who wishes to ascend it. Jocasta desperately needs a champion to ensure her security and status when, lo and behold, here is her champion—the man who has vanquished the Sphinx and liberated Thebes. Who this may have been in the moment of his birth does not matter to Jocasta. Her concern is for her survival, rather than for the sanctity of the young man's soul (or her own, for that matter). And besides, he adores her so much! In the end, we can suppose, Jocasta comes to love Oedipus as many devoted

---

*The Sphinx herself has an illuminating history, one with which Sophocles' original audiences were surely familiar. She was originally sent by the goddess Hera to punish Thebes for the death of the boy Chryssipus, who was a favorite of Hera's. Chryssipus had been abducted by King Laïos, who had forced him to serve as his catamite—a sexual enslavement that eventually led to Chryssipus's death. The more we get to know about Laïos and Jocasta, the more it seems merciful of the Fates to have reared Oedipus outside of his family of origin. But then, as Jean Bolen has observed, there are no good marriages or happy families in classical mythology.

women love their champions, even unto the most terrible consequences.

We can also imagine what a boon Jocasta's love must have been for the ambitious young Oedipus—a queen and a kingdom, ripe for the rescuing! What champion, particularly a champion already given to hubris, could resist the offer? The queen and the Theban people are only too happy to encourage the champion's inflation so they can benefit further from his largess of life force—the more blood he pumps, the more they can reap the fruits of his power. And just in case all this adoration is not sufficiently alluring bait, Oedipus is attracted by one more powerful motivator thrown into the deal—the pulsing promise of sexual gratification by the beautiful Queen Jocasta. The importance of sexual heat cannot be overstated with regard to the dance between feminine vampires and masculine victims. It is the crux of the feminine vampire's ruse that her victim will experience sexual transcendence—an epiphany for the champion that is simply a projection of his own unrecognized sacred sexuality.

The seductive prowess of the feminine vampire may be one of her most noteworthy aspects in the global vampire myth. Historically, feminine vampires were described as "voluptuous and wanton, irresistible, heartlessly cruel. Like the male vampire she has full red lips—supposedly the result of sucking blood, but also traditionally regarded in folk belief as a sign of excessive sensuality. Even the pure must succumb to her macabre charms" (Farson 1976, 42). Bram Stoker was well aware of the sexual allure of the feminine vampire, as evidenced by his sensual description of Jonathan's encounter with Dracula's wives and by his choice of names for the boat that bears Dracula home to Transylvania: *Czarina Catherine,* the notoriously promiscuous empress of Russia. More recently, the archetype of the feminine vampire surfaced in the 1920s, when she was described as "an adventuress who leeched onto helpless men and sucked them dry of money and material possessions. Abbreviating her name to *vamp,* the cinema

of the twenties offered a classic example of the feminine vampire in Theda Bara, an actress who took as her name an anagram of 'Arab Death' and who was photographed with skulls and bones to epitomize her victims" (Cooper 1974, 32). Given the potency of the feminine vampire's sexual deception and predation, it seems fitting that the only mention Jung makes of the vampire in his entire collected works is when he asserts that the vampire is the succubus of a man—that is, the feminine demon who comes upon him in his sleep to suck his semen and blood.

All of these images convey the blood-hot sexual power that throbs in the voice of the feminine vampire when she softly beckons her champion. Power, adoration, and transcendent sex—all in a tidy package that lies in the vampire's lap. A perfect scenario . . . until the dark truth rudely thrusts itself into the charade. In the story of Oedipus, the dark truth arrives in the form of his biological origins, but for most of us, the seductive duet between a champion and his adoring vampire tends to darken it quite another way. Here's how it went for one such couple.

In the beginning, the man was happy to rescue the pathetic damsel, who, coincidentally, had just one or two more little traumas that she hoped he would be kind enough to rectify. Thus began a long series of heroic rescues, each of which was appreciated by the woman only long enough to resuscitate her hero before his next valorous deed. Eventually, the man could not shake off the growing suspicion that he was being used, and he began to simmer with resentment and anger. Of course, he did not want to wound the poor woman, so he tried in the gentlest way possible to regain a little of his power. But when the woman's sugary tactics foiled his efforts, the former champion was transformed by his rage and frustration into a control-hungry abuser. On the receiving end of this ugly transformation was the vampiric damsel, who was reduced by the man's fury into an epitome of the long-suffering though undeserving martyr. At the sight of her eloquent pain, the man was wracked with remorse and self-recrimination,

and he vowed never again to turn on the pathetic creature whose rescue was his very purpose in life. The man submitted a humble apology to his beloved, then retreated into his original heroic position, mumbling to himself that he was lucky to have such an appreciative, deserving audience.

But just because the man had apologized did not mean that the duet immediately reverted to its original form. His mate, skilled at this particular dance, realized that a whole new ration of blood could be sucked out of any remorseful champion who was attempting to apologize: as long as the woman refused to accept the man's apology, she could remain in the role of a righteous martyr whose suffering could demand any price in return for her gift of absolution. So the woman always maintained her injured, unmollified state for as long as possible.

In the course of this guilt game, the woman used many strategies to extract her mate's life force, but her most effective tactic was to punish him with a siege of shunning. Anyone who has been subjected to the "silent treatment" knows the anguish that this tactic can induce. Our anguish is immobilizing because we know that nothing we can say or do will penetrate the wall of disdain we have unwittingly erected around our beloved with our own reprehensible behavior. We feel that, short of separating ourselves from our beloved completely, we have no choice but to linger alone near the wall of disdain, desperately performing acts of penance in the faint hope of winning back the vampire's "love." We bleed our life force into our penance, right up to the moment when we are about to abandon the whole notion of earning the vampire's pardon. And then suddenly, just at the very last instant before we pack up our meager resources and leave, our pardon is handed down from the vampire's pinnacle of magnanimity, and we are permitted back into our beloved's arms.

A detailed picture of this shunning duet between a masculine victim and a feminine vampire occurs in *The Glass Menagerie*. Laura is not her mother's only victim. More nutritious, at least for as long as she can keep him by her side, is Amanda's son, Tom. By the time we meet the Wingfield family, mother and son have been dancing their vampiric duet for years. We can imagine that Tom originally tried to be his mother's champion after his father abandoned the family. In those first few years, we can suppose, Tom tried to acquiesce to all that his damsel requested of him, for the pathetic images of feminine distress are burned deeply into Tom's psyche. At the end of the play, when he speaks across the time and space that separate him from Amanda and Laura, Tom still yearns to rescue his vulnerable sister. We can also see the traces of Tom's old heroic stance toward his vampiric mother as she tries, with increasingly obvious and unsuccessful tactics, to engage her son in the dance. For example, in one scene, Tom apologizes to his mother after he has leveled an explosion of frustration at her and she has subjected him to the silent treatment. But his peace is short-lived:

TOM: Mother. I—I apologize, Mother. [*Amanda draws a quick, shuddering breath. Her face works grotesquely. She breaks into childlike tears.*] I'm sorry for what I said, for everything that I said, I didn't mean it.

AMANDA: My devotion has made me a witch and so I make myself hateful to my children! . . . I've had to put up a solitary battle all these years. But you're my right-hand bower! Don't fall down, don't fail!

TOM: [*gently*] I try, Mother.

AMANDA: Try and you will *succeed!* Why, you—you're just *full* of natural endowments! Both of my children—they're *unusual* children! Don't you think I know it! I'm so—*proud!* Happy and—feel I've—so much to be thankful for . . . ! (Williams 1945, 48–49)

Once Amanda has magnanimously admitted Tom back into her good graces, she pursues the scheme that underlies her "merciful" pardon:

AMANDA: I sent out your sister so that I could discuss something with you. . . . I mean that as soon as Laura has got somebody to take care of her, married, a home of her own, independent— why, then you'll be free to go wherever you please. . . . [*catching his arm—very importunately; then shyly*] Down at the warehouse, aren't there some—nice young men? . . . Find out one that's clean-living—doesn't drink and ask him out for sister! . . . To *meet*! Get *acquainted*!

TOM: Oh, my *go-osh*!

AMANDA: Will you? . . . *Will* you, dear?

TOM: *Yes!* (49–54)

THE ESSENCE OF THE FEMININE VAMPIRE

In *The Glass Menagerie* we watch as a feminine vampire fashions a web of importuning vulnerability, a web that is as fragile in appearance and as resilient in reality as a spider's web covered with droplets of mist. The deceptive fragility of the feminine vampire's web lures many of us into a sticky tangle of heroism and guilt. When we first catch sight of the mesmerizing lacework suspended on tenuous threads, we long to protect and caress the delicate lace. We carefully touch the shimmering strands, dazzled by the glistening dewdrops that cling to them. After an age of enchantment, we stir to leave the astonishing wheel of light, but we find that the web cannot bear to let us go—it clings to us with a powerful adhesive of adoration and need. At first we are flattered and gratified that our presence is so essential to the happiness of another, and we feel that we are finally appreciated in a way that we have always longed for.

And yet, even as we savor the gratitude of the web, we feel a growing uneasiness that something is not quite as idyllic as it seems. The web is sweetly appreciative, but cloying and demanding as well. Our uneasiness evolves into something like dread, though we cannot say exactly what is so dreadful about the web's grateful embrace. And then, perhaps after many years (though

sometimes not at all), a moment may come when we awaken to the presence that lurks on the edge of the gossamer wheel. While we had previously seen nothing but silken rainbows, we now realize that something else is on the web. Something is making the web tremble, and we find ourselves trembling along with the strands to which we are bound. Now the presence is moving onto the web from which we cannot break free. Softly, deliberately, she is coming, picking her way across the lacy mandala, bearing her great mass gently upon her bent and spindly legs. She is savoring her moment, for she knows that we have entered into an endgame that we've already lost. Indeed, she has refined this endgame to an art as intricate and complex as her web. As she delicately edges toward us, we recognize with sinking horror the truth of who she is.

She is Spider—the incarnation of the Terrible Mother as a devouring weaver of fate and a bringer of inevitable death. Her symbol is global and ageless, and although she is seldom linked explicitly to the vampire, there is an undeniable similarity in their styles of predation. (One notable exception is in Stoker's *Dracula*, when Van Helsing compares Dracula to a mythic spider of immeasurable age.) J. R. R. Tolkien describes the Great Spider when she appears as the dreadful matriarch Shelob in *The Lord of the Rings*:

> There agelong she had dwelt, an evil thing in spider-form. . . . How Shelob came there, flying from the ruin, no tale tells, for out of the Dark Years few tales have come. But still she was there, who was there before Sauron . . . *and she served none but herself, drinking the blood of Elves and Men, bloated and grown fat with endless brooding on her feasts, weaving webs of shadow; for all living things were her food, and her vomit darkness.* Far and wide her lesser broods, bastards of the miserable mates, her own offspring that she slew, spread from glen to glen. . . . But none could rival her, Shelob the Great, last child of Ungoliant to trouble the unhappy world. (Tolkien 1954, 422–23, my italics)

It is hard to believe that a monster like this could create the lovely web that entices us to linger and serve. But without her skill at the loom, with only her horrific essence as lure, the feminine vampire would, like Shelob, surely starve.

The image of the Great Spider on her dew-covered web leads us to another essential aspect of the feminine vampire. In *A Dictionary of Symbols* (1971), J. E. Cirlot interprets the image of the spider at the center of her web to represent the Gnostic notion that "evil is not only at the periphery of the Wheel of Transformations but in its very centre—that is, in its Origin" (51). Cirlot adds that the image of the Great Spider on her web is symbolically synonymous with another ancient image of the negative Feminine, one that is found at the center of many weblike labyrinths. The image is that of the Gorgon Medusa, whose gaping mouth, glaring eyes, and mane of vipers had the power to turn to stone all living things who looked upon her. (The appearance of Medusa in this discussion of feminine vampirism was anticipated in chapter 2 by the quotation from *Dracula* that described the Lucy vampire in explicitly Medusan terms.)

Medusa's story is of critical significance here, not only because it enlarges our understanding of the feminine vampire's nature, but also because it also provides us with a positive model for deactivating the feminine vampire who preys on masculine victims. In *Oedipus Rex,* Jocasta is destroyed when Oedipus holds up a mirror to the vampiric truth of their marriage, but the hero himself is reduced to a "great wreck and hell" in the process, so we can hardly consider Oedipus's approach to be a successful deactivation of the feminine vampire. And Tom Wingfield, like so many of us, simply flees his feminine vampire, who pursues him across space and time and haunts him in every corner of the world.

Why is it so difficult for us, even when we are empowered, to kill the feminine vampire? One reason may be that the ethic of nobility in our patriarchy asserts that the strong should protect the weak. The patriarchy punishes those (particularly men) who

fail to be dominant, yet insists that dominators champion those whom they have dominated. How are we champions to reconcile these contradictory roles? The answer turns out to be quite elegant and very old. In fact, we've had a culturally codified version of the answer since the Middle Ages, when the modern notion of romantic love was born. In the medieval recipe for romantic love, the hero was a noble warrior who slashed, burned, gutted, and slew, all for the sake of the fair, helpless lady whom he championed. Domination for the sake of one who is dominated proved to be such a perfect recipe that it has survived intact to this day, claiming responsibility (along with a similar recipe involving heroism for the sake of God) for some of the most noble acts of humankind, and the most heinous as well.

The elegance of romantic love's domination-for-the-dominated recipe has led to its enduring popularity in the patriarchy, which meant that it could not go unexploited for long, given the virulence and cunning of the human shadow. The duet of feminine vampire and masculine victim is simply an insidious perversion of the myth of romantic love. We champions serve and adore our beloved, who bestows upon us approval and appreciation. We feel our existence is thereby justified and ennobled, even if our beloved is actually using us to feed her vampiric hunger. And it is not only in the mother-son dyad that such a duet may arise. There are innumerable men and women whose inner champions have been enlisted to serve the "vulnerable" feminine vampires in their fathers, lovers, children, and colleagues of both genders.

In all these cases, the empowered victim perceives that life has bestowed on him or her some opportunities that the feminine vampire never had. For the pitiful vampire's sake, the victim strives to excel in ways that are not personally meaningful, because turning aside to other, more meaningful pursuits feels like a deadly abandonment of the poor, disadvantaged vampire. Clearly, this vampiric duet is insidious and pervasive, which is why a model for its deactivation is very important to our psychic health.

This brings us back to the story of Medusa the Gorgon, whose life and death can tell us much about the nature of the feminine vampire and her deactivation by an empowered victim.

PERSEUS, THE GORGON-KILLER

Once upon a time, there were three lovely sisters named Stheino, Euryale, and Medusa. The sisters were Gorgons, whom some say were the daughters of the sea and others the daughters of the moon. Two of the three sisters, Stheino and Euryale, were immortal, while the third sister, Medusa, was half mortal, which meant that she could be killed. Mortal or not, death was far from Medusa's mind on that fateful evening when she went to worship at Athena's temple. Medusa was young and lovely and full of herself, as all frisky young women should be. She was especially proud of her beautiful hair, which she wore like a golden, flowing crown. As Medusa mounted the steps of Athena's temple, her beauty attracted the attention of the sea god, Poseidon. Poseidon wooed her with his oceanic passion, so it was only natural that Medusa should yield to his charms. The problem was that, in her ignorance or hubris or simple ecstasy, the beautiful young Gorgon allowed Poseidon to make love to her right in Athena's temple.

The concept of sacrilege is not a modern invention; the ancient Greek deities took offense just as angrily as our modern deities do. Athena's rage at this sort of violation was among the worst, for she was the honorary male among the goddesses—the first offended and the last appeased whenever a woman (or even a goddess, such as Aphrodite) allowed her passions to overcome her good sense. At the sight of the lovely Medusa locked in a brazen embrace with Poseidon (also not a favorite of Athena's) on the very steps of her sacred temple, the goddess became enraged. She hurled a terrible curse upon Medusa, which transformed the beautiful Gorgon into a creature so hideous that to look upon her would turn any living thing to solid stone. Leonard Wolf offers

this image of the transformation as Medusa might have experienced it:

> There Medusa was, lovely and young and proud of her golden
> hair, lying in the very bliss of love—when she heard what at
> first seemed a distant, slithering sound; and then a nearer hiss
> of serpents sprouting in her hair . . . and the agonizing change
> began, seething and scalding, as the woman was slowly twisted
> into the monster we have seen: serpent-haired, boar-tusked,
> scaly skinned, brassy and cold. (1975, 190)

In order to protect the living things of earth, the gods placed Medusa on a deserted island with her sisters for company. The island soon became decorated with an odd assortment of uncannily lifelike sculptures—all those who had lucklessly stumbled upon the horrible Gorgon, Medusa.

And so things stood for a very long time, until the day when a young warrior named Perseus came to the island with the purpose of killing Medusa. Perseus was the son of Danaë, who had conceived him when she was impregnated by Zeus after the god appeared to her as a shower of gold (nice technique, eh?). Unfortunately, Danaë's father did not believe her shower-of-gold story. He thought that she had been seduced by another guy, which was not unreasonable, since it had happened before. Danaë's father was extremely upset with her, but he did not dare to kill her outright, so he locked her and her new baby, Perseus, in a wooden coffer and put them out in the open sea.

The wooden coffer floated to another kingdom, where Danaë and Perseus were rescued by a fisherman and brought to the court of the king. The king of that land raised Perseus, and eventually he wanted to marry Danaë, but she refused his proposal (rather ungracious, but she probably had her reasons). The king, not a little miffed, pretended that he was going to marry someone else and demanded that all his subjects donate one horse as a wedding present. Since Danaë and Perseus had no horse to donate, Perseus

boldly offered to bring to the king the head of Medusa. The king was delighted with this plan, since it rid him of the brash young man. (Kings are often, and not without reason, desirous of eliminating the brash young men in their midst.) So the king sent Perseus off to behead the Gorgon.

Now, killing Medusa was a dangerous task, as you can imagine. But Perseus was determined, and what's more, he had some powerful friends, being the son of Zeus. Among Perseus's friends was Zeus's daughter Athena, whose feelings about Medusa had not improved one bit since the infamous temple rendezvous with Poseidon. Athena appeared before Perseus and gave him a brightly polished shield, warning him to look only at Medusa's reflection in the shield and never at the Gorgon herself. Then Athena enlisted the aid of Hermes, the trickster messenger god, who gave Perseus an adamantine sword with which to decapitate Medusa. Hermes also loaned Perseus a pair of winged sandals, a magic wallet to hold the Gorgon's head once he had severed it from her body, and a helmet of invisibility that belonged to the underworld god, Hades.

Armed with these powerful tools, Perseus flew to the Medusa's island, where he found the Gorgon sisters asleep among the statues that were Medusa's victims. Watching carefully in the mirror of his shield, Perseus backed toward the sleeping Medusa and decapitated her with a single stroke of his sword. Immediately, the winged horse Pegasus flew out of the pool of Medusa's blood. (Apparently, it was Pegasus whom Poseidon had fathered that fateful night on the temple steps). As surprised as Perseus was by the winged horse, he did not hesitate in his purpose and quickly stuffed Medusa's head into the magic wallet. Clamping the helmet of invisibility on his own head, Perseus took off with his winged sandals just before Stheino and Euryale, who had been awakened by Pegasus, could catch him.

Perseus's flight led him to the land of Philistia, where he found the maiden Andromeda chained to a rock, wearing nothing but a

few sacred jewels and awaiting her death at the jaws of Poseidon's sea monster. Perseus beheaded the monster and saved Andromeda, which should have pleased her parents (who had gotten her into the sea monster mess in the first place). But they favored another suitor, and eventually Perseus was forced to turn Andromeda's parents, the other suitor, and all their party guests into stone by showing them Medusa's head. Perseus then returned with Andromeda to his homeland, where he found that the king had imprisoned Danaë and the fisherman who had rescued them from the sea. So Perseus promptly turned the king and *his* party guests to stone, after which he installed Danaë and the fisherman on the throne as the new queen and king. Perseus then gave the Gorgon's head to Athena, who mounted it on her shield, and he returned the sandals, wallet, and helmet to their owners. He got to keep the sword and shield for his own, which seems only fitting, since he certainly deserved some nice prizes for the ordeal he had just endured.

And here was the fate of Medusa. She who was once lovely and unaware, and then hideous and vengeful, served out all of eternity with her head mounted as a weapon of the utmost mortality on the shield of her immortal enemy, Athena. Little more is known of Medusa, although some say that Athena made herself a shield out of the Gorgon's skin. And one more thing: It is said that Asclepius, the mythic founder of medicine, obtained from Athena two vials of Medusa's blood. With the blood from her right side, he could kill someone instantly, but with the blood from her left side, he could raise the dead to life.

From maiden to lover to hag, as divine destroyer and a bringer of life, Medusa is a particularly potent image for the shadow of the Great Feminine, and therefore, for the feminine vampire. In the story of Medusa's horrific activation by Athena and her deactivation by Perseus, we have a portrait of the birth and death of a feminine vampire.

Medusa's horrible punishment is the fate that befalls many innocent souls who worship the divine daughter of the patriarchy, Athena, but offend their goddess with an indulgence of passion. For example, I once knew a woman who had devoted herself passionately to serving men and the patriarchy, only to find many years later that her personal power had been exploited, leaving her with nothing but society's derision for having been victimized. As this woman writhed in her humiliation and fury, a menacing hiss slipped into her voice, a harsh glare crept into her eye, and a bitter rage seemed to chill her blood to a reptilian soup. Some vestiges of the woman's charm remained, enabling her to lure the occasional distracted champion, but her core had become wholly Medusan. Driven by her hunger for revenge, this woman wound up doing whatever she could to appropriate the happiness of others, or she would befoul their joy if she could not make it her own. Although the myth does not explicitly address Medusa's motivations once she has been cursed into hideousness by Athena, it is my sense that the Gorgon both fears her victims and *wants* to turn them to stone. This, too, is consistent with the Medusan woman I knew; she seemed terrified of showing her pain and shame to others, but once someone had caught sight of her hideous wounds, it seemed she felt compelled to petrify the witness with a blast of her frozen, embittered rage.

Because the archetype of Medusa, like that of the feminine vampire, is as complicated as it is dangerous, it may be helpful to identify a simpler image that captures her essence. Although we might compare Medusa to many things, the creature who best embodies her nature (and therefore, the nature of the feminine vampire) is the needle-fanged, cold-blooded, venom-spewing serpent. The serpent is a symbol whose scope and power are enormous:

> There is no cult more universal or ambivalent than that of the
> serpent, and few creatures have been regarded with more awe,

reverence and fear than the snake, with its strange sinuous movement, the rapidity with which it can strike a death-dealing blow, . . . its underground dwelling which puts it in touch with the powers of the underworld and its ability to cast its skin with apparent renewal of life. (Cooper 1974, 202)

In some cases, the serpent represents the most life-generating powers in the universe. For example, in Tantric philosophy the life force is called *kundalini,* literally "snake," and the snake appears in temples of the ancient Great Goddess as the embodiment of her generative power. The serpent can also represent energies of comparable darkness and destruction, however. It is Nidhogg, the Dread Biter of Norse lore, who nibbles away at the Tree of Life and brings all evil into the world; it is Ahriman, the Zoroastrian symbol of tyranny and disorder; and it is best known to us as an incarnation of Satan, the Judeo-Christian symbol of evil incarnate, who brings death and darkness to the Garden of Eden. In addition to these images of absolute evil and good, the serpent's ambiguity has occasionally been integrated into a single symbol. This occurs in the Chinese yin-yang symbol, where the opposing and complementary forces are depicted by two intertwining snakes; it emerges in the Gnostic symbol of the Ouroboros, the snake who swallows its tail as an image of the integrated duality in life and death; and it appears in Hermes' caduceus, the healing staff on which two snakes intertwine to symbolize the balance of creative and destructive forces.

Medusa evokes the darkest aspects of the serpent. The Medusan vampire slithers up in silent hunger behind her unwary prey, freezing her target with her cold-blooded stare, sinking her fangs into the petrified victim, and spitting out the venom of her embittered rage. Then, leaving the lifeless body behind, she gathers her sinuous force about her in coils of deceptive lethargy as she sniffs the air for the hot scent of blood, waiting for the next living soul who will prolong her immortality. While the sharklike Draculan vampire may seize its prey in a calculated show of explicit power,

the Medusan vampire relies on snakelike subtlety to capture her prey. It is easy to understand why the vampire lore asserts that "of all of nature's creatures, the serpent vampire is the most to be feared" (Bunson 1993, 241), and why we have abhorred the serpentine feminine vampire, from her earliest appearance in ancient mythology to her Judeo-Christian incarnation as the serpent who tempted Eve in paradise.

Although the serpent of Eden is widely interpreted as a male Satan, in early Judeo-Christian mythology the serpent was a symbol of Lilith, who can be seen either as a symbol of the feminine principle or as a symbol of the matriarchal culture that predates our patriarchy. Lilith appears in Hebrew lore as the first wife of Adam, who might be seen as a symbol of the masculine principle or as a symbol of the patriarchal culture that prevails today. Because Lilith believed that she and Adam had been created equally by God, she refused to obey Adam's command that she always assume the subordinate position during their lovemaking. Adam, incensed by her refusal to defer to him, appealed to Yahweh, who sided with His man and ordered Lilith to submit to the rule of her husband. Shocked and enraged by this prejudice, Lilith flew out of the Garden, uttering Yahweh's name (which was forbidden) and cursing her husband. Yahweh fashioned His next woman, not out of the same stuff as Adam, but out of Adam's rib, so that she would always be subordinate to her husband and his father god. This new and "improved" woman was Eve. But Lilith was not so easily disposed of. With the apple business in the Garden, she introduced Eve to her own feminine knowledge and power. For this, Yahweh sent His angels to destroy Lilith, but she nimbly escaped and fled howling into the night, screaming in her wounded fury and cursing the progeny of Adam and Eve. To this end, it is said, Lilith drinks the blood of the patriarchs' children, even unto the generation that is ours.

Clearly, Lilith is an early form of the feminine vampire. She might also be said to embody the Terrible Feminine, the part of

the Great Feminine that has been so grievously wounded by the patriarchy that it feeds on its innocent offspring in a disempowered effort at revenge. We may sympathize or even empathize with Lilith's outrage and fury. We must recognize, however, that in the external reality of our lives, Lilith and Medusa live on in the serpentine archetype of the feminine vampire, whose wounding has led her to prey upon innocent souls, drinking their blood in a self-righteous but unholy rage. While the story of Lilith may reinforce our resolve to rectify the sins of the patriarchy, we must also acknowledge that Lilith's acts of revenge, as perpetrated by the feminine vampire, are so monstrous that they require deactivation.

Deactivating the Feminine Vampire

There are several requirements for those of us who wish to emulate Perseus in deactivating the feminine vampire. The first is that we must be able to sense the Medusan viper who lurks under the veil of imploring vulnerability, just as we must detect the ravenous shark that lurks underneath Dracula's cloak of sensual sophistication. Note that I use the word "sense" rather than "see": the myth tells us that it is extremely dangerous to look directly on the truth of this entity, for the vision will immobilize and destroy us, just as mice are immobilized by the serpent's gaze. In this sense, Perseus had an advantage over us; he took care not to look at Medusa because her curse was a matter of general knowledge in his time. In our culture, however, the Medusan power of the feminine vampire is unrecognized by our patronizing attitude toward most things feminine. So we might be tempted to stalk her in the highly focused manner of Dracula's hunters—a steely-eyed tactic that would be deadly with a Medusan vampire.

The key is to approach the vampire as Perseus does—reflectively. If we have spent time in the company of someone who is infected with the feminine vampire, we already have some Medusan behavior on which to reflect. By engaging in reflective exer-

cises, we can safely bring the light of our consciousness to bear on the monster we wish to deactivate, without looking her full in the face and risking petrification. In reflection, we may ask ourselves a few illuminating questions: Have there been any moments of rage in which she has turned us to stone with a glare? Does a serpentine hiss ever creep into her voice, no matter how sweetly the words were spoken? Has she looked on us with a reptilian coolness to germinate the seeds of our guilt? Have we been pulled by our compassion to give more than we can afford to this pathetic being, who seemed to be suffering unfairly? If the answer to any of these questions is yes, then we are probably dealing with a feminine vampire.

If these images evoke your compassion, remember that Medusa's story is a pathetic one, too, but that does not lessen her dangerousness. Whenever we feel the itch of pity for a feminine vampire, we would be wise to recall the image of Perseus as he backed slowly toward the Gorgon's cold, reptilian hiss. We can feel his heart pounding as he relies on the invisibility of Hades' magic helmet to protect him. We can sense the electric tension as he yearns to fly off on his winged sandals. We can watch him reflecting carefully on the contents of his mirroring shield. As we approach our feminine vampires, we must hold the image of Perseus close to our hearts and remember that if he had dropped his guard, let his attention waver for a moment, or glanced backward out of guilt or compassion, then he would have been transformed into yet another of Medusa's yard ornaments.

An awareness of the feminine vampire's nature is critical to her deactivation, but it is not sufficient. In the stories of Perseus and Oedipus, the call of a greater good kept the champion from yielding to the ruses of the feminine vampire. The cause for which Perseus persevered was the redemption of a positive feminine power that was not vampiric—a power symbolized by his mother, Danaë, and later by Andromeda. The positive feminine energy that Oedipus championed was the health of his land, since nature

had been diseased by the sacrilege of his marriage. The masculine victims in both these cases, much like the feminine victims in the last chapter, must hold the Great Feminine to their hearts as they stalk the feminine vampire.

Once again, we touch the positive Great Feminine whenever we feel safe in the world, whenever we feel accepted and appreciated just as we are. When we are connected to the Great Feminine, we know that the feminine vampire's directives are not answers, that her contrived grooming of us is not real comfort, that her possessiveness is not protection, and that her ravenous surveillance is not love. Undeceived by the vampire's lies, we can persevere in deactivating her. In this way, the disease of nature drove Oedipus past Jocasta's objections toward the terrible but redemptive truth, and the gifts of Athena protected Perseus from the seductive gaze of the Gorgon, which might otherwise have lured him into a stony death.

Perseus was also aided in his quest by Hermes, the persuasive messenger of the gods. When Perseus came within striking distance of Medusa, it was largely Hermes' cunning that guided his feet and shielded his acts to keep him safe from the Gorgon's stare. Hermes is of critical assistance when we attempt to deactivate a feminine vampire. Consider, for example, the feminine vampire's apparently innocent question, "Are you still seeing that interesting person you were dating, dear?" Without Hermes by our side, we might actually respond to this question by embarking on a discussion whose purpose and ends are known only to the vampire. At its end, we could find ourselves bleeding out a glut of information mingled with guilt and shame. In contrast, with Hermes by our side, the feminine vampire's fangs can be deflected with a bright shield of questions such as "Well, that's an interesting question; why do you ask?" or "Gee, I didn't realize you liked Chris that much; was I wrong?"

Or suppose we are confronted with the heart-rending plea of "What am I going to do, now that I'm all alone and can't pay the

rent? Will you still come and see me when I'm living in the home-less shelter?" Without Hermes to help us out, we might dive in and bleed out an unending stream of resources in an effort to rescue this waif in distress. But with Hermes close at hand, we can first assess the underlying situation by asking, "What ideas have you already come up with, in addition to the homeless shelter? What is your complete list of resources? And how long would you need to remain there before you could get on your feet again?" or "What would you tell someone to do who was in your same situa-tion, if they couldn't come to me for help and advice?"

The presence of Hermes does not preclude our eventually as-sisting a person in need, nor does it prevent us from answering an honest question. The messenger god simply helps us to know ex-actly what is being asked underneath the apparently innocent questions. Once we know the *real* questions, we can decide ex-actly how we wish to respond before we unwittingly commit our life force to the vampire. Anyone who has been questioned by a lawyer knows how easily we can be drawn by a line of seemingly innocent questions into an incriminating position that may bear no relation to the truth. If you think that this technique of ques-tioning is mastered only in law school, think again. The skill of guileless cross-examination is a prime tactic of most feminine vampires, because information is one form of power that is avail-able to everyone. Information is empowering because when you have information about people, you have a means of exploiting them—which, as we know, is the prime directive of every vam-pire. As long as Jocasta has more knowledge about the situation than Oedipus, she can perpetuate her vampiric dance. Only when Oedipus's knowledge equals hers is her vampire deactivated. When we find ourselves playing information management games with a feminine vampire, Hermes is our invaluable ally.

In addition to his talent for seeing behind manipulative ques-tions, Hermes shares with Perseus four other gifts. Three of these are only on loan, which suggests that they should be used only for

Gorgon-killing purposes and events of similar importance, but not for everyday activities. The three loaned gifts are the winged sandals, the magic wallet, and Hades' helmet of invisibility. The winged sandals enabled Perseus to leap swiftly about, making him difficult to corner and stare down into submission. The gift of nimble movement is important because innocent passersby can only be lured by the sweetly vulnerable mist when they stop and stare directly into her depths. A nimble target who responds with "Gee, that's a good question; why do you ask?" is much harder to immobilize and bleed dry than the plodding target who obediently answers until he is backed into a corner by the vampire. Similarly, we must be nimble in spirit as well as in words. Champions who jump in predictable ways when their buttons are pushed make easy prey for the vampire.

As attractive as the sandals' power may be, however, to wear the winged slippers all the time would prohibit the wearer from ever being grounded. Many masculine victims who have relied excessively on their winged sandals to protect them from feminine vampires eventually find themselves flying around in perpetual solitude, unable to come to root in the sustenance of intimate relationships. Indeed, an overreliance on the winged sandals seems to be epidemic in our culture, given the prevalence of the phenomena we refer to as "emotional unavailability" and "fear of commitment."

The second of Hermes' loans, the magic wallet, serves to keep Perseus's power safe from prying eyes and to keep innocent bystanders safe from his power. The wallet is metaphorically present when information is held as sacred and safe until the owner is certain it can be shown without exploitation or theft. The wallet also permits Perseus to use Medusa's head as a weapon, as long as the vampiric power can be safely contained by a metaphorical wallet. If the wallet user is not extremely conscious, however, or if he is given to a little vampirism personally, then the wallet can easily become the vehicle for further vampiric predation. For ex-

ample, Perseus petrified quite a few people, some of them innocent party guests, before he handed the Gorgon's head over to
Athena. What might we, of weaker will and less noble purpose,
do with such a weapon? We must be extremely careful, conscious,
and skilled before we can "borrow" the vampire's tactics for our
own purposes, however noble they may be.

The magic wallet also implies another important issue. Right
after Perseus beheaded Medusa, he had to grasp the viperous head
and pop it in the sack, even as he tried desperately to avert his
gaze and wrestle with his shield and sword. Given the difficulty of
the task, it seems likely that Perseus may, in his revulsion and
haste, have inadvertently stuffed a few flowers and blades of grass
into the wallet along with the head, just as those of us who have
struggled with the feminine vampire may have thrown the baby
and the bathwater into the psychic pockets that contain our
bloodier mementos of the struggle. For example, we may fear relationship with anyone who is blond or musical like our vampiric
mothers or ex-mates. Lost bits of foliage such as blond hair and
musical talent are not too worrisome, as long as their inaccessibility causes no harm to our psyches. But what if we have thrown an
essential flower, such as "women's love" or "men's feeling," into
the wallet along with the Gorgon's head? In that case, we will
have to do some unpleasant fishing about in order to retrieve the
gold of human happiness from the offal of psychic vampirism.
And this fishing expedition must be done blind—by dint of feeling, hearing, and smelling, but not focused *seeing*—just like most
of the therapy work that addresses our wounding by the feminine
shadow.

The third of Hermes' loans, the helmet of invisibility, enables
Perseus to vanish altogether, like the shaman who protects himself
by disappearing while he performs his magic. The helmet, too, is
a risky tool. Because it belongs to the innerworld god, Hades, we
must assume that the helmet's use transports the wearer into a
realm of internal reality. Connecting with one's inner truth is a

crucial aspect of deactivating the feminine vampire, who would have us sacrifice our personal truth for the sake of her hunger. If we are tempted to dwell perpetually in the inner world, however, we may lose our effectiveness in dealing with the external reality. This is what Laura Wingfield attempts to do—to escape into the invisibility of her inner dreamscape in order to avoid her vampiric mother. But since Laura's body remains in the outer landscape, she is condemned to remain in Amanda's thrall as long as she relies solely on Hades' helmet.

The gifts that Perseus gets to keep are the adamantine sword and the brightly polished shield. The shield and the sword are two traditional weapons of the vampire killer, but in this case the shield serves as a mirror. This use is intriguing, since vampires cast no reflection in mirrors. If we pursue the analogy of Medusa as vampire, what exactly is it that Perseus sees when he looks in the shield? It is always assumed, though not explicitly stated in the myth, that Perseus sees the Gorgon in her serpentine deformity. But perhaps it is something quite different that Perseus must reflect upon when he backs toward Medusa with his sword raised high. Perhaps what he sees is the lovely young woman who caught the sea god's eye on the temple steps so long ago. As the hissing of Medusa's snakes fills Perseus's ears, as the stony evidence of her petrifying gaze stands motionless around him, as his sword falls to behead the monster, it may be no monster that Perseus sees, but a lovely, dreaming maiden with a crown of golden hair.

And isn't this how it must be for those of us who attempt to deactivate a feminine vampire? I once knew a man who seemed powerless to confront his wife about her biting derision of his work. The only time he felt motivated to challenge her was when she was in the middle of a tirade, at which point she would respond to his objections with another scathing verbal assault. Finally, the man realized that he would have to approach his wife in one of the blessed moments when she was calm. As he contemplated what words he would use to censure her attacks, the echo of her serpentine hiss filled his ears and the memory of her immobilizing rage seemed to freeze his heart. But what was worse for the man was that, even as he raised the sword of his intent to set some limits on his wife's criticism, he could not ignore the sweet innocence of her soul, which emerged in the absence of her vampire. Nonetheless, the man knew that he had to set his limits decisively and deactivate his wife's vampire with a single stroke of his words, for a tentative scratch would only lead to one of their usual skirmishes and his continued victimization. And if the man tried out of fairness to approach his wife while her vampire archetype was alert, or if he focused directly on the beast, then he knew he would be petrified with remorse and surrender. From this man's story, we might say that the mirroring shield represents our clear, complete consciousness of the vampire's wiles, which we may sometimes attain only through the consciousness of a third person (such as a friend or a therapist) who continually reflects the vampiric truth of the duet in which we are engaged.*

Once he has slain Medusa, Perseus becomes a hero and the father of heroes. He finds and weds a positive incarnation of the feminine, Andromeda, and he champions the positive feminine, Danaë, against a repressive patriarch. In this sense, the myth suggests that we who succeed in deactivating the feminine vampire can become important and noble allies of the feminine without losing our masculine power. We will be able to experience healthy love—the integration of masculine and feminine energies—as if

---

*Of course, I could not write this passage without recognizing that its imagery was strongly evocative of a current legal case in which a famous athlete is being tried for the murder of his wife and her friend. From the admittedly murky accounts of this couple's marriage, it seems that the husband and wife were deeply infected with masculine and feminine vampiric energies, respectively. This image of mutual vampirization and victimization is reminiscent of Adolf Guggenbühl-Craig's suggestion that all archetypes are polarities seeking integration, or if they have been split, reintegration. More to the point, however, this modern Perseus-gone-wrong teaches us that one should check in the mirroring shield for one's *own* reflection before proceeding with the murder of a Medusan vampire. If the would-be Perseus cannot see himself in the mirror, then he is probably acting as a vampire himself, and no beheadings should occur.

for the first time, just as Perseus experienced with Andromeda. Riding the power of our newly reclaimed love, we can be carried aloft on the wings of our pure instinct, deep creativity, and healthy carnality, just as if we were mounted astride the glorious Pegasus. What better reward for the perilous and heart-rending task of destroying the feminine vampire?

Of course, we are not vampiric every time we look for a champion to aid us in our distress. We all have known moments in which we have yearned for someone's aid. Sometimes no champion appears and we must aid ourselves, but sometimes we find a champion who can rescue us from the pit. Similarly, we are not catering to a vampire every time we aid someone. Sometimes we simply help people or they help us, and we both go on about our lives. And there are many times when no one is either champion or damsel. But someone who is possessed by the feminine vampire cannot comprehend this fact. She requires that someone else be the champion and be it all the time. She will do anything to keep another person in that rescuing role, for without a champion, she feels that she will cease to exist. This desperation leads to one of the distinguishing traits of a feminine vampire: she erupts with contempt or rage when the person who has served as champion tries to show another side of his personality. From her point of view, the person who tries to expand his repertoire beyond the role of champion is depriving her of her sole source of sustenance.

One thing common to all the victims of the feminine vampire in the stories we've heard—Oedipus, Snow White, Gypsy, Perseus, Tom and Laura Wingfield—is the absence of a strong father figure. Robert Bly reminds us that strong, healthy father energies have been unavailable to most people born in the postindustrial West. While I can't say exactly how the absence of a positive paternal figure makes us more susceptible to the feminine vampire, the stories suggest that it does. What's more, the absence of the Good Father archetype makes even the most powerful among us susceptible to the Draculan vampire, who preys upon the strong

as well as the weak. How this can happen will be made clear by the last of our vampiric duets—the story of a masculine victim who fell prey to a masculine vampire and so became a vampire himself. Let's follow these two monsters as they embark on a feeding frenzy so voracious that, in the end, it is hard to tell who is the more vampiric. Once more into the night.

MASCULINE VAMPIRES AND MASCULINE VICTIMS

ONCE UPON A TIME, in a place and time very much like ours, there lived a young man named Dorian Gray. Dorian was many things that we would all like to be: rich, charming, and very goodlooking. The handsome young man had known his share of pain, however. Dorian was the grandson of the wealthy Lord Kelso, who was called a "mean dog" by all the gentlemen in London—harsh language from a group known for its clannishness and courtesy. Lord Kelso was reviled by his peers because when his daughter, Margaret, married a soldier of low rank (who would become Dorian's father), the elitist Lord Kelso hired a hit man to provoke Dorian's father into a duel. In short, Dorian's father was murdered at the order of Dorian's grandfather. Old Lord Kelso hoped to reassert his control over Dorian's mother, but his victory was an empty one because Margaret never spoke to her father again. She died within a year of her husband's murder, leaving behind the defenseless infant Dorian to become the detested ward of his father's murderer.

Dorian grew up in the care of nurses and governesses, who took pity on the lonely child whose exceptional beauty and winning ways had conquered their hearts. His caretakers spoiled Dorian as if he were their own little darling. Nor were his nurses and governesses the last of Dorian's conquests. As he grew older, his allure was unparalleled: "There was something in his face that made one trust him at once. All the candour of youth was there,

as well as all youth's passionate purity. One felt that he had kept himself unspotted from the world" (Wilde 1891, 33).

Dorian's charms were especially cherished by Basil Hallward, a gifted painter who described how he became Dorian's devoted admirer:

> "Dorian, from the moment I met you, your personality had the most extraordinary influence over me. I was dominated, soul, brain, and power, by you. You became to me the visible incarnation of that unseen ideal whose memory haunts us artists like an exquisite dream. I worshiped you. I grew jealous of every one to whom you spoke. I wanted to have you all to myself. I was only happy when I was with you. . . . I had seen perfection face to face, and the world had become wonderful to my eyes—too wonderful, perhaps, for in such made worships there is peril, the peril of losing them, no less than the peril of keeping them." (128)

These words paint Dorian as perfection itself, and perhaps that's how Basil felt when he was in Dorian's hypnotic presence. But when he was not held captive by Dorian's mesmerizing charm, Basil offered another description of the young man, into which there creeps a sinister tone:

> "I turned half-way round and saw Dorian Gray for the first time. When our eyes met, I felt that I was growing pale. A curious sensation of terror came over me. I knew that I had come face to face with some one whose mere personality was so fascinating that, if I allowed it to do so, it would absorb my whole nature, my whole soul, my very art itself. . . . I find a strange pleasure in saying things to him that I know I shall be sorry for having said. As rule, he is charming to me. . . . Now and then, however, he is horribly thoughtless, and seems to take a real delight in giving me pain. Then I feel that I have given away my whole soul to some one who treats it as if it were a flower to put in his coat, a bit of decoration to charm his vanity, an ornament for a summer's day." (24, 29)

Sinister or not, Dorian's magnetism inspired Basil to paint a portrait that would capture the young man's allure. Basil savoured the hours he spent painting the portrait, for it seemed as if Dorian's transcendent beauty enabled the painter himself to transcend the drabness of his life. On the day that Dorian arrived for his last sitting, Basil received an unexpected visit from Lord Henry, a debonair gentleman who loved to tweak the blue noses of London's elite and then dance away under the protective shield of his poetic banter and enormous wealth. At first, Lord Henry listened indifferently as the smitten Basil recounted Dorian's story. But when the iconoclastic lord saw Dorian's startling beauty, he immediately hatched a new plan to feed his lust for power. Lord Henry realized that if he could seduce Dorian Gray into his crusade of contempt, he could perform acts of psychic vandalism that he could never accomplish by himself. What's more, Dorian's compliance and adulation would validate Lord Henry's campaign of cynical depravity:

> Yes; he would try to be to Dorian Gray what, without knowing it, the lad was to the painter who had fashioned the wonderful portrait. [Lord Henry] would seek to dominate him—had already, indeed, half done so. He would make that wonderful spirit his own. (52)

Thus, for the sake of exploitation and gratification, Lord Henry introduced into Dorian's cloud of aristocratic innocence a few serpentine tendrils of mortal fear:

> "Yes, Mr. Gray, the gods have been good to you. But what the gods give they quickly take away. You have only a few years in which to live really, perfectly, and fully. When your youth goes, your beauty will go with it, and then you will suddenly discover that there are no triumphs left for you, or have to content yourself with those mean triumphs that the memory of your past will make more bitter than defeats. Every month as it wanes brings you nearer to something dreadful." (39)

Having raised the specter of death, Lord Henry quickly exploited the young man's newfound desperation to escape the curse of his mortality:

> Let nothing be lost upon you. Be always searching for new sensations. Be afraid of nothing. . . . I believe that if one man were to live out his life fully and completely, were to give form to every feeling, expression to every thought, reality to every dream—I believe that the world would gain such a fresh impulse of joy that we would forget all the maladies of mediaevalism, and return to the Hellenic idea. . . . a new Hedonism—that is what our century wants. You might be its visible symbol. With your personality there is nothing you could not do. . . . You are the type of what the age is searching for, and what it is afraid it has found. . . . The world belongs to you for a season." (35, 39)

With seductive imagery, Lord Henry painted for Dorian a portrait of shadow and light, in which the shadow was composed of decay and death, and the light was to be attained only by gratifying the desires of body and heart. Lord Henry purred to Dorian that to resist one's desires on the basis of conscience or morality was counterproductive to the point of destruction:

> "We are punished for our refusals. Every impulse that we strive to strangle broods in the mind and poisons us. The body sins once, and has done with its sin, for action is a mode of purification. Nothing remains then but the recollection of a pleasure, or the luxury of a regret. The only way to get rid of a temptation is to yield to it. Resist it, and your soul grows sick with longing for the things it has forbidden to itself, with desire for what its monstrous laws have made monstrous and unlawful. . . . Good resolutions are useless attempts to interfere with scientific laws. Their origin is pure vanity. Their result is absolutely *nil.* . . . They are simply cheques that men draw on a bank where they have no account." (35, 114)

In reaction to Lord Henry's words, Dorian was not appalled, repulsed, or even uneasy. No. Dorian Gray was the child of a self-gratifying family that had sunk from defiant passion to murderous revenge. His soul dwelt in the shadow cast by his loveless childhood, leaving him ripe for Lord Henry's plucking with the deft fingers of seductive words:

> [Lord Henry's] praise of folly . . . soared into a philosophy, and philosophy herself became young, and catching the mad music of pleasure, wearing, one might fancy, her wine-stained robe and wreath of ivy, danced like a Bacchante over the hills of life. . . . Facts fled before her like frightened forest things. . . . [Lord Henry] felt the eyes of Dorian Gray were fixed on him, and the consciousness that amongst his audience there was one whose temperament he wished to fascinate seemed to give his wit keenness and to lend colour to his imagination. He was brilliant, fantastic, irresponsible. . . . Dorian Gray never took his gaze off him, but sat like one under a spell. . . . With his subtle smile, Lord Henry watched him. He knew the precise psychological moment when to say nothing. . . . He had merely shot an arrow into the air. Had it hit the mark? How fascinating the lad was! (57, 36)

Dorian's mind whirled in the kaleidoscope of Lord Henry's images. This was a view of life that initially seemed to transcend the young man's wildest dreams. But then Dorian discovered a hidden room of his heart in which there lived a familiar echo of Lord Henry's dazzling vision:

> Yes; there had been things in his boyhood that he had not understood. He understood them now. Life suddenly became fiery-coloured to him. It seemed to him that he had been walking in fire. Why had he not known it? . . . It had been left for a stranger to reveal him to himself. (38)

And so Dorian Gray fell into the luxuriant folds of Lord Henry's nest, where he brooded on the yearnings that had been spawned

in his heart. The incubation of these new desires required only the time it took for a leisurely stroll in Basil's garden among the fleeting blooms (only a season and no more!). As Dorian breathed the intoxicating perfume of the doomed flowers, his fear of death and his hunger for gratification exploded into resolve. When Dorian returned to Basil's finished portrait, which was rosy and glowing in its youthful perfection, his eyes narrowed under their new veil of contemptuous lust, and he hissed:

> "I am jealous of everything whose beauty does not die. I am jealous of the portrait you have painted of me. Why should it keep what I must lose? Every moment that passes takes something from me and gives something to it. Oh, if it were only the other way! If the picture could change, and I could be always what I am now!" (43)

When Dorian spoke these words, Lord Henry knew he had succeeded in his seduction, and he swept his new acolyte off to the opera. Basil, however, remained alone in the darkening studio, disturbed at the change in his beautiful young friend. But he kept his unease to himself and sent the glorious portrait to Dorian's home. Dorian hung the portrait in his living room, but it did not initially have much effect on him. Lord Henry, on the other hand, affected Dorian greatly. The more time he spent with the hedonistic lord, the more Dorian devoted his life to sensory indulgence. There was no texture he did not reach for, no morsel he did not taste, no hue unseen, no tone unheard. Dorian gorged on experience with an apparently bottomless appetite:

> That curiosity about life which Lord Henry had first stirred in him . . . seemed to increase with gratification. The more he knew, the more he desired to know. He had mad hungers that grew more ravenous as he fed them. (141–42)

Among the hungers that Dorian discovered in his feeding frenzy was the hunger that we call passion. Her name was Sybil

Vane, and she was a gifted young actress hidden away in a second-rate theater. Once Dorian saw her, he could not get enough of her performances. Juliet, Ophelia, Desdemona—each was more exquisite than the last in his eyes. Under the spell of the lovely young actress, Dorian found that he was ravenous in a way he had never been before: "I get hungry for her presence; and when I think of the wonderful soul that is hidden away in that little ivory body, I am filled with awe" (69). Dorian was so consumed by his passion that he begged Lord Henry and Basil to accompany him to the theater to see Sybil perform. The two gentlemen were intrigued by Dorian's invitation, particularly when they learned that Dorian had just proclaimed his sentiments to Sybil that very afternoon.

Given their state of anticipation, you can imagine the shock of Dorian and his friends when Sybil's performance that night was atrocious. She moved like a wooden puppet and mouthed her lines mechanically. Dorian was mortified. What on earth was wrong with her? Why was she doing this to him, right after he had pledged his devotion and promised to bring his cherished friends to see her? Lord Henry and Basil left as promptly and discreetly as possible, but Dorian forced himself to remain through the whole dismal production. When the final curtain rang down, he hurried backstage and demanded from Sybil a reason for her horrible performance. With glowing eyes and a full heart she explained that next to Dorian's love, the rest of life, including her work, seemed unbearably drab and empty:

"I knew nothing but shadows, and I thought them real. You came—oh, my beautiful love!—and you freed my soul from prison. You taught me what reality really is. To-night, for the first time in my life, I saw through the hollowness, the sham, the silliness of the empty pageant in which I had always played. . . . You brought me something higher, something of which all art is but a reflection. My love! My love! Prince Charming!

Prince of my life! I have grown sick of shadows. You are more
to me than all art can ever be." (100)

Sybil's plaintive adoration was despicable to the humiliated Dorian. In the same chilling tone he had used in addressing his portrait, Dorian informed Sybil:

> "you have killed my love. You used to stir my imagination.
> Now you don't even stir my curiosity. You simply produce no
> effect. I loved you because you were marvelous, because you
> had genius and intellect, because you realized the dreams of
> great poets and gave shape and substance to the shadows of
> art. You have thrown it all away. You are shallow and stupid.
> . . . You are nothing to me now. I will never see you again. . . .
> I wish I had never laid eyes upon you! You have spoiled the
> romance of my life. . . . I would have made you famous, splen-
> did, magnificent. The world would have worshiped you, and
> you would have borne my name. What are you now? A third-
> rate actress with a pretty face." (101)

In response to this devastating rebuke, Sybil "crouched on the
floor like a wounded thing, and Dorian Gray, with his beautiful
eyes, looked down at her, and his chiseled lips curled in exquisite
disdain. There is always something ridiculous about the emotions
of people whom one has ceased to love" (102). Dorian turned on
his heel and left the theater. He felt as if his life would never be
the same, that it would never again be right. His honeyed passion
for Sybil, which had promised to satisfy his burgeoning hungers,
had turned to mold in his mouth, and the stupid girl was to blame
for it all. At dawn, Dorian arrived home and sulkily roved around
his living room. He threw himself on a couch, but his gaze still
wandered restlessly about the room, settling at last on the portrait. A shiver of disbelief ran through him, and he averted his
eyes, but the picture seemed to pull him back, and he rose to examine it carefully: "In the dim arrested light that struggled
through the cream-coloured silk blinds, the face appeared to him

to be a little changed. The expression looked different. One would have said there was a touch of cruelty in the mouth" (104). Even when Dorian threw back the curtain, attempting to dispel the illusion with the morning light,

> the strange expression that he had noticed in the face of the portrait seemed to linger there, to be more intensified even. The quivering ardent sunlight showed him the lines of cruelty round the mouth as clearly as if he had been looking into a mirror after he had done some dreadful thing. (104)

Dorian's mind sprinted back to the sunny afternoon in Basil's studio, when he had cursed the portrait and condemned it to experience the decay of his life so that he could remain forever fresh and young. With a lurch of terror, Dorian realized that some dark magic had transformed his outburst into reality. He turned desperately to a mirror and saw that his mouth was the mouth of an innocent youth—it did not mirror the cruelty of the mouth in the portrait. Dorian was horrified to realize that each of his sins against body and soul would be indelibly recorded on the painting for everyone, including himself, to see. Most of us can hide or deny the dark lumps of our psyches, but the portrait forced Dorian to confront his darkness in a most painful, immediate way.

At first, Dorian was transfixed with self-loathing. He had never thought himself cruel! His remorse was excruciating—until a new thought rescued him:

> Cruelty! Had he been cruel? It was the girl's fault, not his. He had dreamed of her as a great artist, and given his love to her because he had thought her great. Then she had disappointed him. She had been shallow and unworthy. And, yet, a feeling of infinite regret came over him, as he thought of her lying at his feet sobbing like a little child. . . . But he had suffered also. During the three terrible hours that the play had lasted, he had lived centuries of pain, æon upon æon of torture. His life was well worth hers. (105)

To Dorian's credit, he could not wallow long in the easy comfort granted by this line of thought (which was, not surprisingly, inspired by Lord Henry). Dorian looked sadly at the portrait whose loveliness had been flawed by his cruelty toward Sybil, and he thought again of Sybil's pleading face and devoted heart. Bravely, Dorian vowed to abandon Lord Henry's crusade of hedonism and marry Sybil Vane. It was a noble sentiment, and sincere in the moment. But the shadowy life that Dorian had spun like a sensuous cocoon about himself was stronger than it looked, and it would not permit his casual departure. Before he could act on his noble resolve, Dorian fell asleep, and when he awakened in the afternoon, Lord Henry himself arrived to deliver the verdict of the fates—Sybil Vane had killed herself during the night.

Dorian did not need to rescue himself from pain this time; the same fates who supplied the awful news had also supplied Lord Henry, who spread his hedonistic balm over the shreds of Dorian's conscience. In Lord Henry's presence, Dorian was made exquisitely aware that the birds still sang, the sun still shone, and elegant ladies were waiting for him at the opera. Assured by Lord Henry that indifference was the most reasonable response to this messy and uncomfortable situation, Dorian relaxed with palpable relief:

> "I am glad you don't think I am heartless. I am nothing of the kind. I know I am not. And yet I must admit that this thing that has happened does not affect me as it should. It seems to me to be simply like a wonderful ending to a wonderful play. It has all the terrible beauty of a Greek tragedy, a tragedy in which I took a part, but by which I have not been wounded."
> (114)

And with those words, Dorian rode off in Lord Henry's shining carriage, while Sybil Vane's body lay, unburied and still warm, in a poorer part of town.

Thus began Dorian's long, deliberate journey into darkness. In

the world of Dorian Gray, as long as the sun shone and the birds sang, there would also be an endless number of women and men for him to entice and consume. The destruction and dissipation took an awful toll, of course, but it was not recorded on Dorian's body. That resplendent sculpture in flesh remained a monument to the light, a thing of glowing vitality and unsullied youth. No, it was the portrait that recorded the shadow of Dorian's depravity—the portrait, which was locked away in Dorian's old schoolroom, shut away from view as effectively as any soul's putrescence can be. Most of the time, the portrait was an abomination to Dorian, and he loathed it as virulently as any of us loathe our shadowy sides. He shuddered at the very thought of entering into its presence, and he tried to pretend that it had ceased to exist. At other times, however, Dorian dreamed of redeeming the portrait's decay, of returning its hideousness to its original beauty by performing a series of heroic good works. Doing penance, Dorian thought, might right his wrongs and earn some spiritual salvation. Why should this only be a one-way path to damnation?

> Why should he watch the hideous corruption of his soul? He kept his youth—that was enough. And, besides, might not his nature grow finer, after all? There was no reason that the future should be so full of shame. Some love might come across his life, and purify him, and shield him from those sins that seemed to be already stirring in spirit and in flesh. . . . Perhaps, some day, the cruel look would have passed away from the scarlet sensitive mouth, and he might show to the world Basil Howard's masterpiece. No; that was impossible. Hour by hour, and week by week, the thing upon the canvas was growing old. It might escape the hideousness of sin, but the hideousness of age was in store for it. (135)

Defeated in his attempts at redemptive reverie, Dorian would take refuge in his good fortune, and at these times, he would relish the portrait's continuing deterioration:

He would creep upstairs to the locked room . . . and stand, with a mirror, in front of the portrait that Basil Hallward had painted of him, looking now at the evil and aging face on the canvas, and now at the fair young face that laughed back at him from the polished glass. The very sharpness of the contrast used to quicken his sense of pleasure. He grew more and more enamoured of his own beauty, more and more interested in the corruption of his own soul. (141)

Dorian's unblemished beauty hardly formed an impenetrable camouflage over the murky truth of his deeds. On the contrary, only those who beheld him from a safe distance were fooled. The people who drew closer to Dorian came to react quite differently:

It was remarked that some of those who had been most intimate with him appeared, after a time, to shun him. Women who had wildly adored him, and for his sake had braved all social censure and set convention at defiance, were seen to grow pallid with shame or horror if Dorian Gray entered the room. (154)

But the painful consciousness of Dorian's victims was no match for the gilded standards by which society evaluates its members:

Yet these whispered scandals only increased in the eyes of many his strange and dangerous charm. His great wealth was a certain element of security. Society—civilized society, at least—is never very ready to believe anything to the detriment of those who are both rich and fascinating. (154)

Despite the norms of that superficial society, one person was *not* dazzled by Dorian's mesmerizing persona—his old acquaintance Basil Hallward. Although Basil's worshipful infatuation with Dorian had begun the whole nightmare, it now seemed to the painter as if Dorian had become devoid of conscience. Dorian, for his part, had come to hold Basil responsible for any queasy moments of conscience he still had—moments when Dorian would suspect that the growing decay of the portrait was still, in

some terribly unjust manner, a part of himself. Dorian fought off his conscience with a furious recommitment to his pursuit of pleasure, and this strategy was adequate to silence his inner tormentor temporarily. But there came a day when Basil himself arrived and dared to mouth aloud the words of Dorian's conscience:

> "One has a right to judge of a man by the effect he has over his friends. Yours seem to lose all sense of honour, of goodness, of purity. You have filled them with a madness for pleasure. They have gone down into the depths. You led them there. Yes: you led them there, and yet you can smile, as you are smiling now. . . . They say that you corrupt every one with whom you become intimate, and that it is quite sufficient for you to enter a house for shame of some kind to follow after." (163–64)

Once these words were spoken, it made no difference that Basil asked Dorian to deny his charge. It made no difference that he reached out to Dorian with the love and admiration that was born in his studio long ago. These facts made no difference because Basil had held up to Dorian a mirror in which the portrait's face was reflected. Dorian responded to what he saw in the mirror by resolving to take revenge on the man who had created his merciless canvas accuser. He smiled ruefully and said, "Come upstairs, Basil. I keep a diary of my life from day to day, and it never leaves the room in which it is written. I shall show it to you if you come with me." The old painter followed Dorian up the grand staircase and into the musty schoolroom. Dorian pulled the drape back from the portrait, and Basil gasped with sick horror.

The depraved face in the frame was his painting, but it was not his Dorian. The painting gave no sign of the fresh innocence that still shone in Dorian's face. And yet the painted face was precisely that of the person whose actions Basil had just attributed to Dorian—a monster without conscience who drank the essence of those who adored him and left them with only the stench of shame and loathing. As Basil reeled away from the appalling por-

trait, he begged Dorian not to lose hope, to pray for repentance and forgiveness, saying, "I worshiped you too much. I am punished for it. You worshiped yourself too much. We are both punished" (170).

Basil's compassion might have moved someone who had not lived for years behind the ironclad invulnerability of a perfect persona. But Basil was talking to a man who had spent his adult life projecting and disowning all of his shadowy traits, assigning them to the horrible canvas in the schoolroom. After so many years of abdicating his shadow, and thereby deepening its power to do evil, Dorian was adamantly unable to embrace it as his own. Instead,

> Dorian Gray glanced at the picture, and suddenly an uncontrollable feeling of hatred for Basil Hallward came over him, as though it had been suggested to him by the image on the canvas, whispered into his ear by those grinning lips. The mad passions of a hunted animal stirred within him, and he loathed the man who was seated at the table, more than in his whole life he had ever loathed anything. He glanced wildly around. Something glimmered on the top of the painted chest that faced him. His eye fell on it. He knew what it was. It was a knife that he had brought up, some days before, to cut a piece of cord, and had forgotten to take away with him. He moved slowly towards it, passing Hallward as he did so. As soon as he got behind him, he seized it and turned round. Hallward stirred in his chair as if he was going to rise. He rushed at him and dug the knife into the great vein that is behind the ear, crushing the man's head down on the table and stabbing again and again. . . . Something began to trickle on the floor. . . . He could hear nothing but the drip, drip on the threadbare carpet. . . . Had it not been for the red jagged tear in the neck and the clotted black pool that was slowly widening on the table, one would have said that the man was simply asleep. (170–71)

It would be too easy to imagine that Dorian had become a beast without soul or consciousness, that he could blithely com-

mit his act of murder and waltz off to a night at the opera. But a descent into evil is not as effortless as the fundamentalists would have us believe. Even after years of a life dedicated to predation, Dorian was stricken by the sight of Basil's blood dripping from his hands—a sight that, even after he had washed his own hands, appeared with fresh liquidity on the hands of the portrait. He quickly drew a heavy drape of velvet over the painting, and he tried to draw a heavy drape of denial over the blot of truth that was staining his soul:

> He felt that the secret of the whole thing was not to realize the situation. The friend who had painted the fatal portrait to which all his misery had been due had gone out of his life. That was enough. . . . He felt that if he brooded on what he had gone through he would sicken or grow mad. . . . It was a thing to be driven out of the mind, to be drugged with poppies, to be strangled lest it might strangle one itself. (172, 175)

If the blood on his soul had been the only stain to wipe away, Dorian might have been able to resume his campaign of self-gratification, with never a backward glance at Basil's murder. But there was the supremely inconvenient fact of Basil himself. The decay of Basil's body, unlike the decay of the portrait, could not be ignored for long. Dorian needed help. He realized that no one would help him out of devotion, but devotion was not the most powerful weapon in Dorian's arsenal. No—Dorian's best motivator was fear. He sent for a young chemist who was among those who "were seen to grow pallid with shame or horror if Dorian Gray entered the room," and he threatened him with exposure if he did not dispose of Basil's body. Dorian then locked the poor man in the schoolroom with the body. When the chemist emerged after several hours, a stench of nitric acid hung in the air but the body was gone. It seemed as if the acid had dissolved Dorian's anguish along with Basil's body, and he graced that evening's dinner party with typical panache.

Certainly no one looking at Dorian Gray that night could have believed that he had passed through a tragedy as horrible as any tragedy of our age. Those finely shaped fingers could never have clutched a knife for sin, nor those smiling lips have cried out on god and goodness. He himself could not help wondering at the calm of his demeanor, and for a moment felt keenly the terrible pleasure of a double life. (187)

Thus the portrait protected Dorian's golden persona for years. Even when Sybil Vane's brother finally caught up with Dorian in the darkness of his favorite opium den, the portrait stepped between Dorian and the grave. Just as James Vane was about to blow Dorian's brains against the grimy wall of the den, Dorian protested his innocence and demanded that Vane bring him into the light. Vane did so, and fell back in shock. The man he had expected to see would have been nearly forty, but the man whose neck he gripped was a mere lad of no more than twenty. Vane released Dorian, who fled into the night, leaving Vane to stand bewildered in the darkness, frozen with horror at the possibility that he had nearly murdered an innocent man. Then a small dark woman crept up behind Vane and informed him that the man he had just released was indeed Dorian Gray, the man who had "sold his soul to the devil for a pretty face."

A week after Vane's attack, Dorian was attending a fox hunt at the estate of a friend, strolling with an older man who had sighted a hare and prepared to shoot. Without knowing why, Dorian exclaimed, "Don't shoot it, Geoffrey. Let it live." "Nonsense," replied the old gentleman, and fired. Two death cries pierced the air—one from the hare, and the other from a man who had been in the bushes and been shot in his chest. Later, Dorian went to see the man's body and recognized James Vane. A cramp of guilt clutched at Dorian's heart, and for a moment his soul resurfaced. He realized that the country air was pure and gentle, as was the heart of the country maid that he had intended to deflower that weekend. In a moment of grace, Dorian resolved not

to meet the maid, and with this act of mercy, he intended to change his life. His resolve lasted three days, until his next meeting with Lord Henry. "Hypocrisy," concluded Lord Henry. "You cannot change to me, Dorian. You and I will always be friends" (228).

After Lord Henry had gone, Dorian roamed his house in a fog of doubt. He felt that he had been doomed by his beauty and youth, and that the evil he had committed was closing in about him. But wait! There was the young maid he had saved. Could it be that his mercy toward her had redeemed the portrait in the same way that his acts of depravity had eroded it? Dorian rushed upstairs to the locked schoolroom and pulled the drape from the painting. His lovely blue eyes widened in horror and his beautiful mouth uttered a cry of indignation. The portrait was unchanged, save that the cruel smile had acquired a tinge of hypocrisy and the blood had spread to the feet as well as the hands. Dorian felt himself sinking irreversibly into the pit of pain.

> Time seemed to him to be crawling with feet of lead, while he by monstrous winds was being swept towards the jagged edge of some black cleft of precipice. He knew what was waiting for him there; saw it, indeed, and shuddering, crushed with dank hands his burning lids as though he would have robbed the very brain of sight and driven the eyeballs back into their cave. It was useless. The brain had its own food on which it battened, and the imagination, made grotesque by terror, twisted and distorted as a living thing by pain, danced like some foul puppet on a stand and grinned through moving masks. Then, suddenly, time stopped for him. Yes: that blind, slow-breathing thing crawled no more, and horrible thoughts . . . raced nimbly on in front, and dragged a hideous future from its grave, and showed it to him. He stared at it. Its very horror made him stone. (178–79)

Was there no escape? Would this vile lump of canvas and oil haunt him mercilessly all his life, to betray and eventually annihi-

late him? As Dorian Gray stood before his portrait, it became the incarnation of the Enemy. His eye caught the glint of the knife he had used to kill Basil.

> As [the knife] had killed the painter, so it would kill the paint-er's work, and all that that meant. It would kill the past, and when that was dead, he would be free. It would kill this mon-strous soul-life, and without its hideous warnings, he would be at peace. He seized the thing, and stabbed the picture with it. (234)

The servants who lived in Dorian's house heard a dreadful shriek emanate from the old schoolroom. Because it took them a while to open the locked door, they had several minutes to imag-ine the terrible sight might greet them. But nothing could have prepared them for the truth:

> When they entered, they found hanging upon the wall a splen-did portrait of their master as they had last seem him, in all the wonder of his exquisite youth and beauty. Lying on the floor was a dead man, in evening dress, with a knife in his heart. He was withered, wrinkled, and loathsome of visage. It was not till they had examined the rings that they recognized who it was. (234)

PSYCHIC VAMPIRISM AND OUR SEARCH FOR PERFECTION

When life darkens around us and we darken along with it, our most normal human wish is to cast away all of the darkness. We feel sure that if all the evil were expunged from life, we could start anew with a clean slate, a pure heart, and an innocent soul. Absolved of our shadows, we could soar to the peaks of ecstasy and glide into vales of contentment. How lovely to be like Dorian Gray, with all the accumulated nastiness of our lives locked up in a fusty old schoolroom, leaving us free to live only in goodness and light!

This alluring notion of self-reinvention has inspired countless

myths and rituals. From the scapegoating Hebrews in the Book of Leviticus to the complete makeovers at the Golden Door, from the purifying words of the confessional priest to the excising scalpel in the surgeon's hands, from the ethnic "cleansing" of so many wars to the purging waters of the baptismal font—using means both healing and harmful, we strive for self-redemption through the banishment of evil. We cast off the bad old job, the bad old lover, the bad old body, the bad old leaders, the bad old way, and we dive into the good and the new, hoping to become good and new ourselves in the process. We resist acknowledging the possibility that the bad old way contained some nuggets of good, and the good new way may contain some nuggets of bad. For the bad must be unilaterally bad and the good unilaterally good—any other arrangement is too troublesome and confusing. And when the darkness reemerges in the good (as it eventually must), we feel as if we have been duped by badness masquerading as good. Again we scurry about looking for the *truly* good job, lover, body, leader, or way, in an endless effort to reinvent ourselves by banishing the darkness and cleaving only to the light.

The myth of self-redemption through the banishment of darkness is what enchants and repulses us in Oscar Wilde's *Picture of Dorian Gray*. In a twist of supernatural fate, Dorian is granted the self-redemptive dream—he can cast aside each bit of darkness as it occurs and live in perpetual light. The darkness is conveniently scapegoated onto a secret piece of canvas, while the man himself is born anew each day, with no mark remaining of the evil that has touched him. Unfortunately, the tale, like the story of human history, tells us that self-redemption through self-reinvention is an illusion. Indeed, it seems that when we human beings are handed a clean slate, we scribble something obscene on it, and when it won't come clean, we try to throw the slate away and begin all over again. It rarely occurs to us that we would do better to read whatever we have written on our slates rather than trying

to dispose of them—in other words, to reclaim our essential selves rather than trying to reinvent them.

Even the most cursory review of the human psyche shows that turning our backs on our darkness only makes it increase in power and size. Unpleasant as the prospect may be, the only way out of our darkness is through it. Only when we acknowledge, understand, and transform—that is, discover the positive incarnation of—the darkness in our jobs, our relationships, our lives, our bodies, and our psyches, will we be freed from reliving that darkness in each new good that we find. Unfortunately, the ethic of our culture perpetuates the myth of self-redemption through self-reinvention, exalting the sort of illusory good fortune that Wilde describes in *The Picture of Dorian Gray*. Dorian Gray epitomizes (as long as the magic of his portrait endures) some of the most cherished ideals of our age. He is the quintessential celebrity, the vampiric synthesis of all the fair-haired boys who have ever been groomed by a Draculan patriarch. Dorian represents, as Lord Henry tells him, "what our century wants . . . what the age is searching for" (39). Today, more than one hundred years after Oscar Wilde created Dorian Gray, the world continues to idolize what Dorian represents: immeasurable wealth, irresistible beauty, eternal youth, and a vampiric capacity for consumption.

Who among us has not been mesmerized by a Dorian Gray? And who among us has not, while marveling at a Dorian's meteoric flight, envied that path? We may sneer at the foibles of the Dorians who fuel the tabloids, and we may assert that we would not be as corrupted as those Dorians have been by their good fortune. We may even tell ourselves that we wouldn't want those sour grapes anyway. But mostly we ogle and drool. We faithfully tune into television programs that glorify the rich and famous. We furtively purchase the gossip rags that eavesdrop on our Dorians, and we fantasize about communing with those quasi-celestial beings.

To some extent, when we dream of our Dorians, we are only

doing what the Greeks did—we are projecting the same archetypal energies onto our media celebrities that the Greeks projected
onto their Olympian celebrities. We, too, try to emulate the gods,
but unlike the Greeks, we seem dangerously ignorant of the peril
of hubris. Not that we blindly aspire to godhood from stupidity
or arrogance; rather, we aspire to godhood because the modern
demigods we revere are themselves mortal, so we quite reasonably
feel that their enviable fate might just as well be our own. What's
more, celebrity in our culture is supposed to be available to all
who have the guts to seek it, which implies that those who do not
attain it are somehow deficient in the skills of self-reinvention.

In our eyes, the Dorians who have attained godhood have
earned it. When we look at our modern Dorians, we see only their
abundance of gifts and their occasional glimmers of pain, which
seem to us endearing and incidental. We cannot or will not see the
price that our Dorian Grays pay for their godly status, and in any
case, their decaying portraits are rarely unveiled before anyone
but their lovers, lawyers, therapists, or physicians. The dark portraits behind the legends are securely locked away in the dusty
attics of the Dorians' lives. And yet sometimes the mask of a rein-
vented self slips—when a football player is on trial for murdering
his wife, when a financier is convicted of insider trading, when a
politician is indicted for taking bribes. At these moments, when
the Dorian's rotting portrait is accidentally unveiled, we catch a
glimpse of our idol's shadow—a shadow that has moldered in its
seclusion and grown to the same monstrous proportions as the
Dorian's larger-than-life persona.

The agonies of our modern Dorians suggest that the dangers
to mortals who play god have not diminished one bit since the
time of the ancient Greeks. The only difference is that hubris,
which for the Greeks was a deadly spiritual violation, for us has
become a cultural imperative. The crucial trick is to know the
difference between emulating a deity and believing that one has
become it, which is essentially the same as Marion Woodman's

distinction between relating to an archetypal force and identifying with it. In the first case, we see our wealth, beauty, youth, or talent as transitory possessions that may grace our souls but are not integral to our souls; we know that we exist independently of such godlike gifts. In the second case, we see ourselves as defined by our gifts and indistinguishable from them; any sense that those gifts might be taken from us—whether by age, illness, misfortune, or death—leads us to feel that our very essence is threatened. This distinction between identifying with the gods and relating to the gods is also a distinction between hubris and humility, the knowledge that one is a simple and sacred soul who, for unfathomable reasons, has been temporarily blessed by godlike powers. And this distinction leads us back to the vampire: when the vampire is tyrannizing our soul, we are more likely to identify with our gifts because the soul's inaccessibility leaves no other way to define ourselves.

I once knew a man like this. Desperate to attain some sense of self, he entered a vicious cycle in which he fiercely sought to protect and augment his gifts, usually at the expense of others, even though every one of his gifts was doomed to decay. When one gift with which he identified would begin to wither, he would either go to extreme lengths to preserve it (such as seducing younger women to refute the warnings of his aging body), or he would shift his identification to another gift (such as placing more emphasis on his wealth than on his aging appearance). While the new gift may have been less immediately threatened, it was no more stable or meaningful as a basis for his sense of self.

As death loomed nearer to this man, and the gifts with which he identified threatened to decay in the most final way, he was faced with three alternatives. First, he could accelerate into a frenzy of gift-hoarding to bolster his poorly founded sense of self. Second, he could collapse into a de-selfed sense of despair. Or third, he could turn from the gifts with which he had identified (or from the despair into which he was falling) and look for a

sense of self that was independent from the transitory gifts he had enjoyed. When I last saw this man, he was still pursuing the first alternative, accumulating money, power, and women as a way to conquer death. However, the last alternative—looking away from our gifts and to the self for our sense of identity—holds the most promise for a reconciliation with our mortality.

In order to find a sense of self that is independent from our transitory gifts, we need not disown our gifts and become reclusive mystics. Rather, we must simply become aware that we are something more than the sum of our gifts—that while we may enjoy our gifts, they are not *us*. This is what Aldous Huxley was trying to tell us as he lay dying of cancer in 1963:

> The world is an illusion, but it is an illusion which we must take seriously, because it is real as far as it goes, and in those aspects of the reality which we are capable of apprehending. Our business is to wake up. . . . We must not live thoughtlessly, taking our illusion for the complete reality. . . . We must be continually on our watch for ways in which we may enlarge our consciousness. We must not live outside the world which is given us, but we must somehow learn to transform and transfigure it. . . . One must find a way of being in this world while not being of it. A way of living in time without being completely swallowed up in time. (1964, 279)

Huxley no doubt would have said that Dorian Gray and the man I have described were swallowed up in time, that they were "of the world" rather than "in it." Both Dorian and my acquaintance took their transitory gifts as if they were the whole of human experience, to the exclusion of their core selves. Dorian lived this way because he was a true child of his culture, which, like our own, emphasized immediate sensory gratification and disdained all matters of the soul. Eventually this cultural value system led Dorian Gray (as it led my acquaintance and so many others) to embark upon a vampiric rampage in an effort to repudiate the impermanence of his divine gifts.

Dorian was raised in a family where the masculine energy was embodied by a distant, angry patriarch who ruled in the absence of the child's true father, a simple soul whom the patriarch had killed off because he was deemed an insulting threat to the patriarch's domain. Similarly, many of us have been raised in families where the only masculine energy we have known is the detached authoritarianism of fathers who have killed off their simplicity and passion in an effort to preserve their threatened patriarchy. To make matters worse, all the feminine energy in Dorian's childhood was embodied in the disempowered serving women who raised him in the absence of his true mother, a grieving wife and despairing daughter whose spirit had been crushed by the patriarchy. We, too, have commonly been raised by mothers who functioned as doting serving women under the cold patriarchal hand that had crushed their vitality.

Dorian survived his grim childhood as many of us do—by relying on his gifts to prove his worth. So it is not surprising that he came to his adulthood as many of us do, with an image of himself that was founded largely on his transitory gifts and almost not at all on his timeless self. We who maintain self-images based on such gifts are much more likely to believe that we can wholly reinvent ourselves. We don't have to navigate around an awareness that our immutable core selves will persist through all of our reinventions. For those of us who have that awareness, however, the notion of self-reinvention is impossible.

Self-reinventors are more susceptible to vampiric infection both in the role of predator and victim. Whenever we define ourselves according to superficial attributes—as the smart one, the beautiful one, the funny one, or the dutiful one—we don't allow ourselves to experience anything that is incompatible with our role, and thus we lose connection with those parts of our souls. For example, I once knew a woman who defined herself only in terms of her intellect and who cut herself off from most of her soul's feeling capacities. The disconnection from any aspect of our soul is always experienced as a loss, and we usually project that loss onto the external reality. So it was not surprising that this woman frequently felt she was in danger of losing (or had already lost) the things about which she might have cared most deeply, had she allowed herself any depth of caring. Following closely her feeling of loss was the impression that other people owed her something, and that her exploitive behavior (which proceeded from her sense of their indebtedness) was simply a righteous insistence that they compensate her for her loss. Whenever we feel that others should compensate us for the life force that we have sacrificed by identifying with our gifts, we are, like this woman, at great risk of vampirizing other people. What's more, we are likely to become a vampire's victim, because we are abdicating a great deal of power to those who are supposed to compensate us, and vampires are usually the first in line to apply for these positions of interpersonal power.

As we look more closely at Dorian's childhood through our vampire-sensitive eyes, we can conclude that he was probably bitten by the psychic vampire at an early age, particularly since he lived with his grandfather, Lord Kelso, a man who, in his effort to maintain absolute domination, savaged everyone around him, including his only daughter. But the vampire is not yet the master of Dorian's psyche when we first meet the young man. There are hints that he is capable of cruelty, but every one of us is unwittingly cruel at least once in our young lives, treating another person as if he or she were simply there for our amusement. When the story begins, the vampiric seed has been planted in Dorian, but it has not yet come to full flower. For that to happen, Dorian has to meet the insidious Lord Henry.

THE GROOMING OF A VAMPIRE

Now that you are becoming something of an expert on psychic vampirism, you will probably have recognized in Lord Henry a

quintessential psychic vampire. Sensual gluttony, interpersonal exploitation, and even intellectual flimflam serve to feed Lord Henry's psychic appetite, and when wealth, sex, and fame grow tasteless on his jaded tongue, he turns to novel treats, including the corruption of Dorian Gray. But Lord Henry's motives in targeting Dorian for vampiric conversion extend beyond his need for psychic sustenance. Dorian is not just another adoring victim among the Lord's mesmerized fans. He is a victim of substance, equaling or exceeding Lord Henry in all his vampiric allure, and is thus a perfect heir apparent to Lord Henry's vampiric vocation. The lord feels compelled to convert Dorian to the vampiric way, for just as the vampire's parasitic feeding is an unholy parody of self-renewing life, so the vampire's lust to contaminate substantive souls is an unholy parody of the human desire to procreate. (The vampiric parody of procreation is also implied in Anne Rice's *Interview with the Vampire,* where the vampire Lestat initiates the young Louis into his twilit existence. Converting Louis to the vampiric path ensures that Lestat will have companionship, validation, and self-perpetuation, all rolled into one convenient package.)

As Dorian yields to the paternal mentorship of Lord Henry (who probably exudes more father energy to him than anyone he has ever met), he is quickly transformed from an innocent youth with a vampiric seed into a full-blown Dracula. Even without the supernatural gift of the portrait's decay, Dorian would have been an apt pupil at Lord Henry's knee. He was already well embarked on a spree of hedonism and emotional exploitation long before he realized that the portrait was holding his shadow. Thus, the portrait only facilitates Dorian's vampirism; it does not spawn it. In this sense, the Dorian we meet at the beginning of the story resembles many empowered people who are vampires waiting to happen. Usually these people are harboring the vampiric seed because they have been victimized by a vampire in their early lives. And because their souls are not yet completely numb, they continue to search for the love they never received. Specifically, these potential vampires are seeking the Beloved Parent, and in Dorian's case particularly (as in the case of many empowered young men), the sought-after object is the Beloved Father. What an opportunity one of these hungry puppies can present to a Draculan vampire! Here is the progeny that the vampire thought he would never enjoy—a fine young cannibal who is eager to learn the vampiric way, a devoted acolyte who is anxious to emulate the master, an intimate comrade in the mentor's campaign of predation.

I use the word "intimate" deliberately, for a profound intimacy suffuses the relationship between Lord Henry and Dorian Gray. Although Wilde's sensual terminology had a more explicit meaning, the myth of Dorian Gray can be read in a broader way regarding the intimacy between masculine vampires and their masculine victims. Dorian Gray resembles the fledgling vampires in movies such as *Wall Street* and *The Firm*, where an ambitious young man selects as his mentor a patriarchal power lord who dominates his profession. The fledgling vampires in these films (played by Charlie Sheen in *Wall Street* and Tom Cruise in *The Firm*) submit themselves with lusty fervor to the tutelage of their mentors (played by Michael Douglas and Gene Hackman, respectively). Side by side, young by old, these pairs of masculine vampires stalk the realms of professional and personal relationship in search of bloody conquest. In the most heartless manner possible, they close deals, exploit friendships, and dominate their loved ones. These men are comrades in arms at the hunt, partners in the crime of predation, mates in a life of conquest. Eventually, the sense of communion within such a pair can come to surpass the intimacy of any other relationship in their lives.

Of course, these vampiric men would abhor any explicit acknowledgment of their quasi-erotic intimacy. But in fact, what greater thrill do either of them feel than the joint exploitation of others? The younger man basks blissfully in the acceptance of his potent mentor, while the mentor savors in many complex ways

the virile power of his student. The mentor takes pride in the product of his vampiric loins, who will carry on his mentor's bloody crusade, providing new prey (he believes) when the master himself is too old to hunt. Ah, but here is the rub. The vampire parent is like any optimistic victim: he is inclined to ignore the hard fact that devotion is no protection against another vampire, even one's own carefully groomed vampiric progeny. The vampire child will turn on the vampire parent as soon as he feels that he can safely prevail.

This may not surprise us, given our new expertise in vampirism, but senior vampires are frequently surprised when their heirs turn on them. Even a vampire can be betrayed by his own capacity for deception. (When we begin a campaign of deception, it is ourselves whom we should most fear to deceive, since that is what will eventually happen.) In the case of Lord Henry and other vampiric mentors (such as Dr. Frankenstein), the deception is that the mentor will be able to control the monster he has created. In truth, the only deterrent the vampire child will respect is the possibility that his mentor may still be stronger or wilier. So the progeny waits, knowing that it is only a matter of time before the hunter will become the hunted. And in that movement, the young vampire will be the first to pounce upon his creator. This is how the story unfolds for Dorian Gray and many people in the external reality, where carefully groomed young vampires suddenly turn upon their mentors and commence to feed—emotionally, energetically, or financially. In some ways, this is also the story that Oedipus unwittingly plays out as he feasts upon the life of the dead King Laïos, and it is the story that many young executives play out as they feast upon their aging corporate mentors. Indeed, although I have framed the duet between masculine vampire and masculine victim in the metaphor of parent and child, the most explicit renditions of this dance are actually found in organizations.

For instance, a senior manager once selected one of his most

talented subordinates as the heir apparent to his little realm. The younger man was ambitious and devoted to his boss, and he deployed his formidable talent to serve him. Together, the experienced captain and his loyal lieutenant triumphantly marched up the corporate ladder, with the lieutenant always hanging one rung behind. Always, that is, until the day when a corporate shuffle enabled the elder man to help his protégé attain a position equal to his own. The mentor assumed that he would engage in a friendly rivalry with his former lieutenant, and rivalry there was, but it grew progressively less friendly as the younger man perceived himself to be less capable than his former mentor. Finally, there came a grim day when the younger man saw his chance to strike. In the whirlwind of another corporate shuffle, he was given a position superior to his former mentor.

One week later, the same young turk whom the mentor had so carefully groomed terminated the older man's employment. The mentor was shocked by the betrayal. But Lord Henry would not have been surprised. He would have recognized that the fledgling vampire, having found his wings (and fangs) à la Dorian Gray, had learned his teacher's lessons so well that he had finished by consuming him. I don't know what the corporate mentor thought at the moment of his betrayal, but perhaps he muttered the same thing that other older vampires have muttered as they felt strong, young fangs sinking into the soft skin of their necks—the same sentiments that Lord Henry mutters in bitter envy to Dorian at the end of the story, "I wish I could change places with you, Dorian. The world has cried out against us both, but it has always worshiped you. It will always worship you" (227). But here Lord Henry was wrong. The world would cease to worship Dorian as it had ceased to worship the aging lord. New young vampires would come along and supplant them both, and the legacy of predation would continue.

CHILDREN AS PSYCHIC VAMPIRES

The fostering of younger vampires brings me to another aspect of vampirism that I have not yet explicitly addressed—the notion of children as vampires. The archetype of the child vampire is a tricky one, since children are inherently needy. Children's neediness may make them look like vampires when, in fact, they are only following the path of normal human development. This reminds me of a dream I heard from a woman acquaintance years before I pursued Jungian study. The dream has echoed in my psyche many times since, perhaps because it often reflected a psychic truth that I was wrestling with. This is the dream, as I remember hearing it:

> I am sitting in a grassy meadow, enjoying the warm breeze. There is a movement in the grass nearby. When I look that way, I see a baby crawling toward me. It is a beautiful baby— all blue eyes, blond curls, and pink and white skin. Then I notice another beautiful baby crawling toward me, as adorable as the first. I am trying to decide which baby I should pick up first when I see a third baby, and then a fourth, and then many babies, all crawling happily toward me through the green grass. All are endearingly beautiful, with bright, liquid eyes. And then I notice their mouths. They are all making sucking motions with their soft, wet mouths. Surrounding me are dozens of little lips, round and pink as roses—sucking, sucking, sucking. Suddenly, I realize that the babies are hoping to suck on *me*. My joy is transformed into a sick horror. What if they all suck on me at once? I'll be drained! And still they crawl toward me because they must suck to survive. I wake up screaming as I feel dozens of soft, sucking mouths touching my defenseless skin.

An exhausted parent once suggested to me that the voracious neediness of children might be evidence that we all start out as vampires, and that we evolve with greater or lesser success into

nonvampiric souls. While I can sympathize with the frustration of this parent, I do not think she was right. The fact is that most children will strive to protect the beloved parent, even to the point of their own destruction, and this energetic position is completely antithetical to the conduct of the vampire. It is more likely that children's neediness escalates when they are met with vampiric caretakers, and the more they are treated as objects, the more vampiric they become. Eventually, such children manifest an arrested kind of primitive psychic hunger, and when we meet them as vampiric adults, they still display a childlike or infantile quality in their unremitting neediness. These childlike adults may gurgle and coo as they beguile us, or they may pout and whine when they are rebuffed, or they may rant and scream when their hunger for psychic energy exceeds our ability or willingness to provide it. Whatever form it takes, the childlike neediness of this kind of psychic vampire is likely to elicit from us a variety of parental responses.

One response can be overindulgence, in an effort to placate the vampire's demands. Unfortunately, this response only exacerbates the demands and our depletion, just like it does in the child-parent dyads where the parent offers indulgent placation instead of healthy boundaries. Another response is to erect a wall of rejection or abandonment against the vampire, when we reach our limit of exasperation. This response is like the wall of negligence that some parents construct to shield themselves (however abusively) from the profound neediness of their children. A third response is to erupt in anger, spewing a torrent of abuse at the childlike vampire in an effort to silence his or her demands, like the torrential abuse with which some parents inundate their children out of overwhelming fatigue and frustration. All of these responses can be contrasted with the more constructive response of setting healthy boundaries with a loving attitude. Unlike the first three, this response can deactivate the vampire archetype, or at least slow its growth in the childlike vampire's psyche.

The growth of the vampire archetype in a child's psyche is particularly dangerous, because children's growth (psychic as well as physical) is explosive as compared to that of adults. A child's vampirism can eventually grow to such proportions that its parents (vampiric or not) will themselves become the victims. Here we return again to the story of Dorian Gray, who turned to feed upon the very people—the members of the British elite—who helped to foster his vampirism. And are we so very different from Dorian? When we dare to examine our behavior, many of us will find that we are most likely to vampirize our parents and our mates as well as our children.

One of the most famous depictions of the child-vampire-turns-on-parent-vampire scenario is provided in Alfred Hitchcock's classic thriller *Psycho*. In this film we meet Norman Bates, the eccentric young manager of a wayside motel, who has evidently spent his childhood as the victim of a vampiric mother with whom he lives. We hear Norman's rebellion in his heated arguments with the old harridan ("Shut *up*, mother! *Shut up! SHUT UP!!*"). But we also sense that he is, on a deeper level, still feeding his mother's unholy hungers "A boy's best friend should be his mother, don't you think?" he asks the luscious young female guest. Later, we watch as the same guest is stabbed to death in her shower by a motherly figure. Poor Norman, seemingly the typical male victim of a maternal vampire, is left to dispose of the young guest's body, as he must later dispose of the investigator who is searching for her.

The punchline, of course, is that the vampiric duet between Norman and his mother was reversed long before we ever meet Norman. At the end of the film, we learn that Norman has long since killed his mother in a jealous rage, and that he has literally sucked her personality into his own, perhaps as a way of dominating her once and for all.

We may sympathize with vampire children who suck the life out of their vampire parents, but these offspring are vampires

nonetheless. Once the vampiric parent is vanquished, the hunger will drive the child vampire to seek new victims. This is the story of Norman Bates, and it is the story of Dorian Gray. Long after Lord Henry is eclipsed by his former protégé, many other victims will perish in Dorian's insatiable embrace. And the more innocent his victims are when he encounters them, the more Dorian savors their downfall and relishes the energy he can suck up in the process.

In this sense, Dorian resembles one of literature's earliest vampires and the first of his kind who was both deadly and desirable—the treacherous Lord Ruthven in John Polidori's 1819 story "The Vampyre." Polidori was a brilliant young doctor from Edinburgh who had been assigned to attend the fabulously wealthy and hedonistic poet Lord Byron. Byron was a charismatic psychic vampire who preyed on anyone he could seduce, including the naïve Polidori. Outraged by Byron's cruelty to him, Polidori plotted revenge. After Byron's famous visit in Switzerland with Percy and Mary Shelley (during which Mary Shelley created the story of Frankenstein), Polidori absconded with one of Byron's story fragments—a vampire tale that Polidori then completed and published under Byron's name. Lord Ruthven, the main character in "The Vampyre," according to Bunson's *Vampire Encyclopedia* (1993), "was patterned on Lord Byron himself, a means of achieving literary revenge for the indignities that Polidori had once suffered at the hands of the noble poet. The vampire parodies Lord Byron in many ways, both being pale-faced, exceedingly handsome, astoundingly successful with women, and utterly cruel, particularly to those who love him" (228).

Ironically, history proved Byron to be an even greater vampire than Polidori had dreamed. Despite Polidori's explicit intention to lampoon the vampiric Byron, his tale of Lord Ruthven continued to be attributed to Byron himself, to the extent that Goethe referred to "The Vampyre" as "the best thing that Byron had written." Thus, Byron even succeeded in sucking up the energy

from the well-powered (but fatally misaimed) blow by Polidori's literary stake. Byron's vampiric, debonair energy has endured into the present, in the form of the Byronic Dracula. And the vampirism of Dorian Gray and Lord Henry bears such an unmistakable resemblance to that of Lord Ruthven that one looks to Polidori's tale for Wilde's inspiration. Compare this description of Ruthven, for example, with Basil's denunciation of Dorian quoted on page 168: "To enhance his own gratification after the seduction, Lord Ruthven required that his companion in sin be hurled from the pinnacle of virtue to the very lowest abyss of infamy and degradation" (Polidori 1819, 11). For both Ruthven and Dorian, the more innocent the victim, the more important the kill. In the tale of Dorian Gray, the most graphic example of this behavior is Dorian's destruction of Sybil Vane.

AUDIENCE/PERFORMER VAMPIRISM

Although she comes from impoverished circumstances, Sybil resembles Dorian in several important ways. She is charismatically attractive, she is uniquely gifted, and above all, she needs an audience to make her feel that she is truly alive. Sybil and Dorian quickly come to serve as audience and performer for each other. The vampiric dance between audience and performer comes easily to all of us who have been appreciated for what we did, rather than for who we were. This kind of upbringing leads us to fear the black void that we believe underlies our gifts—a void that we fear will open and swallow us if we are "unmasked" as the pretenders we feel ourselves to be. Desperately, we try to dazzle the members of our lifetime audience, hoping that they will not detect our black void (which is in fact not a void at all, but the place where our unacknowledged core self dwells, right next to our yucky old shadow). The members of our audience offer or withhold their applause, which puts us at their mercy and makes us ready prey for any vampires lurking among them. For their part,

the audience vampires feed off our superhuman efforts to per-
form, while we attempt to hold their projections and bring their
dreams to life, so that we may vampirize their energy in return.

This is the duet that every performer and audience risks whenever the curtain goes up (which in our age can be all the time)—a
duet in which Sybil and Dorian engage. Dorian loves Sybil because she "realized the dreams of great poets and gave shape and
substance to the shadows of art." Sybil is Dorian's beloved muse,
the projection of all that he cherishes in himself but cannot explicitly acknowledge. In this sense, Dorian is a typical vampiric member of the audience. Nor is Sybil innocent of vampirism, for
Dorian fuels her with his projections and sustains her with the life
force that he offers on the altar of her performance. Sybil cherishes the audience that reflects back to her the image she wishes
to see, validating her hope that she is much more than she fears.
But no matter how flattering the applause may be, it is based on
Sybil's gifts, not on her self—a painful fact that she does not realize until it is too late. Once Sybil believes in and relies upon Dorian's projections of her godliness, she lets the mask of her gifts fall
to her feet, only to realize her worst fear: she is disgusting to her
beloved audience member, who sees only a void behind her gifts.
Dorian's venomous repudiation—"Without your art, you are
nothing"—undermines Sybil's weak sense of self and drives her to
suicide.

No wonder we are terrified of letting our masks slip, even a
little, when such a fate may await us at the hands of a vampiric
audience. So we dance ever faster while the vampire feeds, believing ourselves to be appreciated and loved. And with every step we
take, we feed as well on the vampiric audience whose applause
keeps our gift-based self-image afloat.

Naturally, it is possible for performers to perform and audience to admire without the vampire archetype entering the relationship. I can recall one particular instance in which an image
was created by a performer and received by her audience without

any vampiric need to maintain the projection beyond the context of the performance. When the curtain rang down, the archetypal images may have lingered in the psyches of the performer and the audience, but the performer did not feel compelled to continually enact the archetypal story, and the audience did not continue to project it onto the merely mortal performer. In a nonvampiric performance such as this one, audience and performer are in implicit agreement that they have collaborated in the invocation of the archetypal energies, but no one believes that the performer *is* the energy itself. On the other hand, when a performing relationship is vampiric, the burden of archetypal projection turns the performer into the vampiric toy and tormentor of the audience, rendering him (in the words of Aldous Huxley) "a mixture between a god, a naughty child and a wild beast. The god must be worshiped, the child amused and bamboozled and the wild beast placated and, when aroused, avoided. The courtier who, by an unwelcome suggestion, annoys this insane trinity of superhuman pretension, subhuman ferocity and infantile silliness, is merely asking for trouble" (142–43). A vampiric performing relationship will also turn an assembly of otherwise noble souls into a ravening mob that capriciously exalts or vilifies the performer. In the worst case, it brings the stalkers out from the woodwork, since they are obsessively (albeit erroneously) trying to suck up the energy of the person onto whom they have projected divinity.

It is difficult to break the vampiric cycle between an audience and a performer, both in the public kinds of performance and in the private performances of our relationships. Doing so can occur only in the rare moments when a performer reveals his or her imperfect human truth, which underlies the audience's projection, and the audience accepts the performer's truth with compassion and grace. In these moments both performer and audience are freed from the vampiric dance and are permitted to rest in their simple humanity. Unfortunately, judging by our media headlines and relationship traumas, such moments of compassionate grace

are not the norm. A performer's release of the audience's projection more often results in a soul-ravaging tirade like the one that Dorian unleashes on Sybil. In the face of such abuse, some of us bury our despair and redouble our efforts to perform, while others abandon our gift-based self-images and seek a healthier foundation for our sense of self. In a few cases, we give up completely on both our façades and the possibility that there is anything beneath them, and we sink, like poor Sybil Vane, into a deadly despair.

VAMPIRIC PERFECTIONISM

In the years following Sybil's death, Dorian grows increasingly obsessed with the portrait in the schoolroom. At times he shuns it completely, while at others he is fascinated by its decay and revels in the difference between himself and the man on the oiled canvas. Similarly, when we think we have entered a new state of goodness, we reflect back on the ugliness we have disavowed and sneer at our former badness, which we think we have locked safely away in the shadowy attic of our psyche.

The image of shadow is critical here. The vampire myth tells us, not only that vampires detest mirrors and cast no reflection in them, but that they cast no shadow as well. Moreover, some myths state that a person whose shadow is stolen (by being nailed to a wall, for example) will become a vampire. The shadowlessness of the vampire has particular relevance to the Jungian use of the term *shadow*, which denotes the traits in ourselves that we do not acknowledge as ours. As we come into contact with the external world in early childhood, we learn that some of our innate potentials are good and others are bad in the terms of our early environment. Quickly we learn to consciously display the traits for which we are rewarded, and to hide (and eventually deny) the traits for which we are punished or ignored.

The way in which our potential traits fall into the two catego-

ries of display and denial depends largely on our socialization and temperament. For example, one man I know had learned to display proudly his discipline and reserve, and to hide his flexibility and expressiveness (which he had learned to call by names such as "weakness" and "melodramatics"). With a different kind of socialization and temperament, however, this man might just as easily have learned to display his flexibility and expressiveness, and to hide his discipline and reserve (which he would have learned to call by names such as "rigidity" and "coldness"). There are as many arrangements of traits in these two categories as there are permutations of personal experience. Still, the basic Jungian view is that every human psyche is composed of a *persona*—the traits which we have learned to consciously display—and a *shadow*—the traits we have learned to hide and deny.

This arrangement is fine so far as it goes, but it doesn't go the distance of a lifetime. Eventually, the traits that are stuffed into the shadow want out, and out they will come in a variety of forms, few of which are pleasant. It is not as if we make a calm, logical decision to put any trait—"expressiveness," for example—into the shadow. Our shadow lessons are learned early, unconsciously, and with primal emotion. The man who was trained to hide his emotions had thrust "expressiveness" quickly and fervently into his shadow, where he had learned to refer to it as "melodramatics." Once a trait has been forced into the shadow, it lives like a child locked in a closet—it is likely to retain an immature or feral quality that is laced with feelings of fear and anger. We do all we can to suppress the shadow trait, but eventually it will erupt into our lives, wreaking mischief or havoc in the orderly house of our conscious persona. The man's rejected shadow trait of "expressiveness" finally began to sabotage his persona of calm reserve with eruptions of inexplicable emotionality.

If we have been victimized by vampires in our childhood, as Dorian Gray was, our shadow closet probably contains the feel-

ings associated with not having been loved enough at some crucial point. To become conscious of these painful feelings, which usually include desperate longing, innocent love, and bottomless despair, would require us to relive the horror of the earlier time. The pain of such an experience cannot be comprehended; it felt like death before, and revisiting the experience will feel like psychic annihilation. What's more, our shadow feelings often retain the primitive quality of their original form, which makes them capable of erasing any sense of control that we might have developed since their incarceration in the shadow closet. Therefore, most of us refuse to acknowledge any feeling that lives in our shadow unless it breaks free of our control and erupts into our external lives. When it does, we usually see the erupting shadow as awful evidence of our "real" selves. This is unfortunate, since the shadow traits we detest are no more real than the persona traits we love. Nonetheless, we fear their "reality," and in order to defend against our perceived terribleness, we blame others for our shadow eruptions by projecting the traits onto them. For example, my calmly disciplined acquaintance would become enraged any time his wife or a co-worker displayed strong emotions. Once the shadow is projected onto someone else, we can feel free to hate its unlucky host, rather than hating ourselves.

When the vampire lore tells us that vampires cast no shadow, and that the loss of shadow can actually lead to vampirism, it suggests that whenever the vampire is activated in our psyches, we will be especially determined to render our shadows invisible to ourselves and others. This makes sense, for how can we fulfill the vampiric destiny of immortal perfection if we have to contend with our rejected shadow parts? Better to conceal or project our shadow instead, and base all of our self-image on the lovely mirror of goodness we have purchased with our denial. When our goodness mirror shows a tinge of darkness, we try to ignore it. And when the tinge becomes an unignorable blot, well then, it is time to look for a new mirror and banish the old one to the heap

of decaying images in the attic. We don't care what happens to the putrid old mirrors. We just want their darkness to leave us alone with our latest illusion of our unsullied goodness.

Not surprisingly, the badness rarely departs like an obedient child. Usually, it loiters in the corners of our psyches like an annoying tormentor whose sole purpose is to irritate and offend us. Tormentors of this type reside in Dorian Gray's psyche, and he attempts to banish them with a variety of hedonistic drugs. Other tormentors arrive in his outer world, however, and these are not so easily banished. The first of these is Basil Hallward, who inadvertently reminds Dorian that he remembers his painting, which Dorian knows is the hard evidence of his badness. This is irritating enough to Dorian, but Basil goes on to suggest that Dorian's behavior resembles the corrupt image that only Dorian knows is hidden in the old schoolroom. Dorian's reaction to Basil's insight is not unlike Oedipus's reaction to Teiresias's truthseeing: he takes out his rage on the messenger. Oedipus was afraid to harm Apollo's messenger, but Dorian is not similarly constrained. He shows Basil the secret of the portrait and then, with an eerie calm, murders the painter. Like the psychic vampires we know, he slashes in cold fury at anyone who holds up a mirror to reveal his shadow.

Dorian Gray's method of killing Basil—by stabbing him in the throat and leaving the blood to drip and pool on the carpet—could hardly be more vampiric. And just as any vampire drinks up the victim's life force, so Dorian drinks up the satisfaction of believing that he has destroyed yet another source of darkness in his life, even though the darkness that Basil described was only a reflection of what Dorian carried within. Later, with the chemist's extorted assistance, Dorian banishes the evidence of his badness as it is revealed by Basil's body, just as he has banished its revelation in his own body. And yet, as Dorian becomes increasingly aware, that evidence is not truly banished. The portrait is hidden in the locked schoolroom, but echoes of its accusation are prolif-

erating in Dorian's daily life. Here, too, Dorian's quandary is identical to that of the mythic vampire. In legend, the vampire is a creature with a wide variety of irritants and enemies, many of which, like mirrors and shadows, are common parts of daily life. And because the external world frequently confronts us with mirroring information about our imperfections and disturbing evidence of our shadowy parts, psychic vampires must maintain a vigilance bordering on obsession in order to banish from their presence the ordinary objects they abhor.

Psychically, this vigilance is manifested in an attempt to be perfect—to be as attractive, accomplished, admired, or adored as is superhumanly possible. It should be noted that the need to be perfect has other origins besides the vampiric. Perfection has historically been associated with completion (from the Greek tradition) and with divinity (from the Judeo-Christian tradition). Thus, our quest for perfection can reflect our yearning to be psychically complete and connected to the divine. Because we are rarely conscious of these spiritual motives in our concrete world, however, we tend to seek perfection in concrete ways. We try to achieve the perfect weight, find the perfect job, and be perfectly well behaved. Of course, it is sometimes helpful for us to engage in concrete activities that symbolize our less tangible psychic pursuits. But we can get into trouble when we try to substitute concrete accomplishments for the spiritual kind. Our quest for perfection is spiritual in essence, and concrete achievements alone are not capable of providing what we seek. It would be like trying to satisfy emotional hunger with literal cookies, or trying to obtain spiritual wealth by accumulating a large bank account.

I once knew a woman whose quest for perfection lacked any psychic foundation, and as a result, it assumed a cold rigidity. In other words, the flexibility and compassion that distinguish a spiritual pursuit of psychic completion and divinity were absent from her literal pursuit of concrete perfection. Instead, the woman become fiercely, even mercilessly, invested in her literal accom-

plishments. With wafer-thin modesty, she proclaimed her noble efforts at struggling toward whatever kind of perfection she was currently pursuing—profit, thinness, parenting, tenure—and she tallied her victories with lines through a "to do" list. Her psychic vampire was activated, which meant that efficient accomplishment was godly to her as she exchanged the potency of love for the illusory power of control. Eventually, this woman was forced to adopt the inevitable stepchildren of a psyche bent on control—obsession and compulsion. Although obsession and compulsion can be useful in moderation, and although they are not always indicative of an active vampire archetype, these traits have been mythically associated with the vampire.

This perfection-seeking woman soon found out that obsession and compulsion are fickle companions. Initially, these traits helped her navigate through daily life with remarkable efficiency and competence. But somewhere along the way, her trusted servants turned on her. Over time, it seemed that she, who was formerly the master of her obsessions and compulsions, became their slave, and she found find herself laboring endlessly to meet their demands. Never rich enough, nor thin enough, nor loved nor safe nor accomplished enough. She felt she was never, never enough. Just one more deal, just one more pound, just one more conquest, just one more finished list. Then she would be the best. Then she would truly be loved. Then she would finally be perfect. The sad truth for this woman, as for us all, is that when the vampire drives us, there is no satisfaction in whatever we compulsively seek, no refuge from what we obsessively fear. There is only the momentary illusion of control and the inevitable return of the terrified hunger. In *Vampires, Burial, and Death* (1988) Paul Barber observes:

> If one excepts his craving for blood, [the vampire's] power-lust is his sole passion and is seldom explained or analyzed. To be a vampire, it seems, is to be power-mad, in the grip of a com-

pulsion not unlike that of our folkloric revenants counting their poppy seeds. . . . His acts are explained as the result of compulsions: we are told that he "must," not that he "likes to." He is singularly lacking in options. (83, 58)

A less publicized but globally acknowledged trait of the vampire is its obsessive-compulsive nature. Barber's remark about poppy seeds refers to the lore, common to many cultures, that the most effective way to escape a vampire is to scatter poppy seed, mustard seed, or (in Asia) rice grains between oneself and the monster. The vampire will be compelled to stop and count all the grains, giving its intended victim sufficient time to flee the vampire or kill it.

As Dorian Gray becomes aware of all the seeds of evidence that his portrait seems to have sown, he desperately tries to eradicate each dark truth, one by one. At first, he tries to reverse the bits of darkness by making up for his sins with good deeds. This exercise provides an interesting corollary to the clean slate myth, since it proceeds from the belief that one's badness might be erased by acts of compensatory goodness. Without an acknowledgment of our darkness and a commitment to its transformation, however, our good deeds accomplish only what Dorian achieved when he tried this trick—instead of indulging in blatant, obvious vampirism, he indulged in a new, pernicious kind that reeked of hypocrisy. Behaviors that qualify as hypocritical vampirism include doing favors for someone whom we secretly have wronged, donating resources to groups whom we otherwise disdain, patronizing subordinates whom we secretly exploit, and mouthing beliefs that we secretly desecrate with our behavior.

If we try to convince ourselves that we have obliterated our darkness with an extravaganza of self-conscious good deeds, we risk being confronted with the hypocrisy of our altruistic crusade. Like Dorian Gray, we must face the portrait of our dreaded shadow, and like Dorian, we may detest the task. But we ignore the detested mirror at our peril. If we refuse to look, then it will

seem to us that the psychic vampire is active only in others (as Dorian felt when he looked at Basil and the hideous portrait). And again like Dorian Gray, if we sharpen our self-righteous stakes for the purpose of killing only the vampires in others, then we risk sharpening our own fangs with the same strokes. As Leonard Wolf observes about *Dracula,* "Stoker's achievement is this: he makes us understand in our own experience why the vampire is said to be invisible in the mirror. He is there, but we fail to recognize him since our own faces get in the way" (1975, xviii).

We must hold up the mirror to ourselves, not only to protect other people, but for our own protection as well. When our inner vampire speaks, it sounds like our own voice, so we believe everything it says and quickly become its cowering slaves. What's more, the vampires in other people will often enlist the aid of our inner vampires. For example, think back to the vampiric mother who manipulated her daughter by inducing guilt. Whenever the mother would invoke the terrible things that would happen if the daughter didn't comply with her wishes, the tactic would awaken the daughter's inner vampire, which constantly whipped her into a quest for concrete perfection anyway. When the mother's vampire spoke, the daughter's vampire (which she heard as her own inner voice of truth) joined in for the chorus and drove her on mercilessly, long after the mother had stopped speaking. Because the daughter was much less conscious of her own vampire than she was of her mother's, she was continually trapped in its jaws, which made it, therefore, the more dangerous of the two demons.

The vampire lore tells us that holding up a mirror to a literal vampire is a dangerous task. Similarly, holding up a mirror to someone (including oneself) in whom the vampire archetype is activated is not to be attempted lightly, because the human capacity for soulful compassion is not accessible when a vampire archetype is activated. As Wolf observes, "the folklore of mirrors holds that the images people see of themselves in the glass are relations of the human soul. Dracula, who is merely a corpse in motion is not, in a proper sense, animated, and therefore makes no reflection" (1975, 27). If activating the vampire archetype leaves the psyche compassionless, then it is risky to reflect someone's truth to him while he is acting in a vampiric way. For example, as any abuse survivor knows, reflecting to the abuser the implications of his behavior in the middle of an abusive episode is only likely to escalate the nightmare. Sometimes it is even dangerous to reflect back a person's vampiric behavior when they are *not* in the clutches of that archetype. If acknowledging the abuse is too painful, the vampire may be reawakened to obliterate the pain of remorse. In any case, the act of reflecting on our own vampiric behavior places us at a terrible crossroads where we must choose among the paths of denial, growth, or despair.*

When Dorian arrives at this place of confrontation, he sinks into a profound despair. I have often wondered what would have happened if Dorian had chosen a different path in this crucial moment, one in which he dragged out the rotting canvas for all to see. Of course, doing such a thing would have required superhuman courage, but the feat is not impossible, for it is exactly what people in therapy do on a regular basis. With many fewer resources than Dorian Gray, many brave souls drag their portraits out of the attic and into the light of the therapy room, where they shudder with fear at what they will see. I can't speak for everyone, but I believe that my clients never see anything as horrible as what they have feared. And in my eyes, what they have dragged out of the attic is often not horrible at all. Usually, their portraits simply depict some normal human traits that have been bent and discolored by pain but that can be reclaimed for their essential beauty and value.

The process of reclaiming one's dark portrait it not simple or quick, but it is possible for most of us to accomplish with less

---

*Vampires in legend are reputed to loiter at crossroads—a sign that we are susceptible to vampiric invasion or predation when we are confronted with the doubt, insecurity, and fear that accompany our most difficult trials and changes of life course.

anguish than our fears would have us believe. If Dorian had brought his ugly old portrait downstairs and had shown it to someone who was as compassionate as Basil (but wiser in the ways of the psyche), he might have transformed both the portrait and himself. Eventually, they would have reintegrated, with Dorian becoming more receptive, more approachable, and more human than the deceitful mannequin he had become, and the portrait becoming more appealing, more illuminating, and more sympathetic than the monster it had become. Of course, Dorian would have had to sacrifice his ability to glide above the grimier aspects of human existence, but he would also have been able to dig beneath his fickle beauty and discover the true gold that was hidden in his soul. In the end, he could have nestled contentedly into the life he was born to live. And he would have survived.

As it was, Dorian could not give up his illusory perfection and celebrity status. He could not disentangle his sense of himself from the transitory gifts of the gods. He felt that he *was* his beauty and his youth, and that they were the essence of him. Without his illusion of perfection, he felt he was nothing. And since the horrible portrait was the repository of his imperfection, he felt that he could only survive by destroying its darkness. He aimed his knife at the hideous portrait, hoping to watch the portrait's (that is, his) putrescence drip and pool on the floor just as Basil's blood had done. Once and for all, he would banish his darkness and live in the light. He tightened his grip on the metal stake of his knife and drove into the heart of the detested image. And in so doing, he died.

Dorian Gray meant to kill only his darkness. If he had understood that his darkness was a part of him, he would have realized that in killing it, he was killing himself as well. And perhaps some part of Dorian Gray was aware of precisely this fact, just as Westley Dodd wished to be executed so that his dark self would not have the chance to murder again. But it is more likely that Dorian simply thought, as so many of us do, that he was going to redeem himself and live only in goodness and light by eradicating his darkness. He had projected his darkness onto a human image and now he would destroy it.

We do this, too, although we usually project our darkness onto a real human being rather than a piece of canvas that bears a human image. And sometimes, if our darkness seems too great for a single human to bear, we project it onto a whole group of human beings. The projection of our darkness onto a group gives us one advantage over Dorian Gray: since our friends and neighbors usually have similar darknesses that they want to unload as badly as we do, we can all agree about the group on whom we wish to project. That way, we don't have to hide our dark portraits in the attics of our psyches, but rather, we join our friends and neighbors in a public orgy of projection in our media, our streets, our businesses, and even our places of worship. We feel we have nothing to hide, for it seems clear to us that the darkness lies in the poor, the homosexuals, the immigrants, or the Jews. Having collectively projected our darkness, we feel collectively purged, and we can all be fresh and new and perfect together. Our own darkness grows in this miasma of vampiric revelry, of course, and soon we find that the darkness we perceive in the persecuted group has grown, too. In the end, we may feel compelled to annihilate the offensive group, just as Dorian Gray tried to annihilate his portrait. What we fail to realize is that whenever we attempt to exterminate the detested people who hold our projected shadow, we, like Dorian Gray, are killing our own souls as well.

I would like to note that enlisting another person's energy for one's own benefit, in the manner of Dorian Gray, is not always vampiric. We all need to feel the shape of other people's energy in order to balance our own. In a nonvampiric relationship, the balancing of energy is a mutual offering. If I need to feel the shape of your energy today in order to regain my balance, we both know that at other times I will willingly extend the shape of my energy to balance yours. In contrast, when a relationship is vampiric, one

or both partners will recognize over time that the energy flow is fundamentally unequal. One person is extending himself far more than the other. Another difference is the degree of compassion with which the two members approach the relationship. In non-vampiric relationships, we balance each other's energy with mutual concern for each other's well-being. In contrast, psychic vampires have no capacity to see the exploited person as anything more than an extension of themselves.

This cautionary note notwithstanding, it may seem from the preceding stories that nearly all relationships are vampiric, and that our yearning for love is doomed to deliver us into the vampire's jaws. Don't despair. Stay by my side for a final round of musing and myth, in which we will learn how love can be redeemed and redemptive, even in the jaws of the vampire. This final leg of our journey will lead us into the deepest danger, but it is a peril we must encounter before we can greet the dawn. Forward into the night.

THE REDEMPTION OF LOVE
GIVING UP DRACULA FOR SIR GAWAIN

AT ITS CORE, every vampire story is really about the dark shadow that falls across our path as we seek our perfect Beloved. Ah . . . the Beloved! We all seek that divine entity who will bring our dreams to life and lift us into a state of transcendent bliss. We feel the essence of the archetypal Beloved in every myth, every fairy tale, and every celluloid concoction that shines before us in the perpetual night of the movie theater. For most of us, the search for a loved one is the most compelling pursuit of our lives—the only pursuit that can drive us beyond ourselves as we journey to hell and back. But here's the bad news: the path we walk on our search for our true love makes a perfect hunting ground for hungry vampires. In the tale of *Dracula,* for example, every character is looking for a being who will bring transformation, completion, and redemption. Jonathan Harker seeks in Dracula a prize client whose largess will enable the young clerk to transcend his mediocrity and achieve professional success. Lucy Westenra seeks among her many suitors the one who will provide her with conjugal and connubial nirvana. Lucy's suitors seek in Lucy the traditional prize of vulnerable, adoring womanhood. The mad pariah Renfield seeks in Dracula a savior who will decimate Renfield's contemptuously sane society. And the child victims of the Lucy vampire seek a mother figure who will love them utterly. All these characters believe that their heart's desire can be incarnated in another individual, a belief that leads them to fervently and perilously seeking their perfect, archetypal beloved in imperfect human beings.

In its simplest form, the search for the Beloved is born of our fierce human drive to commune with an entity whom we love, and who will love us in return. Love, in this sense, is more than a conglomeration of respect, honor, affection, and devotion. These qualities proceed from love, but they are not its essence. This kind of love is what we experience when we connect with a being that is greater than ourselves. And here is born a dangerous illusion—we believe that something larger than life can be incarnated in a single person. This is only natural, since we must use the finite shapes of our external experience to comprehend an infinite internal experience. But true love is really much more complex, profound, and transcendent than the repertoire of any mere mortal.

The essence of the archetypal Beloved is as sacred, as vast, and as intimate as the soul, which means that our relationship to the Beloved is most potent when it is not distorted by the human limitations of an external person. In other words, we are most likely to commune with the true Beloved when we turn within and touch that in ourselves which resonates with all that is sacred. This is the part of us that Jung called the Self, but we may also call it the soul or the divine. Ecstatic mystics regularly enjoy this kind of intrapsychic soul love, but it is more difficult for the rest of us to achieve because we pay more attention to finite external reality, which is full of compelling sensory distractions. Most of us are not inclined to maintain the mystic's internal focus and spiritual discipline, which are requirements for communing with the Self, so we spend the greater part (if not all) of our lives looking to other people, rather than to our own souls, for our sense of ecstatic communion. This is why most of us come to expect and demand perfect love from the imperfect human mortals on whom we've projected the image of our divine Beloved.

This is not to say that an interpersonal love between two people cannot approximate the potency of communion with the true Beloved. In fact, our feelings of interpersonal love are the experiences that teach most of us how to recognize and nurture, when it finally appears, the small green shoot of intrapsychic love with our true Beloved. We also have a great opportunity to encounter the perfect Beloved during the lonely spaces between our interpersonal love relationships, since these are the periods when we are least distracted by the illusion that some finite human being is our sacred Beloved. Thus, our feelings of interpersonal love can teach us, both by their presence and absence, invaluable lessons about how to commune with the inner Beloved, and therefore it seems appropriate and even necessary for us to devote some energy to seeking our Beloved in external reality.

Unfortunately, when we embark on an external quest for someone to incarnate our Beloved, our path is fraught with several kinds of peril, much of which is vampiric. When we look outside ourselves for a love that will make us whole, we are likely to see our chosen loved one as stronger and healthier than is humanly possible and thus, as capable of rescuing us and making us whole. Psychic vampires adore this setup because they see in it our vulnerability to vampiric seduction. Let's look at exactly how this seduction works by considering the story of a talented professional woman whom I once knew—a gifted architect who sought her sacred Beloved in a series of external men. This woman, like so many of us, could not believe that she herself possessed the magical traits that she perceived in her lovers. It wasn't that she had a poor self-esteem—she just couldn't imagine how she could feel so enchanted by her lovers' traits if she already possessed them herself. The woman was most enchanted by the *otherness* of her lovers, by the traits that seemed to be absent in her own psyche: tenderness, playfulness, and a carefree attitude about life, traits that were incompatible with her upbringing and work.

In truth, all of these traits were very much present in the woman's psyche, but she did not experience them as hers. It may seem odd that this smart, accomplished architect could have been so blind to her own psychic wealth, but there were good reasons for her impaired inner vision. In some cases, she didn't perceive a cherished trait in herself because she had learned in her childhood that it was not appropriate for her gender, age, or cultural role. In other cases, she recognized her potential for the trait, but didn't own it because it had caused her pain when she had displayed it in the past.

Odd as it may seem, the architect experienced her lovers' magical traits as being sometimes splendid, at other times awful. The reason is this: the most magical traits of any loved one are always the traits, good or bad, that we don't acknowledge in ourselves—in other words, our shadows. Think for a moment. Didn't it ever strike you as odd that some of the people we most adore at one instant are those whom we most detest at another? It is a wry joke of the psyche that our loved ones frequently embody our unacknowledged darkness as well as our unacknowledged light.

Because the architect had been forbidden as a child to express her emotions freely, as an adult she always sought lovers who could express their feelings with fluid ease. Sometimes she found her partners' expressiveness lovely, while at other times she cursed their "moodiness." This duality turned each of her partners into a perfect vehicle for her psychic needs, since she could press him into service as either her savior or her scapegoat. Unfortunately, as long as the woman projected any of her traits—positive or negative—onto her partner, she was incapable of living out the trait's desired aspect herself, nor could she mitigate its destructive potential in her own psyche.

Whenever the architect projected her traits onto an external loved one, she increased her vulnerability to vampiric invasion in three ways. First, as long as some of her energies were projected onto someone else, she did not have access to the whole of her power, which left her in a weakened and yearning state. Second, as long as she was desperate to find an external loved one, she was inclined to project her power onto any warm body that would hold the projection (even if the body was only warmed by stolen blood). And third, once the woman had securely clamped her projection onto a new loved one, she felt as if she were psychically welded to this man (who, after all, seemed to be her only means of connecting with the energies that she had hidden from herself). In this enmeshed state, the woman opened wide her psychic windows to any man who could hold her projection of the archetypal Beloved.

This bundle of circumstances is the perfect setup for the vampiric attack. To begin with, all predators target the vulnerable members of the herd, and when we are projecting a portion of our strength onto any external person, we are vulnerable. Moreover, the most lethal predators are those who can make themselves attractive to the intended prey; posing as the perfect Beloved is the best disguise of all. Finally, a predator can do the most damage when the prey has dropped its defenses and admitted the predator into its inner sanctum. Thus, a psychic vampire had only to detect the architect's fervent search for a screen onto whom she could project her inner Beloved. Once he had smelled her desperate yearning, the man could easily metamorphose himself into the kind of man who would meet her criteria for a projection screen. This is easy work for vampires, both mythic and psychic, since all vampires have the predator's keen senses and a talent for shape shifting. And psychic vampires are especially adept at masquerading as the Beloved, since

> the vampire appears empty, like a shadow, and we, the human observers, may project whatever form will grip our imagination most. . . . In this complex and disturbing fashion the process of depletion begins, and through this balance of fantasy and reality the vampire sucks not only blood, but the psychic energy which controls our mental and physical functions, slowly but surely becoming a perfect projection of our desires. (Maschetti 1992, 46)

Once a vampiric man was the bearer of the architect's projections, she was in his thrall, because she had abdicated to her beloved vampire the traits for which she most yearned. Ironically, these became the very traits that could have released the woman from the vampire's control, for if she could have recognized them in herself, the beloved vampire would no longer have been able to hold her captive. Instead, because the woman perceived that her lover held her unclaimed power, she granted to one psychic vampire after another the key to her heart's desire, and she willingly paid in blood for a chance to turn that key. The irony of this illusion was that the vampires' bait was simply the reflection of her own gifts.

In *Dracula,* the vampire seems to possess a plethora of enviable traits that are actually reflections of each observer's own inherent (but initially unrecognized) gifts. Jonathan Harker envies Dracula's invincibility and wealth, though in the end, it is Jonathan who prevails over the vampire by dint of his fortitude and affluence. Similarly, Van Helsing waxes eloquent about Dracula's wisdom and intelligence, though it is Van Helsing's wisdom and intelligence that leads to the vampire's destruction. Quincy, Seward, and Holmwood are aghast at Dracula's sexual presumption with Mina, though they have aspired to similar conquests with Lucy. And Lucy herself is ravished by the vampire's sexual charms in the same way that she has ravaged her suitors with her own unconscious sexuality. As for Mina, her strength and intelligence are greater than Lucy's, but she does not initially claim these traits as hers, so Dracula seems to grow in strength and intelligence as he stalks her. What's more, Mina seeks a true love who will, unlike Lucy's suitors, grant her the empowerment that she can enjoy only as a married woman in the patriarchy. And Dracula seduces Mina with the "empowering" prospect of vampiric marriage. Mina, interestingly enough, does a much better job of resisting the vampire's empowerment lure after she has been bitten by him: once Dracula bites her, Mina must finally turn away from her male allies and rely on her own power, since the men can no longer risk exposing themselves to her vampiric contamination and her projections of empowerment.

Unfortunately, the architect did not have the hard-won advantage of Mina's gory awakening and enforced self-reliance. When this woman projected the archetypal Beloved onto a psychic vampire, she did not have to confront bloodied fangs and a string of mutilated corpses. Her vampiric lovers looked so humanly benign that she was convinced her potency existed only in them, and she never realized that her lovers were exploiting her projections. Instead, she resolutely basked in the reflected glory of the glowing projection screens held by her various lovers, and she cherished each screen as much as (or more than) the screenholder behind it. Not surprisingly, the woman did whatever she could to please her screenholders and ensure their continued presence in her life, and whenever she began to feel discomfort or depletion from the effort of this whole endeavor, she just stifled her irritation and fatigue until they overcame her. In the meantime, the woman shifted her shape continually to accommodate the desires of the men who held her projections of the Beloved.

Sometimes the architect would pause long enough in her frenzy of projection to realize that the man onto whom she was projecting her Beloved was projecting onto her his Beloved as well. When this happened, the woman often found that she had become the thing that her lover was projecting, whether it resembled her innate character or not. This process of transformation through projection is referred to by some Jungians as "dreaming somebody up." We can be fairly sure that we are dreaming up another person when an aspect of his or her personality seems larger than life—more divine or more evil than we would have believed possible in a mere mortal.*

---

*This kind of dreaming up happens not only between lovers but also between enemies. That is why it is so important that we select our enemies carefully, because our duets of hate have the potential for the same intimacy and symbiotic influence that we normally expect from our duets of love.

It is as common for us to be dreamed up by someone else as it is to do the dreaming up. Generally, we are being dreamed up when we find ourselves behaving in ways that feel unlike us. The woman in a couple I once knew had a strong temper, but it usually ran on a long, slow fuse. When she was with her partner, however, her temper flared often and instantaneously. The woman knew that she was capable of anger, but until she met her partner, no one had been able to make her that angry that fast. Finally she noticed an interesting fact: her flashing temper seemed to bother her a great deal more than it bothered her partner. She then realized that she would snarl or snap whenever her partner was bored, frustrated, or anxious. At these moments he would begin by teasing her, which she could enjoy in moderation, but when her partner was feeling upset, he would push his teasing over her edge. The woman would lose her temper, and her partner would retreat in wounded rejection ("I was only trying to *play*"). She would feel like a heel and apologize, and he would then graciously forgive her and trot off, feeling (I imagine) entirely blameless and infinitely better. In retrospect, the game was pretty simple—when the man felt angry, he dreamed the woman up as a kind of peevish mother who was unfairly chastising her innocently playful child. She manifested his anger, he got the release, and he walked away with the innocence as well.

Of course, this is the dreaming-up tale of a relationship well along in years. In the beginning of this relationship, as in the beginning of most relationships with a loved one, the dreaming up was much more pleasant. At first, our loved one seems larger than life in so many delightful ways, and we feel equally transcendent. Both of us experience our capacities to be more compassionate, insightful, and creative than we thought two people could be, freed as we are of our normal capacities to be irritated, demanding, or petty. Our mutual dreaming up elevates us both to be our best selves. It is a blissful exchange of mutual adoration, exaltation, and gratification.

In *Dracula,* Mina describes something akin to this rapturous duet of mutual projection in her heated embrace of Dracula as they drink each other's blood and throb in orgasmic communion:

> I closed my eyes, but could still see through my eyelids. . . . The mist grew thicker and thicker, and I could see now how it came . . . pouring in, not through the window, but through the joinings of the door. It got thicker and thicker, till it seemed as if it became concentrated into a sort of pillar of cloud in the room. . . . Things began to whirl in my brain just as the cloudy column was now whirling in the room, and through it all came the scriptural words "a pillar of cloud by day and of fire by night." (Stoker 1897, 242–43)

John Seward completes the description from the perspective of those who burst in on the couple *in flagrante:*

> Kneeling on the near edge of the bed facing outwards was the white-clad figure of [Mina]. By her side stood a tall, thin man, clad in black. His face was turned from us, but the instant we saw we all recognized the Count. . . . With his left hand he held both [Mina's] hands, keeping them away with her arms at full tension; his right hand gripped her by the back of the neck, forcing her face down on his bosom. Her white night-dress was smeared with blood, and a thin stream trickled down the man's bare breast which was shown by his torn-open dress. The attitude of the two had a terrible resemblance to a child forcing a kitten's nose into a saucer of milk to compel it to drink. (263–64)

The intruders on Mina and Dracula's embrace see nothing in it but coercion and horror. And yet our most passionate sexual embraces, if observed by others, would likely resemble a ferocious struggle. Most cinematic renditions of the Dracula myth interpret this scene as the climax of a frenzied passion that consumes the couple, who attempt to merge with each other in a lustful exchange of passion and blood. Pure symbiosis, pure consummation, pure bliss—these are the hallmarks that distinguish both a new relationship with an external beloved and a vampiric initiation. To borrow from the sensual, romantic imagery of Anne Rice:

> I think I knew what he meant to do even before he did it, and I was waiting in my helplessness as if I'd been waiting for years. . . . I drank, sucking the blood out of the holes, experiencing for the first time since infancy the special pleasure of sucking nourishment, the body focused with the mind upon one vital source. . . . I was dying as a human, yet completely alive as a vampire. . . . The process of transforming a victim into a vampire can only be described in human terms as a kind of "falling in love." (Rice 1976, 19, 21)

Although our initiation into vampirism can feel like falling in love, there are many more kinds of vampiric relationship than the romantic variety Rice describes. Think for a moment of Renfield's exaltation of Dracula—isn't this the political or religious zeal of a newly converted minion who has not yet perceived the master's feet of clay? Think, too, of Jonathan's initial deference to Dracula—isn't it much like the unquestioning devotion that an aspiring professional offers to the powerful superior whose treachery he does not yet suspect? And think of the adoration that the Lucy vampire's child victims must have felt for the sweetly maternal figure—isn't their blind love much like that which many children offer to their subtly vampiric parents? In all of these dyads—romantic, political, religious, professional, familial—the initial experience of projecting onto an external beloved is the same. The encounter seems impossibly fortunate, impossibly marvelous, impossibly gratifying.

It seems impossible because it *is* impossible; no one can really be the divinity that we project on our various loved ones. Eventually, the person's underlying reality must leak past the projection screen. No matter how much we yearn to believe in our loved one's perfection, or how much we would like to be the paragons of humanity that our beloved projects onto us, no mere mortal can maintain the perfection inherent in a projection. A projection reflects an archetypal energy in the projector's psyche, and while it may resemble a piece of the screenholder's psyche, it is more like a deity than a real person and therefore impossible for a mere mortal to sustain.

I once knew a talented physician with an innocent soul who repeatedly watched in surprised horror as his projections of godly Belovedness slipped from the grasp of the human women onto whom he had projected them. Whenever one of his projections failed, the physician felt betrayed by the all-too-human woman behind the screen, and he would condemn her as a deceitful fiend or a pathetic worm. He would cast all blame for his failed projection on his lover, rather than sharing in the responsibility for the projective duet he had been dancing with her. Then, as the physician's outrage dwindled into loneliness, he would crawl back to his lover and attempt to resume the projection, which she would often accept, since she had also lost a projection screenholder in the fray. And so this man experienced intimate relationship as a kind of symbiotic vampirism, a seesaw between projection and rejection that could last for for weeks or months or even years. And although he often felt forced to prolong his vampiric relationships by the familial, financial, religious, and professional pressures that surrounded him, the most insidious pressure was his own sense that his survival relied on his projective interdependence with his latest lover.

We, too, may spend years in a vampiric seesaw with a loved one, and we may repeat the same vampiric exchange of projection over and over with different partners. As soon as our current projection exchange fails with someone, we fire a volley of accusations, then stomp away in a high and righteous dudgeon to look for a more worthy projection screen. A partner who is a psychic vampire will do whatever must be done to maintain the projective exchange, for if we victims see the vampire who stands, like the great and powerful Oz, behind the curtain of our projection, then the spell of interdependent fantasy will be broken. But most of the time, relationship vampires needn't worry that they will be unmasked. We are so convinced our gold lies outside ourselves that we resolutely maintain our projection of Belovedness unless the screen collapses beneath its weight.

Of course, simply being the screen for our projections doesn't make someone a vampire. It's just that a vampire's nose is exquisitely attuned to the scent of a projection trying to happen. When vampires sniff one out, they fly to its source, shifting their shapes en route to fit the budding projection. The vampire arrives, on time and on target, as the perfect loved one for whom we have yearned. That is why it is important for us to identify and deactivate the psychic vampires who feed on our love, no matter how reluctant we may be to engage in the task of vampire killing.

KILLING THE VAMPIRE

Whenever we contemplate killing the psychic vampire, we must remember that "killing" any aspect of the psyche only means that we are transforming its energy into another, preferably healthier, incarnation. For example, through inner work, we can transform what was once an easily provoked, killing rage into a manageable anger that is actually helpful and constructive. Thus, the goal of psychic vampire killing is not really to eradicate the vampirically infected traits in ourselves or someone else, but rather to "kill" their old, contaminated form and give birth to their more healthful incarnations. And whether we find the contaminated trait in ourselves or someone we love, killing a psychic vampire always involves reliving old emotions, acknowledging *all* of what we seek and fear, grieving our losses, and rejoicing in our gains. It requires us to make an ongoing series of ethical decisions that ask us to choose between working toward transformation or surrendering to the vampire. Vampire killing requires us to go back to the moment when we couldn't find love and settled for exploitation, and it challenges us to make the choice again, and again, and again. As Linda Leonard has astutely observed, we can prevail against the vampire archetype only if "we are willing to consciously fight this battle, not just once but daily" (1986, 107).

Several factors make killing the psychic vampire a particularly difficult kind of transformative work. First, pulling back our projection of the archetypal Beloved usually feels like we are losing the external loved one. Under the weight of this depressing illusion, we usually do whatever we can to preserve the relationship, however vampiric it may be. Second, our psychic vampires usually have infected parts of our own or our loved one's psyche, and it feels as if we will kill off those vital parts when we kill the vampire who infects them. But when we kill an infection in our finger, it means, not that the finger will die, but that the finger can now resume its normal and proper function. Likewise, the vampire's death permits the infected traits to regain their health.

We face a third problem when the amount of vampirism in our past has been extreme. We whose childhoods have been haunted by psychic vampires have been the target, not of well-meaning people who hurt us primarily through ignorance, but of people who reduced us to objects and exploited our life force simply to serve their own needs. Consequently, we may have little experience of positive, loving energy to use now as a source of hope and guidance. Our work of searching our adult experience for a model of redemptive love is made difficult because people we trusted in our early years tried to exploit us, and the wounded part of us is now loathe ever to trust anyone again.

A fourth element that deters us from vampire-killing is the fact that our early encounters with vampiric energy were packaged as a lie, and we felt that our survival was dependent on playing along with the vampire. The vampire promised us power as a superior alternative to love, using the words of love to draw us in. Feeling obliged to believe the vampire's deceit, we fashioned a beautiful mask for the monster so we wouldn't have to see its bloodsucking truth. The mask may bear the image of the Beloved Mother or Father or Child or Lover or Leader, all of whom we carry in our hearts and seek in the external world. In order to destroy the vampire, we must focus on the vampiric truth that lies underneath whatever mask we have created. This means giving up our belief that the mask reflected the vampire's essence and that the vampire's truth was a loving truth. In other words, we must give up something we never really had.

In one sense, giving up something we never had is much like giving up something we actually had in the first place. We make the rounds of loss that Elisabeth Kübler-Ross has so insightfully identified. We must rage and grieve and deny and rage and accept and grieve some more, until the loss has been psychically metabolized. But when we give up something we never had, we must also embrace the painful truth that led us to create the lovely mask of illusion in the first place. This is terribly difficult work. At first it seems like a task without recompense (aside from the death of the vampire, which in the moment may feel more like a loss than a liberation). However, there are two huge benefits from the bitter task of killing our comforting but dangerously deceptive illusions about the vampire.

First, the illusions themselves tell us precisely what we need in the way of mothering, fathering, friendship, or love. What we thought we had in the external mother, father, friend, or lover is the image of the energy we need to find in reality—both in our external relationships and activities, and in our internal experience of image and feeling. Thus, when we find ourselves bitterly disappointed in a person, a pursuit, or ourselves, we can use whatever it was we were expecting as a map home to the inner Beloved, who can give us the love we truly want and need. To perform this task, we must bring our idealized images to life by alternately *being* them and *relating to* them.

For example, if your mother was vampiric and your mask for

her was nourishing, then nourish yourself as you thought she was nourishing you. If your father was vampiric and your mask for him was instructive, then instruct yourself as you thought he was instructing you. If your lover was vampiric and your mask for your lover was comforting, then comfort yourself as you thought he or she was comforting you. The ideals that inspire our masks in the first place are part of what Jung called the *collective unconscious,* the deep part of our psyche that holds the elemental shapes of all human experience, including the Beloved Mother, Father, Child, Lover, and Leader. While it is a bitter disappointment to find that our projection of these sacred entities has served as a mask for the vampire, it also can be profoundly comforting to learn that, no matter what, we carry each Beloved entity's true essence inside ourselves.

The second benefit of tearing off the vampire's mask is that it encourages the loving soul of the vampiric person to be reanimated. Because the vampire archetype is rarely activated all the time, the vampiric person's soul occasionally shines through. Often, that soul has inspired us to project the Beloved mask in the first place. But any projection actually muzzles the screenholder's soul, since no one's idiosyncratic humanity can live up to our impossibly perfect projection. When we tear the mask off the vampire, we also tear the muzzle off the person's soul, which may then sing through in its own unique glory, liberated from both its vampiric invader and our impossible ideals. For example, my physician acquaintance was finally forced, through a series of odd circumstances, to remain in relationship with a woman from whom his projection had fallen. Once he had recovered from his outrage, he was surprised to see how much the woman blossomed, for she had been liberated from the gilded cage of his perfect projection. No longer a submissive kewpie doll, she had ceased to vampirize him as well, and the physician realized that she was really quite lovable, in an "oddly human way" (his words). When we pull back our projections and cherish someone's truth (including our own) rather than defending our comforting illusions, we invoke the innate healing power of that person's psyche.

Unfortunately, this beacon of hope may not seem like much of a reward when compared to the peril and pain associated with killing the psychic vampire. Yet the peril and pain are necessary. In all of the vampire lore, there is no account of a vampire committing suicide. Vampires don't just go away. Indeed, it seems that they *can't* just go away. Once they start down the vampiric path, they are compelled to pursue it until they are stopped. No matter how reluctantly a vampire may engage in the hunt, hunt it must until it is destroyed. What's more, the lore suggests that the vampire's victim must be an active party to the monster's destruction. If a vampire is bleeding away our psychic energy, then it is up to us to deactivate it and reclaim our rightful power. If we wait for someone else, including the vampire, to do this work for us, then we are very likely to perpetuate the vampirism.

This aspect of vampire killing is particularly important to remember in light of some therapists' inclination to dwell on their clients' wounds and stagnate the therapeutic process by seeking recompense from the perpetrators. Although it is true that the vampire's soulless predation has wounded, scarred, and sometimes destroyed its victims, it is also true that voluntary self-reform or suicide are impossible for vampires, whose compulsive essence is survival at any cost. Nor can we wait for someone else to kill our vampires and retrieve our power. If we do, we set ourselves up in a terrible way, for our dependence on a rescuer disposes us to feed on the rescuer's power, which in turn disposes the rescuer to start exploiting our neediness, which in turn begins a new cycle of vampirism. Thus, only the vampire's victim can kill the vampire.

Placing the onus of vampire killing on those whom the vampire has most depleted may seem unjust, but the very task of deactivating our vampiric predators and reclaiming our own power is integral to healing our wounds. If, for example, we feel that the pain of our incest experiences will only be healed by compensatory acts by the abuser, then we are continuing to give the perpetrator an unhealthy amount of power over us. Where is the healing retrieval of power in that scenario? Or if we feel that the pain of a parent's rejection can only be healed by the parent's acceptance, then the power still lies with the parent, and not where it belongs—in ourselves. Of course, we can't invoke the appropriate healing force unless we understand the wound we are healing, but if we probe the wound endlessly and wait for someone else to fix the damage, then we are only cooperating with the vampire. As we linger and probe, we only bleed more profusely, and eventually we may be desperate enough to seek "rescue" from the very entity who desires to lap up our blood. Our wounding may be the vampire's fault, but the wound is inevitably ours, and so is the responsibility for killing the vampire.

This is not to say that we must do all this vampire killing alone. Indeed, we are advised, both in lore and in psyche, to seek stalwart allies. Loyal friends, wise teachers, skillful bodyworkers, and insightful therapists can be valuable allies on our journey. But it is up to us, the vampire's victims, to lead the charge, if only in spirit and intent. Although Mina, Dracula's prime victim, is unable to take a leading role in the final pursuit and destruction of the vampire, she nevertheless exhorts her allies to persist in their efforts to kill the monster, and eventually she becomes their most powerful source of inspiration. In the end, it is Mina's men who destroy Dracula, but it is Mina, the vampire's intended victim, who guides and empowers them. What Mina brings to their war against the vampire is her resolve to destroy the monster and her awareness of its bloody truth—an awareness that is as painful as it is intimate, for Mina herself is being turned into a vampire. Those of us who have been victimized by a psychic vampire often feel too depleted to do anything more than Mina does—to remain aware of the awful truth and tacitly resolve that the vampirism should end. Mina's story teaches us that no matter how passive our awareness may feel, the key to deactivating a psychic vampire is our persistent consciousness of the task at hand.

SEEKING THE INNER BELOVED

One rule always applies when psychic vampires haunt our personal relationships: we protect ourselves against vampirism in our relationships whenever we pull back our projections of the inner Beloved and become aware of how our projection reflects the parts of ourselves that we have denied. Let me describe this process by telling you about what a friend of mine did when she finally grew tired of the vampirism she suffered as a result of projecting her inner Beloved onto external men.

First of all, this gracious woman accepted some advice from a nosy friend (ahem) and decided to pull back her projections and seek the Beloved within. This meant that whenever she was caught in the throes of passion, particularly when the passion could not be lived out, my friend reminded herself that she was, in fact, brushing up against a sweet projection of her inner Beloved. In order to get to know her inner Beloved better (and, incidentally, ease the pain of her impossible passion), my friend attempted to *become* the person by whom she was mesmerized. Usually, this meant manifesting in herself the traits which she found most admirable in the object of her affections. Of course, when her obsession was one of hatred, she grudgingly recognized that she had to identify in herself some manifestation, however subtle, of the traits that she detested in the other person. Either way, the purpose of my friend's exercise was to reclaim as her own the traits that she had projected onto an external person. Not only did this resolve her obsession and give her access to the full power of her psyche, but she found it a powerful way to ward off psychic vampires. The more she pulled back her projections and mined her own psychic gold, the less likely she was to select vampiric men in her desperation to find a projection screen.

Although mining her psychic gold was highly rewarding, my friend found that, like the mining of literal gold, it entailed a lot of difficult, unpleasant work in the dark. In plumbing the depths of her psyche for traits that she had previously denied in herself, she had to brave the reasons that she denied those traits in the first place. Because rejected traits are usually stuffed into unconsciousness along with one's earliest, most painful emotions, my friend's trait-reclaiming exercises were often dreary little picnics. What's more, once she had redeemed her intrinsic power, my friend had to see her external projections for what they were—smoke and mirrors that disguised her lovers' imperfect human reality. Initially, this new perspective dropped my friend into despair, since it forced her give up her illusion of a Perfect Lover in exchange for a simple, flawed mortal. Her awakening was no easier when her projection had been a negative one, for she had to give up her illusion of a Detestable Fiend for a simple, blundering human being.

When we are in a vampiric relationship, we are usually ravenous for love (which is why we are being vampiric in the first place), and unfamiliar with love's reality (since it's hard to be familiar with something we have never known). Thus, when we pull back our projections, we are likely to feel as if we have been dropped to a pit of oblivion, for there is seldom more than mutual feeding behind the projections. This is exactly how my friend felt. And since her socialization (like so many of ours) had taught her to view the outer reality as the only reality, the realization that her images of her external lovers were mostly composed of her projections made my friend feel as if she would never meet another man she could love. At all. Ever. The truth was that her inner Beloved was, in many ways, more present for her than the men onto whom she had projected Belovedness (though it took her a while to believe that truth). What's more, once my friend had discovered her inner Beloved, she found that she could savor his reflection (not projection) in real men, whom she no longer felt compelled to love vampirically.

My friend's initial contact with her inner Beloved came in a dream about an enchanting stranger, and later, in her fantasies about a variety of external men. But the source of her images of the Beloved was not the important part. What was important was that becoming familiar with the shape of her inner Beloved enhanced the "reality" of his gifts to her; his words and gestures took on more and more weight as she came to believe in him, which in turn enabled him to show her what it is on the inside that she had been seeking on the outside. When my friend gave me permission to use her story for this book, she told me (with some heat) that words like "becoming acquainted with her inner Beloved" were insufficient to describe the immediacy of her actual experience, and what's more (she said, with greater heat), such words would sound too bland to rival the illusory bliss of vampiric projections. So let me talk a bit about what communion with the inner Beloved can feel like, and how it can lead us into external relationships that are profoundly loving, nonprojective, and nonvampiric.*

The inner Beloved is an archetypal energy that usually appears to us in the form of a person. We may sense the inner Beloved in a dream or a story or a film or an individual, but the archetype's essence is usually a composite of several images. If we want to know the shape of our inner Beloved, we must first do what my friend did—pull together and contemplate several images of the Beloved that we have projected. Not all such images are the romantic kind; they may be parental, professional, even political. For any type of projection, we should focus on the images of all the people whom we have felt could fill us with self-respect and

---

*This issue has also been discussed by the Jungian analyst Linda Leonard in her book *On the Way to the Wedding: Transforming the Love Relationship,* and I urge those interested in doing more work with the inner Beloved to read Leonard's insightful discussion.

self-love. Although they may seem unrelated at first, the energies we perceive in them will eventually coalesce into a coherent, though complex, entity who will symbolize our personal archetype of the Beloved.

For my friend, this work of getting acquainted with her inner Beloved initially felt like an exercise in pure fantasy. As her Beloved eventually assumed a more concrete shape, he came to offer her a wealth of information and support. My friend found that all his input was extremely important and lovingly framed, though some of it was initially difficult for her to accept—sometimes because it showed her something negative that she didn't want to see, and sometimes because it showed her something positive that she was afraid to believe was real. In every case, however, my friend's inner Beloved presented his truth with unswerving love and deep compassion. In the end, he became her constant companion—the lover who would never desert or betray her, who would never deceive or use her, who would never dominate or exploit her. (When any of these ugly behaviors seemed to be creeping into her Beloved fantasies, she quickly checked for vampires.) And the more "real" my friend's inner Beloved became to her, the more he was able to guide her to external men who resembled him, while his love for her kept her from clinging projectively to the men she found.

Of course, this process was a bit trickier than it sounds. For example, my friend initially tried to find her inner Beloved without any outside input, and she was seduced by her inner vampire into believing that he, a demon lover, was her Beloved. My friend found that she was less likely to go astray once she solicited the help of a therapist, which makes sense, since outside observers can often give us a clearer view of our inner Beloved, just as they can for an outer loved one. Because vampires always try to isolate their prey, a third person can help break their hypnotic spell. This may be why vampiric people like to isolate themselves with their victims away from the intruding eyes of the victim's friends.

Once my friend became acquainted with her true inner Beloved—that is, once he seemed more solid and "real"—she began the second stage of their relationship. She now took a bit of time each day to *become* her inner Beloved, and another bit of time to commune with her inner Beloved. Again, this initially felt to her like an exercise in perpetual fantasizing, but then she said to herself, "Isn't this what I do anyway when I am smitten with an external lover? I'm constantly thinking, 'What would he say, think, do, feel, or advise in any given situation, about any given topic? And how would I respond?' " Only this time, my friend was not imagining how an external person might respond. This time, her Beloved actually *was* all she imagined.

Because our inner Beloveds usually look like a person of the same sex as the people onto whom we have been projecting Belovedness, the inner Beloved of my friend appeared to her as a man, while the inner Beloved of the physician I described earlier would more likely appear to him as a woman. Although these human forms are common images of the Beloved, they are by no means its only forms. I have seen clients in whom the Beloved initially appeared in the form of an animal, or a tree, or a geological structure. And our inner Beloved may be reflected in political, religious, professional, or familial relationships, as well as in our love relationships with a mate. To find our personal forms of the inner Beloved, we must first identify the ways in which we expect our lovers, parents, bosses, or leaders to fix or complete us—the ways in which they seem to be more divine than we feel we are ourselves. Seeking those qualities in our own psyches, we then weave our new recognition of our own divinity into a coherent shape of the inner Beloved, using our projective fantasies about our external lovers, parents, bosses, or leaders.

In whatever form or venue our inner Beloved is reflected, he or she bears the same attitude toward us. The Beloved is a being who honors our sacredness, inspires and protects us, offers us dignity and devotion, and helps us to transform ourselves into the people we were born to be. No wonder we seek the Beloved so fiercely, projecting Belovedness onto any serviceable screen in the external reality. No wonder, too, that anyone who attempts to hold our Beloved projection will inevitably fail at the task. And yet, we wonder, must we forgo all projective love so that we and our loved ones will be safe from psychic vampirism? Must we utterly abandon our search for a Beloved in the external world?

REDEEMING PROJECTIVE LOVE

We can begin to form an answer by remembering that no external person can be the true Beloved—the inner reason for our being— and our external loves are not the whole story but echoes of a larger, deeper experience. And when we become captivated by our projections and blind to the psychic vampirism in our relation-ships, we must remember above all that the divinity we perceive is actually our own. This is what I think the Jungian analyst Robert Johnson means when he says, "Romance must, by its very nature, deteriorate into egotism . . . the passion of romance is always directed at our own projections, our own expectations, our own fantasies. In a very real sense, it is a love not of another person, but of ourselves" (1983, 193).

Johnson's words reflect a core truth for those of us who are able to honor the humanity of people who reflect some aspect of our Beloved only after we have reclaimed the Beloved within ourselves. The relationship that we finally achieve in this case, in which we engage with the other person in a profound exchange of respect and affection, but not projective love, is what Johnson describes as "stirring-the-oatmeal love." "Oatmeal love" is usu-ally not as thrilling or enchanting as projective love, but it is a most sacred form of relationship, for as Johnson observes, it "af-firms the person who is actually there, rather than the ideal we would like him or her to be or the projection that flows from our minds" (191). Oatmeal love and projective love, Johnson concludes, "are utterly opposed energies, natural enemies with completely opposing motives" (197).

Certainly, Johnson's words reflect a deep truth about human love, but they do not address the role of love as a facilitator of psychic growth. As much as we may wish to minimize the psychic vampirism in our relationships, it is not always possible or appropriate to eradicate every archetypal dance of projected Belovedness and snuggle into the comfortable simplicity of oatmeal love. For one thing, our inner psychic processes often require some mirroring external manifestation in order for us to work with them. For example, we sometimes need to have an external argument with another person that mirrors an internal conflict in our psyches in order to fully grasp and resolve the nature of that inner conflict. In the same way, some of us can find our way home to the inner Beloved only through the echoes of Belovedness in our external relationships. These external mirrors of our internal reality are particularly important for those of us who are extraverted—that is, for those of us who more easily find meaning in the events of external reality. We who are extraverts by nature or training are more inclined to become acquainted with our inner Beloved when the aspects of that archetype are reflected in our external loves.

In addition, all of us may need to do some projecting in our relationships for spiritual reasons. Communing with our inner Beloved is much like communing with the divine. In contemporary Western society, many of us no longer pursue this transcendent spiritual goal primarily through religious practices. Rather than kneeling at the altar of orthodox religion, as our ancestors did, we kneel at the altar of love, and we practice our new form of ecstatic, mystical worship in our external relationships. We look to our loved ones for our images of a loving divinity, and when we see our projected divinity reflected in their faces, we blissfully commune with its energy until the projection fails. Robert Johnson deplores this development and exhorts us to turn within, back to the altar of our loving souls. In other words, Johnson would have us all seek the inner Beloved, invariably and constantly, thereby forgoing the very real dangers of projective love. This is great work if you can do it, but it is not a path that everyone can take. Some of us must manifest some of our worshipful loving— and our spiritual growth—in the mirror of our external loves before we can experience them within ourselves.

Manifesting our spiritual growth in our external loves presents us with a serious challenge. Any path of spiritual growth (which some call "redemption" or "salvation" and the Jungians call "individuation") can have a heavenly outcome, but it always entails some time in hell. When our loving relationships serve as our paths of spiritual growth, they are likely to entail some hell time as well—a reality blatantly incompatible with our culture's notions of love. As the Jungian analyst Adolf Guggenbühl-Craig has observed, our culture tells us that love is supposed to be a relationship of well-being, in which both people in the relationship feel consistently happy and satisfied. Of course, some sense of well-being is an essential component of every enduring relationship—otherwise it would only be a short-lived tempest of mutual projection. The image of love as a path of continual well-being is problematic, however, when our love relationships are also the arenas in which we must struggle toward individuation, redemption, and salvation, as they must often be, according to Guggenbühl-Craig:

> For us the question is, has [love] to do with well-being or with salvation? . . . Individuation is not individualism. . . . Every single soul has a part in the collective soul. . . . An egoistic individuation of a single person as a private pastime is therefore hardly conceivable. . . . The life-long dialectical encounter between two partners . . . can be understood as a special path for discovering the soul, as a special form of individuation . . . that portion of human motivation that presses toward salvation. (1977, 34, 35, 36, 38, 41)

Guggenbühl-Craig's provocative words combine with Johnson's views to convey a more complete sense about the role of love in our psychic health and development. Oatmeal love is like a foundation of rock on which our relationships may safely rest. Yet, even on the sturdy footing of oatmeal love, some experiences and emotions stand out in their capacity to move us. These exceptional events tell us that some of our unrecognized internal forces are attempting to express and transform themselves. Internal forces of this kind are archetypal processes that we dare not ignore, and in many cases, they can be worked through only within the context of our personal relationships. For example, one man I know had spent years reflecting, with courage and honesty, on his relationship with his vampiric mother, but it was only when he fell in love with a wise, loving woman that he was able to work through (and out of) the destructive patterns of behavior that he had developed in response to his maternal psychic vampire.

Similarly, the patterns of archetypal energy that we manifest in our relationships can be powerful teachers in our pursuit of spiritual growth. Several ways in which this can occur are presented by the Jungian analyst Verena Kast in her compelling book *The Nature of Loving* (1986). Kast describes six mythic couples and discusses how their relationships can be manifested in the relationships of real human beings. In particular, Kast describes ways in which her clients have used these images to comprehend the powerful psychic forces moving in their partners and themselves. Kast demonstrates how a conscious, well-monitored exchange of archetypal projection can illuminate the psyches of both participants in a way that individual reflection and therapy cannot. As you probably know from personal experience, we often find ourselves manifesting feelings and behaviors in relationship that we would *never* manifest in the insular state of emotional detachment. Sometimes we seem to be horrifyingly worse in relationship than we ever could have imagined being in solitude. But sometimes our relationships evoke in us a magnificence of soul that we might never have achieved alone. As Kast observes,

> a secret aspect of love is its power to grant us the vision and courage to see something in a partner which that person may have sensed but perhaps may never have known had it not been lovingly suggested by another. . . . through love, we envision the best possibilities in the beloved and give that person the feeling that those possibilities can be realized. (1986, 5)

The images in Kast's work enable us to understand how an exchange of projection can be a helpful and indeed necessary part of interpersonal relationships that involve psychological and spiritual growth. Only in the projective exchanges of our current relationships can some of us, like the man with the vampiric mother, conjure up our emotional histories and heal the wounds they have dealt us. Our current relationship can help us recognize and resolve any crippling misconceptions and harmful behavior patterns that we unconsciously assimilated in our childhoods. In fact, this kind of therapeutic work is much of what the Freudians and self psychologists talk about with regard to human relationship.

For others of us, only in the projective exchanges of relationship can we consciously resolve the archetypal dynamics that would otherwise torment us in their destructive unconsciousness. For example, our current relationship may enable us to bring to life the archetypal energy of Aphrodite that demands our sexual awakening and maturation—a demand that, as long as we remained solitary, would be locked in our psychic closet, only to wreak havoc in our lives when it escaped. Archetypal work like this is much of what the Jungians focus on when they talk about human relationship.

Finally, some of us find that the projective exchange of relationship is the only forum in which we can constellate what Robert Sardello (1995) has called "the Soul of the World"—an inner calling that can sometimes be brought into external being only within the context of human relationship. For example, the human dyads of Franklin and Eleanor Roosevelt, Sigmund Freud and his daughter Anna, Carl and Emma Jung, and even Bill and Hillary Clinton seem bound as much by their passion for their united vision as by their intimate passion for each other.

PROTECTING RELATIONSHIPS AGAINST VAMPIRISM

In all the foregoing forms of redemptive relationship—familial, archetypal, global—projecting the image of the Beloved is an essential part of the partners' psychic health and development. But whenever we project our internal archetypes onto an external person, we have learned, we are at risk of abdicating our own power, which leaves us vulnerable to vampiric predation and inclines us to vampirize the person who seems to own our divine energies. How can we resolve this dilemma?

Whenever we know that we are entering vampire country, we must always be prepared. Even before we get within killing distance of any vampires, we can protect ourselves with a variety of vampire deterrents. For one thing, we must always travel in daylight, which vampires detest. In terms of our external relationships, this means that we must never project Belovedness onto someone *unconsciously,* for vampiric danger lies in the unconsciousness of night. Traveling in daylight will also insure that we and our partner can both cast a shadow. Because vampires cast no shadow, the instant that the shadow of one or both partners in a projective love cannot be seen by both partners—that is, when one or both appear to be perfect—it's likely that a psychic vampire has been activated. Similarly, we must take a clear mirror into the vampiric realm of projective relationship, so we can constantly reflect upon the truth of our behavior. If our simple, flawed humanity becomes invisible, then a vampire archetype has probably been activated.

Another helpful tactic in vampire country is to spend a lot of time on the rivers and oceans, since vampires hate to cross open bodies of water. Water is an image of deep feeling, and deep feelings terrify the vampire, who must remain cool, detached, and if possible, magnetically unattainable to its intended prey. Given these requirements, anything that stimulates loving warmth and neutralizes one's magnetism will also be anathema to the vampire. The vampire's ally is the immediate *bang!* of a drugged high, not the unpretentious warmth of real humanity. Of course, vampires don't just walk up and announce that they are offering a quick, addictive high in the place of real life and love. They lie in wait and offer their deadly bait under the guise of demidivinity. This means that we should carry into the vampiric realm of projective exchange a substance that will foster in our relationship the warmth, truth, and noncharismatic simplicity of oatmeal love. For instance:

> Garlic is richly and widely praised as a remedy for nearly all the ills of mankind. . . . The Egyptians had so high a regard for garlic that they employed it when taking an oath [of truth]. . . . And the Talmud, too, praises garlic, saying that . . . "it satisfies [and] warms the body" . . . Some add that it fosters love and drives away enmity . . . by the feeling of comfort it engenders. . . . Pliny, an older authority, says of garlic . . . that a magnet, rubbed with garlic, will lose its power. (Wolf 1975, 123)

Is it any wonder that the power of garlic, like that of the mirror, can repulse our psychic vampires?

The symbols of garlic and the mirror are related in another way. One of the traits of the vampire is the foul odor of its breath, which carries the stench of rotting blood and unnatural existence. In contrast, the bad breath we associate with garlic reflects its wholesome powers—powers that appear, even to modern medicine, to nourish the blood organically. This imagery suggests that whatever we do to nourish the life force of ourselves and our partner in a projective exchange will protect us against any vampiric energies by mirroring the odiousness of the vampire's parasitic nature as compared to the essence of self-renewing life.

The last protective tool that we should carry when we enter vampiric country is a medieval addition to the age-old vampire lore—religious paraphernalia. In the oldest vampire tales, as in most modern lore (excluding *Dracula*), vampires are not deterred by religious paraphernalia in and of themselves. Still, they abhor what these objects can represent, which is our intimate connection to our own divinity. Therefore, any time we venture into the vampiric realm of exchanging Beloved projections, we must maintain a conscious devotion to the sacredness of both ourselves and our partner.

Beyond these protective measures, what can we do to reduce the potential for vampirism in our exchanges of beloved projection? Rather ironically, it seems that our external search for the beloved which summons the psychic vampire in the first place, may also rescue us from its jaws. Let us now embark on the final stage of our perilous nocturnal journey, as we learn how love itself, when deployed with great skill and consciousness, can kill a psychic vampire.

SIR GAWAIN AND LADY RAGNELL

I have spent most of this book showing you how our search for love leads us into all kinds of vampiric danger. Sometimes we allow psychic vampires to feed on us, in the illusion that they will love us in return. Sometimes we vampirize other people in a desperate attempt to take by exploitation that which can only be given freely—the pure life force of love. At this point, it may seem as if any form of love beyond the friendly simplicity of oatmeal love puts us at severe risk of vampiric contamination. And yet most of us feel compelled to seek our true Beloved in the external world—a search that, according to Kast and Guggenbühl-Craig, can be an essential part of our psychic and spiritual growth.

And yet we still don't have a model for safely integrating projective (and potentially vampiric) love into our oatmeal loves. Must we adopt an attitude of grimly reluctant heroism for our fearsome forays into projective love? Must we constantly arm ourselves against vampiric attack? Must the Belovedness we project always be the tool of the vampire? No, not always. We may also find, if we are very skilled and very fortunate, that we can kill our psychic vampires with love itself. Here is one final story, in which two wise people accomplished this heroic deed.*

Once upon a time, during the time when Camelot flourished, King Arthur was out hunting in one of his forests. Actually, the ownership of this particular forest was a matter of some dispute: after King Arthur had chased the brutal Saxons out of England, he had fallen into the habit of claiming as his personal property many pieces of land that he had, in fact, only liberated. Arthur was hunting on such a piece of co-opted land when he shot and wounded a white deer. As he was preparing to finish the kill, a gigantic man loomed over the king and threatened to kill him on the spot. Arthur, who was unarmed and unprepared for such an assault, trembled in astonishment before the giant.

"Do you know who I am, sir? And have you no mercy?" the king asked fearfully.

"I have no mercy for you, King. I am Sir Gromer, the rightful owner of this forest, and I see no need to show mercy to the man who has taken from me what is mine!"

"But surely there is something I can do to convince you to spare my life!" cried the king.

---

*I am deeply indebted to the Jungian analyst Polly Young-Eisendrath for introducing this myth in her insightful book *Hags and Heroes: A Feminist Approach to Jungian Psychotherapy with Couples* (1984). Although my interpretation of this myth differs significantly enough from hers to preclude much reference to her book in my discussion, Dr. Young-Eisendrath's compelling interpretation was an essential foundation for mine.

"Well," replied Sir Gromer, with a malicious grin, "I'll give you a reprieve of twelve months in which you must answer a riddle of mine. But if you fail to give me the answer one year from today, then you must submit to your death by my sword!"

The King felt he had little choice but to agree to the arrangement. "What is the riddle you wish me to answer?" he inquired suspiciously.

"The riddle is this," replied Sir Gromer, vastly amused with his game, " 'What is it that women most desire, above all else?' "

The king's heart fell when he heard these words. Where would he find someone who cared enough about such a ridiculous question to learn its answer? But he had struck a bargain and he could not back out. Greatly worried, the king returned to the castle, where he fretted and sulked for quite a while. No one could get him to disclose the reason for his distress until the noble Sir Gawain finally approached him. Sir Gawain was one of Arthur's favorite knights, for he was honest, direct, and businesslike, and he was deeply devoted to his king. Once he heard the riddle, even Sir Gawain was puzzled, for it was such a trivial question that it hardly seemed worth the life of a king. Nonetheless, Sir Gawain reassured Arthur that the riddle would be solved within the space of a year, and he set all the knights in Britain to the task of finding its answer.

Toward the end of the year, Sir Gawain and the knights had filled several books with answers to Sir Gromer's riddle. Sir Gawain felt confident that they had managed to find the correct response, but Arthur, whose life depended on those special words, continued to worry and fret. A few days before the deadline, he wandered back to spot where he had shot the white deer. Without warning, the king was accosted by a dreadful old hag who was so revoltingly ugly and obscenely rude that she made Arthur's stomach turn. But the hag seemed unconcerned with the king's revulsion, and before he had time to speak or run, she cornered him against a tree.

"I am the Lady Ragnell," she grunted, "and I know that you don't have the right answer to the riddle." Arthur was shocked by the impudence of the disgusting hag, but he began to fear she was right when she pressed against him and confided in an insinuating tone that she was the stepsister of Sir Gromer, which gave her access to information that no one else could have. Through his revulsion and despair, Arthur felt a glimmer of hope. He offered the hag a variety of riches in exchange for the riddle's answer, but the Lady Ragnell only sneered at his words.

"What use have I for pretty adornments?" she sniffed, "The only way I will give you the answer is if the noble Sir Gawain agrees to marry me."

"I can't give you a human being!" cried the outraged Arthur.

"I know that, you fool," snarled the hag. "I only want you to propose the matter to Sir Gawain and let him do what he chooses of his own free will."

So Arthur returned to the castle, feeling even gloomier than before. He summoned Sir Gawain to his chambers and presented him with the awful hag's proposal. At the sight of his anguished king, Gawain was moved to pity, and he swore he would marry the Devil himself to save his monarch's life. Together, the king and Sir Gawain rode back to the forest, where they informed the hideous hag that Gawain would marry her in exchange for the riddle's answer.

On the appointed day, Arthur and Sir Gawain rode to meet the vengeful Sir Gromer. As the giant loomed over the king, Arthur stammered out answer after answer from Sir Gawain's books, hoping that he would find the right one before he was obliged to offer Lady Rangell's answer and doom his beloved Gawain to marry the hellish hag. Sir Gromer accepted none of the answers the knights had obtained, however, and with every incorrect answer he raised his killing sword higher and higher in anticipation of the fatal blow. Finally, with a desperate cry, Arthur blurted out the answer that Lady Ragnell had given him: *"What women de-*

sire, above all else, is the power of sovereignty, the right to govern their own lives!"

The moment Sir Gromer heard these words, he bellowed with rage and charged off into the forest, swearing that he would take bloody revenge on his treacherous stepsister, Ragnell. But the lady was safely en route back to the castle with the sober-faced king and Sir Gawain. When the threesome arrived at Camelot, they went straight to the great hall, where Lady Ragnell and Sir Gawain were married. After the wedding, everyone attended the marriage feast, but most of the guests had a hard time enjoying themselves. They were appalled at the sight of the disgusting hag who chortled and belched next to Britain's finest knight. Sir Gawain himself seemed poised and unconcerned, however, and he attended to Lady Ragnell's needs with all the courtesy and care that a loving groom should devote to his bride. Finally, the feast was over and Sir Gawain accompanied his hideous wife to their wedding chamber. Once the door closed behind them, Lady Ragnell turned to Gawain with a solemn look and said, "I am gratified by the way you have conducted yourself today. You have treated me with dignity and you have inflicted on me neither your revulsion nor your pity. Now, my husband, it is time for you to kiss your bride."

Sir Gawain immediately stepped forward with the same grace he had shown all evening and kissed the ugly hag on her cracked lips. Then he fell back with a start, for he saw before him a beautiful woman with shining eyes. Fearing that some sorcery was afoot, Sir Gawain put his hand to his sword, but Lady Ragnell did not give him time to act on his fear. She quickly explained, "My horrible appearance was the result of a curse by my stepbrother, for he hated my forthrightness and honesty. He condemned me to appear as a loathsome hag until the most noble knight in Britain should marry me of his own free will. When I saw the king trembling under my stepbrother's sword, I seized the opportunity to break my stepbrother's curse."

Sir Gawain was overjoyed, as much for Lady Ragnell's sake as for his own good fortune in finding that his bride was a lovely woman and not a hideous hag. But Gawain's joy was interrupted by Ragnell's somber tone. "All is not well, my dear friend, for we have broken only part of Sir Gomer's curse. You must now make a choice. I can be beautiful by day for all the world to see, and hideous by night in our chambers, or I can be hideous by day as I move about the castle and lovely at night in our bed. Choose carefully, my dear."

Gawain considered the dilemma only briefly before he replied. "I am sorry, my beloved, but I cannot make the choice. It is your life, and therefore it is you who must choose the moments of your beauty and pain."

Lady Ragnell's lovely face glowed with contentment as she heard Sir Gawain's words, and she said, "Ah, my love, you have now broken the curse entirely. For the spell commanded that if my noble husband were to grant me full sovereignty over my life, then I could be beautiful whenever I chose!" And with these words, Lady Ragnell and Sir Gawain fell into each other's arms and began their life's journey together.

At the outset of this story, we see the two forms of vampiric energy that we have encountered in this book. On the one hand we have a vampiric king who has arrogantly gobbled up the resources and livelihoods of many of his subjects, including the indigent Sir Gromer, who has lost everything in the king's massive land grab. What's more, Sir Gawain, the fair-haired son of a culture in which it is ludicrous to consider what women might truly want, is so devoted to his master that he will "marry the Devil himself" to please the king. The story paints Camelot as a patriarchy that is riddled (so to speak) with masculine vampirism.

On the other hand, we find Lady Ragnell, a woman whose relationship and response to the patriarchy are reminiscent of Lilith's. Ragnell has been suppressed and cursed by her patriarchal stepbrother, much as Lilith was cursed by Adam and Yahweh. In retaliation, Ragnell plots to avenge herself by betraying her oppressor and taking as her chattel the fairest son of the land. Ragnell's face, like Medusa's, is hideous to behold, so she must use blackmail and insinuation to get what she wants. The story paints Lady Ragnell as someone who is clearly ensnared in feminine vampirism.

Of course, neither Gawain nor Ragnell are purely vampiric. Gawain shows himself quite capable of nobility, and Ragnell eventually reveals her essential grace. The ambiguity of these characters only emphasizes their similarity to most of us as we enter into a relationship involving projective love. We are capable of nobility and grace, but we are also capable of psychic vampirism. The miracle of Sir Gawain and Lady Ragnell is that this couple did not, as so many of us are inclined to do, descend into a vampiric vortex in which their nobility and grace were obliterated by their exchange of projections, leaving only their mutual vampirism to define their relationship. Instead, they succeeded in killing their psychic vampires with a love that could itself be seen as distinctly projective. How did they manage this? The story doesn't tell us exactly what is going on inside their heads as they accomplish their feat, so I'll try to improvise a possible scenario from what has been written about projective love.

As I understand the words of writers such as Guggenbühl-Craig and Kast, there is a precarious but navigable path through the dark forest of projection to the place where we can kill our vampires with love. Using the Gawain/Ragnell story as an example, the path looks something like this: Both Sir Gawain and Lady Ragnell enter into their marriage fully aware of each other's vampiric potential. Ragnell has experienced the derision, oppression, and condemnation of Gawain's patriarchy, and Gawain has been an eyewitness to Ragnell's hideousness, manipulation, and treachery. Yet both these people elect to rise above their dark experiences of the other and focus instead on their personal commitments to nobility and grace; each thus enables the other to show nobility and grace as well. Gawain treats Ragnell as a lovely, deserving bride, and Ragnell shows her deep respect for Gawain by placing her fate in his hands. Neither Gawain nor Ragnell have any concrete reason to trust so fully in each other's nobility and grace. Perhaps their mutual trust is motivated by a deep instinct for truth, but it could just as easily be driven by their projections of Belovedness. Either way, when Ragnell and Gawain each choose to respond as if the other were the projected Beloved, they somehow dream each other up to *become* those noble, graceful souls. By trusting in Gawain's nobility, Ragnell redeems her beauty and sovereignty, and by trusting in Ragnell's nobility, Gawain receives a partner of loveliness and grace.

This miracle is not confined to fairy tales. It is precisely what Verena Kast is talking about when she says that when "we envision the best possibilities in the beloved, [we] give that person the feeling that those possibilities can be realized" (1986, 5). In other words, when we project an aspect of our divine Beloved onto another person, our projection may resonate with some aspect of the person's actual divinity—an aspect that the person couldn't have seen or manifested in solitude. As a result of our projection, the other person's divine aspect might actually be activated as a real force in his or her own psyche; that is, it might "rise to the occasion" of our projection. To whatever degree the other person can maintain the activation of that divine energy, without relying on our projection, the divine energy may serve to vanquish a vampire in that person's psyche. In this case, projection becomes a conscious gift of love, not an unconscious tool of exploitation.

A more explicit example of this process occurs in the cinematic trilogy *Star Wars*. Through three movies (minus fifteen minutes), Darth Vader displays unremitting vampirism. Darth is a space-age vampire par excellence—a robotic man who has purchased electronic immortality at the price of his loving soul. At the end of the second movie in the trilogy, we learn that Darth Vader is the father of the young hero Luke Skywalker. In Darth's human form he was Aniken Skywalker, a noble Jedi knight who defected to the evil Empire, leaving young Luke to search for a replacement father figure. Luke experiences considerable success in his projective search for the Beloved Father, finding first Obi Wan Kenobe and then Master Yoda, both of whom give Luke the paternal Jedi training that he has yearned for. When Luke learns that Darth Vader is his father, he is appalled, for Darth has been his mortal enemy and now is exploiting their familial bond to corrupt Luke. Moreover, since Luke has been devoted to seeking the Beloved Father, Darth's revelation places in question the nobility of his cause. Luke struggles with this quandary throughout the third film, until its final climatic scene.

In this scene, where the evil emperor and Darth are threatening Luke's life if he will not defect to the Dark Side, Luke appeals to whatever shreds of Aniken Skywalker remain in the vampiric Vader. "There is goodness in you, Father—I can *feel* it," he insists. One could make a good case here that what Luke feels is only his projection of the Beloved Father, since Darth Vader has been nothing but vampiric. And Luke's projection of Belovedness, like any other, involves extreme vampiric peril. If Luke is wrong and there is no shred of Aniken Skywalker left in Vader's electronically amplified psyche, or if the shreds that remain are not sufficient to vanquish the vampire in Darth, then Luke will be physically and psychically eviscerated by the Dark Side. But as most of us know, Luke wins this extremely dangerous gambit. At the critical moment, Darth picks up the evil emperor and throws him, and not Luke, into the bottomless pit. At the end of the movie, Luke removes the stormtrooper helmet of Darth Vader and we see the battered but love-filled face of Aniken Skywalker, a face that will later glow beside those of Obi Wan and Yoda as their spirits smile approvingly on the heroes' victory celebration.

Luke's dangerous gambit of killing the vampire with love is implied in several of the other stories we have encountered in this book. Clarice Starling accomplishes a similar miracle with Hannibal Lecter. By gradually entrusting her painful personal story to the vampiric psychiatrist, and by maintaining her respectful dignity in the process, Clarice finds a way through to whatever remains of Lecter's soul. We know this because Lecter not only supplies the information that Clarice is seeking, but he actually touches her without hurting her, and at the end of the film he grants her mercy from his predation. Similarly, when Gypsy finally faces down her vampiric mother, she achieves their autonomy and reconciliation by evincing, along with her deep commitment to her own independence, her profound love for Rose. "You'd really have been something, Mother," Gypsy says at the end of Rose's final song. "Think so?" asks Rose uncertainly. "If you'd had someone to push you like I did," Gypsy offers—an offering of love that reaches through the maternal vampire to Rose's essential humanity.

Of course, the pure power of projected Belovedness cannot by itself kill a psychic vampire, and if projected love is all we come armed with, we will surely be sucked dry in the attempt. Laura Wingfield was filled to the brim with projections of Belovedness, but they only served to cement her subjugation to the Amanda vampire. In the examples we have seen of successful vampire killing, the heroes and heroines came well prepared to the killing ground, particularly when they sought to kill their vampires with love. Their preparation extends beyond the vampiric deterrents of day-bright consciousness, honest self-reflectiveness, shadow verification, oceanic feeling, pungent lifeblood builders, and tokens of our human sacredness.

The first weapon that every vampire killer must carry is the heart-piercing wooden stake, made of living wood and driven through the vampire's heart with a single blow. The characters we have met who killed their vampires with love all used the stake's energy masterfully, as they penetrated through the vampire's defenses and into the loving core of his or her soul. "There is goodness in you, Father—I can *feel* it," declares the fervent Luke Skywalker. "You are very perceptive, Dr. Lecter," observes Clarice gently, "but can you stand to turn that keen vision on yourself?" "I thought you did it all for me, Mama," Gypsy states with sorrow and love. In each case, the brave vampire killer takes careful aim and drives the stake of loving truth home to the soul of the vampiric person.

The second weapon necessary in vampire killing is a noble sword for beheading the vampire. The mind is a dangerous tool of every psychic vampire, for it is that "nimble hobgoblin" whose quicksilver logic can justify unspeakable acts of predation. Vampire killers must cut away all of the vampire's treacherous logic and disembodied values. This metaphorical decapitation has also been done by all the successful vampire killers we have met, often after they have first beheaded themselves. Clarice reaches past Lecter's head and into his heart by moving out of her head and into her own heart as she shares her deepest feelings with him. And it's a good thing she does, for if she had tried to use her intellect to outmaneuver Lecter's, he would have devoured her like all the rest of his victims. Luke similarly rejects a war of disembodied reasoning with Darth, emphasizing instead that he can *feel* his father's goodness behind the inhuman black mask. And Gypsy responds to her mother's assault by declaring her unreasoning love for the flamboyant persona she has discovered in herself, as well as her deep affection for her mother's loving side. When we wish to deactivate the psychic vampires in our relationships, we must move our center of operations from our clever reasoning minds to our feeling bodies and hearts, for they are far less likely to betray us in the vampire's domain.

The third weapon we need on our side is the most reliable and globally endorsed method for killing a vampire, although I have not yet mentioned it in this book. If you want to kill a vampire and be sure that it is dead, you must cremate the monster and scatter its ashes to the four winds. The weapon in this case is fire, but not just any old fire will do. The fire must be a clean flame that produces an intense, unrelenting heat over a prolonged period of time. Quick, hot fires will only singe the vampire. A slow, cold burn will avail you nothing. Fires that are fueled by a hodgepodge of impure materials will falter and die when set to the task of cremation. The kind of fire we need for vampire killing is the kind our ancestors employed to purify that which is unclean. It is the kind of fire the alchemists sought for the holy process of alchemical transformation—a pure and holy flame.

The metaphorical fire that can kill a psychic vampire is the deceptively simple heat generated by the touching of two human souls. If our love can manage to touch the loving soul of the vampiric person, and if that person's soul can be induced to vibrate in resonance with ours, then her vampire archetype can possibly be neutralized. Remember that the vampiric person has settled for exploitation because she experienced a lack of human warmth and compassion. When she encounters the compassionate warmth that is kindled in the fire of connecting souls, she may perceive a new opportunity to choose between love and exploitation. And this time, she may choose differently—she may choose to seek and receive the love that was unavailable the first time she chose.

This process of psychic healing is similar to the process of physical healing invoked in naturopathic medicine. The naturopathic treatments, which include the Eastern practices of acupuncture and ayurveda and the Western practices of homeopathy and chiropractic, are often the most healthful and effective means for repulsing the body's subtle invaders because they heal by invoking the person's essential life force—referred to as the "immune system" in Western medicine and as the "chi" in Eastern medicine. Naturopathic treatment begins with a detailed investigation into the nature of the trouble and the troubled person (both in relation to and apart from the immediate problem). The patient's systems of physical and psychic health are then identi-

fied, invoked, and enhanced. In the physical realm, the chi is fueled through diet, exercise, psychotherapy, and natural
substances. In the psychic realm, the chi is ignited by means of
imagery, instinct, feeling, and creativity. In naturopathic treatment, the external guide and the active client hold the problem in
sight while encouraging the client's chi to transform the problem
into a neutral, or even beneficial, aspect of the client's life. In contrast, traditional allopathic medicine treats the patient as a passive
invalid who is cured by external treatments—scalpels, antibiotics,
and the physician's knowledge of science—which are often employed to the exclusion or detriment of the body's inherent healing force.

Among the many forms of human connection, I see the warmth
of human connectedness as a form of psychic naturopathy. Elicit-
ing another person's love with our own can sometimes reignite
the love-seeking fire of the person's soul, which, like the chi of the
physical immune system, can be the most healthful way to neutralize the vampire archetype. The image of human warmth as a
curative force resonates with the words of Alice Miller in her
book *For Your Own Good*. Miller argues that much of our inhuman treatment of others may be seen as a way to recreate our past
victimization in the external reality, in an effort to externalize and
"master" it, much as traumatized children attempt to recreate and
master their trauma in their play activities. In Miller's view, when
our psyches are structured by childhood abuse to perceive the
world in terms of predator and victim, we will repeatedly create
victims in the external reality so that we can be constantly reassured that we are no longer victims ourselves. Miller asserts that
we will only reduce our inhuman behavior when we have touched
the emotional memory of the victims that we once were.

Integrating Miller's view with the vampire metaphor, we can
say that a psychic vampire will cease to prey upon others only
when he can, through the compassionate intervention of a loving
force, feel his own victimization as a child and, at the same time,

feel compassion for the victim that he was as a child. Once the old pain has been touched and grieved, the vampiric person can revisit his early decision to settle for exploitation over love. Of course, he may choose once more to identify with the cold power of the vampire. But then again, he may choose to recommit to the warmth of human love.

In our external lives, we can ignite the soul-connecting flame whenever we speak sincere words of compassion and love. These words may sound like: "I know you are angry about the loss of your job, and I know you don't mean to hurt anyone else. Still, our children are frightened by your loud voice. They think they are responsible for your pain." Or, "It's hard to remember, when we are each suffering, that the other is hurting, too. But our isolation from each other's love only multiplies our pain." Or, "Your fear is very understandable. And when we are afraid, we can feel as if everyone has sided with the enemy. Remember that I am on your side, and I want to help you succeed in this fight." Or the words may resemble my friend's idea for a new bumper sticker: "Please be kind—everyone you meet is fighting a great battle." Simple words, simple love, simple humanity—a simple, pure fire that can cremate the energy of the vampire.

There is a second kind of fire that can kill a vampire: the blaze of a soul that is burning with the passion of its destiny. This kind of passionate flame is usually ignited by a vision of our inner nature, independent of vampiric influence. When we are moved by this vision, we feel a reverence for the energies in ourselves and others that glow with their own light, untouched by ambition or pride. As we contemplate the glow of these special energies, we become more conscious of the ways in which we and our loved ones exude coldness or warmth, which makes it easier to distinguish between the chill of vampirism and the warmth of human connection. When we choose the warmth of connectedness, we and our loved ones have the opportunity to wear the faces we had before we were conceived.

What do these philosophical words look like in human behavior? Turning to our stories for models, we find the fire of vision in all the characters who killed their vampires with love. It is manifested in Clarice Starling as a passionate devotion to saving helpless innocents from the vampires who would exploit and destroy them. Clarice's passion is part of what touches Lecter's elusive humanity and neutralizes his personal vampire (at least with regard to Clarice). Luke Skywalker is also guided through his vampiric ordeal by a well-honed vision of his destiny as a Jedi knight—a noble vision that he tenaciously views as his father's legacy. When Luke learns that his father is not a dead Jedi but the undead robot Vader, Luke's vision serves to protect his love and redeem his vampiric father. As for Gypsy, she explicitly clings to her newly discovered vision of her destiny when she tells her vampiric mother, "I am *Gypsy Rose Lee!* And I *love* her. And if you don't, you can just clear out now!" Rose is initially furious with Gypsy's passionate dedication to her vision of herself, but in fact, Gypsy's passion frees the older woman to reexperience her own womanhood; in the end, Rose seems to respect and validate Gypsy's vision for her life.

The fire of vision is hard to distinguish from vampiric inflation when it first ignites, but the difference becomes more obvious when the visionary fire settles into a steady inner flame. This constant flame feels nothing like the cold ruthlessness of a vampiric inflation. The flame of a sacred vision can be felt whenever someone is at deep peace with herself and is doing what she was born to do. It might be a veterinarian who deftly ties off one tiny suture after another on the small, clean incision. Or a parent who teaches a simple task to a small child, breathing respect and affection into every word. Or a therapeutic companion who guides the steps that give rise to our healing. These acts reflect our recognition of who we were meant to be and our commitment to developing that side of ourselves.

When we live as the people we were born to be, we are most truly and intensely alive. In contrast, the vampire

> is human anti-matter. He lives only by killing. . . . He does not even die, as a man does: he is undead. He is, in other words, a pure inversion. There is no anomie, no alienation, as great as the vampire's: he is *the* alienation of man, and that alienation is potentially immortal. He is ultimately exploitive—a spreading center of alienation, despoiling others of their very lives and identities too. (Dresser 1989, 161–62)

If the vampire is the antithesis of life, then it stands to reason that the essence of life—that which gives our lives power and meaning—is poison to the vampire. Thus, doing what we were born to do is lethal to our psychic vampires. The more we incarnate our destiny and pursue that which gives meaning to our lives—not through our acquired preoccupations, but through our innate giftedness—the more likely we will be to kill our vampires with the cremating fire of love.

Whether we generate a vampire-killing fire by touching other souls with our own (even in projective love) or by incarnating our innate gifts, the potency of our loving fire lies in its capacity to connect us to that which is greater than ourselves. When we allow ourselves to fully experience our projective love for another person, we sense that we are somehow touching a form of divinity that we cannot control or create. We wonder, Where does this enormous feeling come from? And where might it take us if we allowed it to guide us? Similarly, when we bring an inner passion into the world and retain some humility in the process, we are likely to sense that we are being guided by a vision of what is possible, more than by our notions of what is reasonable. We wonder again, Where does this vision come from? And where is it taking us?

When we are moved by that which is greater than we are, no matter how prosaic our inspired acts may seem, we are experiencing a form of connectedness that is described by religious mystics as a direct communion with the divine. Without this kind of personal connectedness to the divine, say the mystics, our reverence will lose its soul, our divinity will be suffocated by dogma, and our religion will be reduced to the worship of paraphernalia. That is why religious paraphernalia alone are useless against the psychic vampire. In order to imbue our loving fires with vampire-killing power, we must remember Aldous Huxley's injunction that, "in order to know God, to become directly acquainted with God rather than knowing about God, one must go beyond symbols and concepts. These are actual obstacles . . . to the immediate experience of the Divine" (1964/1992, 252). In Huxley's view, when we locate the divine in dogma without a personal connection to the divine itself, we are mistaking the finger pointing at the moon for the moon itself. In other words, our psychic vampires will prevail unless the vampire-killing fires of our pursuits and relationships are infused with the divine powers of vision and archetypal love.

Before I leave the vampire-killing fire in your hands, I should caution you that it is a weapon to be handled with extreme care. Whenever we attempt to touch the soul of a vampiric person, we must remember that some souls have been ravaged beyond our ability to redeem them. If we try to ignite a loving fire in someone whose soul is inaccessibly buried under the vampire's tyranny, our well-meaning flame may simply be enlisted to serve the vampiric tyrant. Many women sat for weeks in the courtroom behind Ted Bundy, hoping to redeem the ravaged soul behind the sociopath's cool smile. Similarly, many husbands, wives, sons, daughters, friends, colleagues, and followers have spent their lifeblood attempting to contact the humanity of an irrevocably vampiric loved one. When we attempt to kill a psychic vampire with the cremating fire of love, we must remember the cautionary lore; the cremating fire will bring psychic death to the vampire when it is properly used, and psychic undeath to the firebearer if it is not deployed with extreme consciousness and preparation.

There is a troubling irony in the use of love to kill the vampire. The picture I have painted implies that some of us will come to commune with the divine only by entering the unholy land of the psychic vampire—the realm of projective love in which we draft innocent souls to serve as our unwitting screenholders, and suffer the life-lumpiness that can proceed from this role. The notion that we may encounter the divine only by entering a pit of darkness is antithetical to our views of good and evil, which, we imagine, must inhabit opposite poles that can never be joined. And yet the name Lucifer is derived from *lucem ferre,* or "bringer of light." The astonishing fact seems to be that the leering, sneering vampire, for all its loathsome predation, may be the unwitting bringer of light. As it lures us onto its killing field of projective love, it can also bring us, despite its foul intent, into the lap of the Divine.

Now, let me say again, and most emphatically, that this journey is extremely perilous, and in order to win our way through to the divine, we must be heavily armed against the beast. But the fact remains that when the vampire lures us into the place where visions and nightmares coexist, we may discover our vision of our divinity and thus come home to ourselves. In this sense, the vampire can occasionally be, as Mephistopheles describes himself to Faust, "a living part of that power which perpetually thinks Evil and does Good," and our journey into its lethal realm can also be the path to our redemption. When I contemplate this perilous journey, I am reminded (as I often have been during the writing of this book) of another perilous journey that was born in the mind of J. R. R. Tolkien during the dark days of the Second World War. It was a journey taken by two men, an elf, a dwarf, a wizard and four little beings called hobbits, who crawled together across a perilous landscape in order to destroy the power of the Lord of the Rings. In Tolkien's story, as in his world, war was being waged between exploitation and love, and in both wars, many souls were irreparably wounded or irretrievably lost.

So it is along our journey through the vampire's realm. For every one of us who finds our way home along the perilous path of love, many others in our ranks will bleed away our lives into the maw of the bloodsucking beast. We will rush into the vampire's arms with a host of hungers—hunger for the Beloved, hunger for perfection, hunger for immortality, hunger for meaning, and hunger, hunger, hunger for the divine. In the realm of the vampire, our hungers will be rendered unholy. They will savage our souls and deplete our life force, even as we seek our living divinity. Only if we can recognize and resist the vampire's seduction, only if we devote ourselves to love instead of exploitation, will our hungers be satisfied in a holy way. In the end, we must come to terms with the fact that the beast has always been with us, and that it will be with us forever, plotting its next bloody feast. This is not necessarily a story without hope, nor is it a night without a dawn. But if we wish to survive the vampiric darkness and savor the light of true love, we must first come to terms with the vampire's unholy hunger.

REFERENCES

Angelou, Maya. 1978. *Phenomenal Woman.* New York: Random House.

Barber, Paul. 1988. *Vampires, Burial, and Death.* New Haven, Conn.: Yale University Press.

Becker, Ernest. 1992. "The Basic Dynamic of Human Evil." In *Meeting the Shadow,* edited by Jeremiah Abrams and Connie Zweig. Los Angeles: Tarcher.

Blackwood, Algernon. [1912] 1987. "The Transfer." In *Vampires: Two Centuries of Great Vampire Stories,* edited by Alan Ryan. New York: Doubleday.

Bolen, Jean Shinoda. 1984. *Goddesses in Everywoman.* New York: Harper-Collins.

———. 1989. *Gods in Everyman.* New York: HarperCollins.

———. 1992. *Ring of Power.* San Francisco: Harper San Francisco.

Bunson, Matthew. 1993. *The Vampire Encyclopedia.* New York: Crown.

Cirlot, J. E. 1971. *A Dictionary of Symbols.* 2d ed. New York: Philosophical Library.

Cole, Joanna. 1982. *Best-Loved Folktales of the World.* New York: Anchor Doubleday.

Cooper, Basil. 1974. *The Vampire in Legend and Fact.* Secaucus, N.J.: Citadel.

Cooper, J. C. 1992. *Symbolic and Mythological Animals.* London: Aquarian/Thorsons.

Dallett, Janet O. 1991. *Saturday's Child.* Toronto: Inner City Books.

Dresser, Norine. 1989. *American Vampires.* New York: Norton.

Farson, Daniel. 1976. *Vampires, Zombies, and Monster Men.* New York: Doubleday.

Fjerkenstad, Jerry. 1992. "Who Are the Criminals?" In *Meeting the Shadow,* edited by Jeremiah Abrams and Connie Zweig. Los Angeles: Tarcher.

Greenburg, Dan. [1964] 1993. *How to Be a Jewish Mother.* Reprint. Los Angeles: Price Stern Sloan.

Guggenbühl-Craig, Adolf. 1971. *Power in the Helping Professions.* Dallas: Spring.

———. 1977. *Marriage Dead or Alive.* Dallas: Spring.

———. 1980. *Eros on Crutches: Reflections on Amorality and Psychopathy.* Dallas: Spring.

Guiley, Rosemary Ellen. 1991. *Vampires among Us.* New York: Pocket Books.

Harris, Thomas. 1988. *The Silence of the Lambs.* New York: St. Martin's Press. 1991. Film directed by Jonathan Demme. Orion Pictures.

Howell, Alice O. 1988. *The Dove in the Stone.* Wheaton, Ill.: Quest.

Hoyt, Olga Gruhzit. 1984. *Lust for Blood.* Chelsea, Mich.: Scarborough.

Hurwood, Bernhardt J. 1981. *Vampires.* New York: Quick Fox.

Huxley, Aldous. 1952. *The Devils of Loudun.* New York: Granada.

———. [1960] 1992a. "Symbol and Immediate Experience." In *Huxley and God,* edited by Jacqueline Hazard Bridgeman. San Francisco: Harper San Francisco.

———. [1964] 1992b. "Shakespeare and Religion." In *Huxley and God,* edited by Jacqueline Hazard Bridgeman. San Francisco: Harper San Francisco.

Johnson, Robert. 1983. *We: Understanding the Psychology of Love.* San Francisco: HarperSanFrancisco.

Kast, Verena. 1986. *The Nature of Loving: Patterns of Human Relationship.* Wilmette, Ill.: Chiron.

Koltuv, Barbara Black. 1986. *The Book of Lilith.* York Beach, Me.: Nicholas-Hays.

Lee, Gypsy Rose. 1957. *Gypsy: A Memoir.* New York: Harper & Brothers.

Leonard, Linda Schierse. 1982a. *The Wounded Woman: Healing the Father-Daughter Relationship.* Boston: Shambhala Publications.

———. 1986. *On the Way to the Wedding: Transforming the Love Relationship.* Boston: Shambhala Publications.

———. 1993. *Meeting the Madwoman.* New York: Bantam Books,

Marigny, Jean. 1994. *Vampires: Restless Creatures of the Night.* New York: Abrams.

Maschetti, Manuela Dunn. 1992. *Vampire: The Complete Guide to the World of the Undead.* New York: Viking Books.

Masson, Jeffrey. 1992. *The Assault on Truth: Freud's Suppression of the Seduction Theory.* New York: HarperCollins.

Masters, Anthony. 1972. *The Natural History of the Vampire.* New York: Berkley.

McNally, Raymond T., and Radu Florescu. 1972. *In Search of Dracula.* New York: Warner Books.

Miller, Alice. 1981. *The Drama of the Gifted Child.* Translated by Ruth Ward. New York: Basic Books.

———. 1990. *For Your Own Good: Hidden Cruelty in Child-Rearing and the Roots of Violence.* Translated by Hildegarde and Hunter Hannum. New York: Noonday Press.

Monette, Paul. 1979. *Nosferatu, the Vampyre.* New York: Avon Books.

Noll, Richard. 1992. *Vampires, Werewolves, and Demons.* New York: Brunner/Mazel.

Olivier, Christiane. 1980. *Les Enfants de Jocaste: L'empreinte de la mère.* Paris: DeNoël/Gontheir.

Polidori, John. [1819] 1987. "The Vampyre." In *Vampires: Two Centuries of Great Vampire Stories,* edited by Alan Ryan. New York: Doubleday.

Preminger, Erik Lee. 1984. *Gypsy and Me: At Home and on the Road with Gypsy Rose Lee.* Boston, Mass.: Little, Brown.

Qualls-Corbett, Nancy. 1988. *The Sacred Prostitute: Eternal Aspect of the Feminine.* Toronto: Inner City Books.

Rice, Anne. 1976. *Interview with the Vampire.* New York: Ballantine Books.

Rule, Ann. 1980. *The Stranger beside Me.* New York: Signet.

Sardello, Robert. 1995. *Love and the Soul: Creating a Future for Earth.* New York: HarperCollins.

Sophocles. 1977. *Oedipus Rex.* Translated by Dudley Fitts and Robert Fitzgerald. San Diego: Harcourt Brace Jovanovich.

Stoker, Bram. [1897] 1979. *Dracula.* Reprint. New York: Jove/MCA.

Tolkien, J. R. R. [1954] 1965. *The Two Towers.* Reprint. New York: Ballantine Books.

Whitmont, Edward C. 1992. "The Evolution of the Shadow." In *Meeting the Shadow,* edited by Jeremiah Abrams and Connie Zweig. Los Angeles: Tarcher.

Wilde, Oscar. [1891] 1962. *The Picture of Dorian Gray.* Reprint. New York: Signet.

Williams, Tennessee. [1945] 1970. *The Glass Menagerie.* Reprint. New York: New Directions.

Wolf, Leonard. 1975. *The Annotated Dracula.* New York: Ballantine Books.

Woodman, Marion. 1982. *Addiction to Perfection: The Still Unravished Bride.* Toronto: Inner City Books.

———. 1992. *Leaving My Father's House: A Journey to Conscious Femininity.* Boston: Shambhala Publications.

Wright, Dudley. 1987. *The Book of Vampires.* New York: Dorset.

Young-Eisendrath, Polly. 1984. *Hags and Heroes: A Feminist Approach to Jungian Psychotherapy with Couples.* Toronto: Inner City Books.

CREDITS

ACKNOWLEDGMENTS

The process of writing this book has repeatedly evoked the image of giving birth. As is often the case in a difficult birthing, many souls have devoted their wisdom and love to a lengthy gestation and delivery. The fact that my newborn turned out to resemble Rosemary's baby only increases the value of my supporters' gifts. These are the people to whom this book owes its existence. I extend my most profound and heartfelt gratitude . . .

To Judith Barr, my mentor, my teacher, my guide, and my friend, who held my soul for safekeeping throughout the long and perilous night. There is no way I will ever know at what cost Judith kept me alive and safe for these many months. I only know that her nurturance and guidance are gifts I can never fully repay, and it is further tribute to her nobility that repayment is explicitly irrelevant in this matter; I can only thank her from the bottom of my grateful soul for her act of devotion and love.

To David O'Neal, my editor at Shambhala Publications, whose gentle suggestions and wry wit have escorted me with grace and good cheer through the publishing process—which, in my case, included a thoroughly beneficial revision of the original manuscript. I owe much to Dave; the chance to meet Gypsy and the opportunity to redeem projective love are only two of the gifts I received from the changes he proposed. But most of all, it was Dave who gave this book, written by an unknown author about a fearsome topic, a chance to speak to the collective soul. I only hope that the book's impact will justify his inspiring faith in the value of its words.

To Sue Fahrbach, who listened to more vampire gloop than anyone else, and who met the gloop with unflagging attentiveness and enthusiasm. To whatever degree this book is accessible and coherent to real people, it is due largely to Sue's generous spirit and diamond-bright clarity.

To Mark Girard, whose feline gaze penetrated by heart and tenderly helped me to tolerate, redeem, and finally embrace my hidden gifts—from the most vampiric to the most divine.

To Christine Glenn, who helped me wrestle to the ground of truth the book's most intransigent concepts. Chris's encyclopedic knowledge, her unflagging optimism, and her simple good sense bolstered me at several precarious moments, and her many precious hours of razor-sharp editing eliminated the chaff from the wheat, with huge benefit to the quality of my work.

To Julie Harrelson, for bathing me in her oceanic energy when I was marooned in the desiccated aftermath of writing this book, and for helping me to *relate* to the book's darkness, after I had identified with it for so long.

To Linda Lobb, who so often and so unselfishly poured the golden light of her soul like a balm over my vampire-sickened spirit.

To Sheila Mitchell, who stood guard over me in the internal and external realities, fending off the intruders with her formidable gifts in both planes of existence.

To Susan Payton, for the crystalline starlight that illuminated my dark path, and for her gentle but remorseless commentary on the conceptual structures within and beneath the book itself.

To Marcia Smith, for the silver sword of her editor's mind, which penetrated to the heart of so many topics in this book, and for her compassionate insight into the nature of the Medusa.

To Janet Harvey, who taught me with firmness, patience, and rare expertise how to hold the correct inner position, no matter how persuasive and persistent the destabilizing forces may be.

To Don Newton, who cheerfully chased the vampire around my aching body and cradled me in his healing hands all the while.

To J. Roxane Russell, who has made it possible for me to conduct my private practice in a manner that preserves my values and beliefs, and whose enduring friendship has been a quiet, constant source of support in so many different ways.

To Jeff Schultz and Mike Louaillier, for their consistently enthusiastic support of this peculiar investment, and for their noble service as my financial gladiators.

To Sallirae Henderson, for her wicked sense of humor and heaven-sent guidance on matters cosmological, cosmetic, and comic.

To Dr. Jean Shinoda Bolen, whose words have so often guided my clinical work and my writing. A wise woman in her own right, Jean exhorted me to claim the Wise Woman in myself. What's more, she made a special effort to support me at a critical moment in my struggle to birth this book into the collective.

To Adolf Guggenbühl-Craig, Verena Kast, Linda Leonard, Alice Miller, and Marion Woodman. None of these people knows me, but I feel that I have come to know them through their numinous words, which I count as some of my most valuable teachers.

To Alice O. Howell, for teaching me (1) why the thirteenth fairy should be invited to every party, (2) how important it is to appreciate her unenviable role in balancing the energy system, and hence (3) why one should not feel maleficent when one is required to incarnate her energy.

To Pamela Birrell and the late Mary Meehan, who respectively guided my first professional and personal steps along the rich and wondrous terrain of my Jungian path.

To Julia McAfee, one of the wiser souls who declined to tread the vampiric road in writing. It was Julia's 1992 workshop that convinced me to write this book.

To Martha Mae Newell, who encouraged me to write about the vampire archetype in the face of dissuading expert words.

To Marty Milner, who taught me that my approach to healing the psyche had a powerful counterpart in the realm of physical healing.

To Joe Soprani, whose expertise has pointed my way along the elegant path of energetic equilibrium.

To Chantal de Montjou, who introduced me to *Les Enfants de Jocaste*, and who convinced me that *vampirize* was a perfectly good verb, no matter what the language.

To Katie Bretsch, who guided me to Verena Kast's heartening book on archetypal loving.

To the many friends, including Beverly Fagot, Mary Leinbach, Mick and Mary Rothbart, Marjorie Taylor, and Marion Underwood, who forgave my long silences and academic inactivity as I bent myopically to my Jungian task.

To my parents, Red and Shirley Hort, who never questioned the dark path I have chosen, even though they may, at times, have wondered if *they* had given birth to Rosemary's baby. The gifts, both learned and innate, and the support that I have received from my parents were crucial in the writing of this book. Thanks, too, to my stepmother, Natalie Hort, for not fleeing in horror when she found that she had acquired a stepdaughter with such peculiar interests.

And finally, and most importantly, to my dear clients—the inspiring, courageous voyagers who have enriched this work in innumerable ways. I can only hope that you will receive in return some worthy portion of what you have given to me and to this book. Although you remain anonymous in its pages, my words owe much of their power to your unique souls, each of which will be forever imprinted upon my heart.

INDEX

Angelou, Maya, "Phenomenal Woman," 106–108
Anger, 215
Anima, 64–65
Animus, 72, 92–93, 111–112
Aphrodite, 67–68, 140
Archetypes: collective, 6, 218; defined, 4–5, 6–7; projection of, 65, 223–224; relating to, 5, 6, 177–178; vampire, activation of, 26–27; defined, 3–8; as infection, 27, 216, 244–245; as shadow of relationships, 33–34
Artemis, 5
Arthur, King, 234–238
Athena, 66–68, 139–143
Audience/performer vampirism, 189–192

Bad versus good, 27–28, 174
Barber, Paul, *Vampires, Burial, and Death,* 197–198
Báthory, Erzsebet ("Bloody Countess"), 83–85
Beloved: appearance of, 225–226; envisioning of best in, 240–241; communing with, 205–206; father, 182, 217–218, 240–241; help in finding, 224; loss of, 216–217, 222; mother, 103, 217–218; parent, 217–218; projection of traits onto, 207–208, 221–222; real people versus archetype of, 225; reclaiming aspect of, 216–218; search for, 204–205,

206–208; seeking the Inner, 221–225. *See also* inner Beloved, love
Blackwood, Algernon, 11
Bolen, Jean Shinoda: *Goddesses in Everywoman,* 5; *Gods in Everyman,* 5; *Ring of Power,* 17
Bram Stoker's Dracula (Coppola), 35
Byron, Lord, 188–189

Championing (a feminine vampire), 113–114, 132–134, 138–139, 154
Charisma: as a vampiric disguise, 14, 24; Dracula's, 37; masculine vampires and, 48–55; example of a psychic vampire's, 7–12; versus wisdom, 53
Children: as psychic vampires, 185–189; vampirism of, 20, 26, 28–29, 124, 187, 193–194, 216, 245. *See also* daughters; fathers; mothers; sons; victims
Cirlot, J. E., *Dictionary of Symbols,* 137
Collective unconscious, 6, 218
Contempt, 19
Creativity, 103–104
Crosses (and other religious paraphernalia), 233, 249

Daughters: as victims of vampiric fathers, 63–66; as victims of vampiric mothers, 56, 82–83, 85–89, 90–93, 104–105, 152. *See also* children; sons; victims